DOG ABOUT TOWN

ACKNOWLEDGMENTS

If a book like this is to be helpful and reliable, it cannot be the result of the efforts of a single person. *Dog About Town* is possible only because so many contributed so much. My deepest gratitude to the following people:

Chris Beaudoin, the superb photographer who shot the cover and most of the pictures in this book, working with amateurs and making it look easy. Other photographers include Richard Browner, Owen Beglane, Jr. and Robert Kuhnke.

Barbara Gonsch owned the first three "city dogs" and served as teacher, model, consultant and supporter. Susanne Fahringer, Elayne Kossuth and Risa Bell were also consultants, resource providers, dog-model suppliers and constant supporters.

The animal professionals who guided, fact-checked and taught — Martha Gerhardt, D.V.M., the standard by which all vets should be judged; Caroline Wilson, founder of the Cape May Obedience Club, an outstanding handler and trainer; plus countless other breeders, handlers, trainers, groomers and other specialists.

Thank you also to The ASPCA and its many staff members, where my consciousness about animal welfare issues was awakened, and who also provided guidance, information and access. On behalf of all of us who love dogs, I also express immense gratitude to "The A" for being there — for advocacy, pioneering new programs, caring and concern.

Extra thanks to the volunteer providers of dog models: Sue Paterson for Mollie and Barkus; Risa Bell for Natasha; Mischa and Alexandra; Richard Browner for Roxie; Susanne Fahringer for Sandy and Abby; Devi Verna for Ebby; Michelle Langevin for Tasha; Richard Murphy for Egg-queena, Barbara Skelly for Chelsea.

And thanks to the human models, too: Alvina Bove Gustafson, Jennifer S. Winters, Devanna Verna, Barbara Skelly and daughters Kendall and Jasmine, Roger Fahringer, Michelle and Corey Langevin.

Finally, to all the friends and strangers who were my "testers," who used drafts of *Dog About Town* to choose and raise their own companions, proving my techniques and strategies repeatedly in New York City; Boston; Chicago; Memphis; San Francisco; Los Angeles; Orlando; Springfield, MA; Boulder, CO; Kingston, NY and beyond.

DOG ABOUT TOWN

How To Choose & Raise An Urban Dog

by Patricia Farley

CAPITAL BOOKS, INC.
Sterling, Virginia

Permissions Department
Capital Books
P. O. Box 605
Herndon, Virgnia 20172-0605

ISBN 1-892123-10-X

Printed in the United States of America

Book and cover designed by Ted Randler,
1609 Claremont Avenue, Richmond, Virginia 23227

LIBRARY OF CONGRESS CIP INFORMATION

Farley, Pat.
Dog about town : how to choose & raise an urban dog / by Patricia Farley.
p. cm.
Includes bibliographical references (p. 263).
ISBN 1-892123-10-X (alk. paper)
1. Dogs. 2. City and town life. I. Title.
SF426.F37 1999
636.7'0887--dc21 99-35323
CIP

To Jenna German Shepard,
Penny Beagle, and Tosca,
Rubi and Mickey M.
American Eskimo, the first
true city dogs, who showed us
the way and are still sorely
missed.

TABLE OF CONTENTS

YES, YOU CAN HAVE A DOG IN THE CITY!

Are you one of those city dwellers who loves dogs but simply doesn't believe a pooch would fit into your lifestyle? ***You're probably wrong!***

Do you believe dogs aren't happy in cities? If so, you're needlessly passing up one of life's great pleasures! Some breeds would hate an urban life, but many breeds have always lived indoors or have adapted to a more-restricted world wonderfully well. You don't have to give up on all dogs, just choose the right one.

Do you think your schedule or lifestyle eliminates a dog? If you're only home two hours out of every twenty-four or travel three hundred days a year, you're right. But if you're like most of us — working hard with some overtime, enjoying a normal social life, traveling occasionally — a dog can fit in. I kept contented dogs for years while working ten to twelve hours a day. I traveled for business and spent many weekends visiting country friends. A busy, active life — something like yours? With a few minor changes and the city's array of support services, you and your dog can *thrive*.

Does your apartment forbid pets? Check again. In many states, judges have ruled no-pets clauses invalid. If anyone in your building or complex has a dog, the clause is null and void. If you see cats sitting in the windows, the clause may also be void. If you're a senior citizen, you may be legally exempted.

Are your objections based on what you see of other city dogs? All too often, dog-owners are the worst advertisements possible for the pleasures of keeping a dog in the city. We've all seen and heard about it — pets who destroy their homes when left alone, who bark constantly whenever their human leaves, who require endless walks through hurricanes and blizzards, who leave sidewalk messes that we've all stepped into. Dogs who require people to race home and break social engagements (even business appointments), who make elevator riding or navigating a crowded sidewalk miserable, even dangerous. Dogs who start fights on the street or frighten us.

Are these signs that dogs don't belong in cities? NO! They are simply proof of my point — these dogs haven't been chosen or trained correctly. That's what this book is all about: How to have a dog in the city *happily* for you, your dog and your neighbors.

So don't reject the idea of a dog companion. A dog can greatly enrich your life, whether it's in an apartment, a condo, a co-op, a townhouse, a townhouse community with strict leash laws or whatever. A dog is even good for you. New research proves that when you pet a dog, your blood pressure and pulse rate drop. Older people with dogs visit doctors 21% less frequently. People with dogs leave hospitals faster and people with dogs live longer! A dog is definitely good for you.

I know you and your city dog can enjoy living together, because I've done it for over twenty years and so have dozens of my friends and acquaintances. Let me show you how.

Chapter 1

A GOOD CITY DOG IS NOT THE SAME AS A GOOD COUNTRY DOG

The city-dwelling dogs who have irritated you, enraged you, frightened you, endangered you and saddened you are solid proof that city dogs can't be chosen by the same standards or trained in the same way as country dogs.

Can you imagine a Teacup Poodle happily and successfully herding cattle on a ranch? Why would you expect a Komondor, who has spent centuries living with and thinking of himself as a sheep, to adjust to city life? You've got to pick a dog who fits into the way you live, and you have a great many choices.

It's logical to expect city dogs to live according to a special set of rules. Think about it. In the country, you may want your dog to bark the moment anyone steps onto your property, but in town you'd be evicted in short order if your dog sounded off every time anyone moved in a nearby apartment.

Country dogs may never need to be on a leash. City dogs have to walk on a lead the first time they leave your living room. Country dogs may never ride in an elevator, in a taxi or on public transportation, stay in a kennel, visit a store, or exercise in a park filled with babies, bikers, joggers and other dogs. Country canines just scratch at the door when the urge strikes them. They don't have to keep things under control for eight or more hours, then relieve themselves only in a very specific, often busy, smelly and noisy area.

The rules aren't hard to teach. They are merely different.

Frankly, I'm amazed that so few people have figured this out. The very bad behavior of so many city dogs makes it obvious that knowing special city manners and street smarts is rare indeed. I've spent over twenty years in city apartments with several dogs including an eighty-five-pound German Shepherd. I constantly received surprised praise from my neighbors, landlords and doormen on my "extraordinary" dogs. They weren't extraordinary except to me; my dogs had just been taught how to be city dogs. It made my life easier and happier. The dogs were always welcome tenants. And my dogs were happier and safer, too.

An urban environment is not the same as a rural one—choose and train your dog accordingly.

How did I learn what my dogs could and should do? My first clues came from a neighbor who owned three beautifully trained American Eskimos also known as Spitzes. They showed me what was possible, and I began my experiments to discover what my dogs could do. As I am a person who doesn't like upsetting others, I tried to make my dogs as untroubling and well-mannered as possible. One of my early dogs made this very difficult. She was a Beagle, one of the most stubborn, hard-to-train breeds in existence. Desperate to gain control, I turned to professional trainers and obedience classes. I enjoyed this training and the people I met enormously, and became much more involved, constantly learning more.

Gradually my dogs became "city dogs" that were at home with a "working mother," crowds, apartments and the rest of urban life.

Soon friends and friends of friends were asking me how they could train their dogs to be as well-behaved as mine. At one point, a man knocked at my door with his Cocker Spaniel beside him. He lived several floors below me and our elevator man had sent the pair to me for lessons!

This book sums up these decades of experimenting, researching and training. Everything here has been fully tested and proven. Relevant sections have been reviewed by vets and trainers to be certain all my information is absolutely accurate. The training techniques and behavior strategies I tell you about are based on my direct experience. I can assure you that in book after book by famous professionals, there are methods of teaching and breaking habits that just don't work. I tried them. So did others I interviewed. These books also provide information on breeds of dogs that's totally inadequate for intelligent decision-making. I give you the information my friends and I wanted, all thoroughly researched with dog-owners and handlers who really know the truth.

I'm going to be very frank about dogs who are not suited to your lifestyle. I know some people do live happily in cities with these dogs. The individual dog may be an exception (after all, every dog is unique) or owner and dog may have worked out good compromises. Fine! But if you don't have a dog now, why ask for trouble? Stick with the breeds we know can be content with the life you lead.

This book covers the city dog in full detail — where to get your new companion, what to teach him when and how, support services, city medical care, the culture shock of taking your dog to the country, traveling with your dog, even how to get through crises and where to find more information or help. Let this handbook be your guide to a happy life with a well-behaved companion who can enrich your world immensely.

One quick word on pronouns. It goes against my beliefs to call a dog "it" and perpetuate the idea that animals are things, yet constantly writing (or reading) "he or she" is very awkward. So when I talk about "dogs," I'll call them "hes." When I speak of specific dogs, I'll use the appropriate gender for that individual. This is not to recommend a gender — in fact all my dogs have been females. It's merely bowing to the tendency to think of cats as female and dogs as male.

And a note about "research." In many places in this book, I will tell you that help, support and services may be available in your area and suggest you research to find out. Unfortunately, you can't pull out the Yellow Pages and look under "getting help in caring for your dog when you have a serious illness."

The Appendix offers information on national organizations and a few regional resources that can be a good starting point, especially in Web searches. Most of your research, however, will be local and the very best places to start are (1) your local humane society, (2) local breed clubs, and (3) your vet. There's an invisible animal world, a network of caring, deeply involved people who support and help and use each other's services — people at your shelters and in your local breed clubs are part of this network.

I've found the people in the animal world to be almost universally caring, compassionate people. They may be opinionated and bluntly direct (animals respond best to this sort of personality), but most are extremely giving folk who go out of their way to help. Many are volunteers. In fact, the phone you're dialing may be to the home of a busy person with a full-time job and a family. So if phones aren't answered, keep calling.

Don't even worry about calling a breed club if you have a 59-breed mutt. Although club people are certain their breed is the very best dog, they care about all dogs...and their owners.

Don't give up if there isn't a service like the one you're seeking. Explain why your need is urgent and ask the people you speak to what they suggest you do. Animal people are so generous that I suspect someone will find a way to help. If your first call doesn't produce what you need, ask that person if there's anyone else you might contact, then make that call...and continue. I can't guarantee it, but I sincerely believe you will find help.

Chapter 2

YOU'RE PICKING A ROOMMATE — BE COMPATIBLE!

Most dogs are social magnets, and walks can become a pleasant round of visits.

You're going to live in very close quarters with your dog. If he gets on your nerves, you can't open the door and shoo him outside for a few hours. He's always going to be there, so you'd better be very sure you don't get on each other's nerves. Think of your dog as a roommate with a twenty-year lease and exercise the same care in selecting him as you would in choosing a human companion.

Consider everything — your personality, your temperament, the various care requirements for different types of dogs and your personal preferences. The dog for you is the one that best matches all of your requirements. That's what we're going to identify in this Chapter, and the Worksheet at the end will help you make your choices.

SUIT YOUR TEMPERAMENT

If you move through life at a half-run, you'll hate the slow-moving Basset Hound and he won't enjoy being dragged down the street while you curse at him to hurry up. If you normally sound gruff and abrupt, you certainly don't want a dog who trembles when you say, "good dog" as some super-sensitive Cockers are prone to do. On the other hand, if you're mild and soft-spoken, you'll be exhausted by a Schnauzer who doesn't believe anything you say until you fake a tough persona.

The Worksheet will help you identify the key aspects of your temperament. Once you have this, match yours to your dog's as closely as possible for maximum happiness — with three exceptions: If you rate yourself as very excitable, high strung, high energy and high speed, your best dog is probably not a dog as hyper as you are — the two of you together could send one or both of you over the edge. For you, a dog who can keep up with you but takes it all with a calmer, somewhat indulgent point-of-view is the smarter choice — like a Beagle or Keeshond.

If you're loud, flamboyant and dramatic, avoid hyper dogs who are known to be mouthy — he'll never shut up around you.

And if you're highly emotional, avoid quick-on-the-trigger dogs who could be confused by your reactions, exaggerate situations and attack.

MATCH YOUR PERSONALITY

Opposites may attract in human relationships, but dogs and owners are happier together when their personalities mesh. If you're social and outgoing, you want a life-of-the-party dog like a Golden Retriever rather than one that hides or attacks. If you like being boss, you want the challenge of a dog like a Corgi. If you're a straight shooter who calls 'em as you see 'em, you want a dog with those qualities rather than a charming, manipulative rascal like a Poodle.

There's an old saying that people look like their dogs, and there's something in it. I suspect people gravitate towards dogs whose appearance matches their inner pictures of themselves. You often find a man who looks like a prize-fighter with a Bulldog and a very fragile, delicate, graceful woman with a Whippet. Certainly, you need to be comfortable with the appearance of your dog, but looks shouldn't be the primary reason for your choice because appearances can be very deceiving. That Bulldog is so gentle, lovable and sensitive that he's one of the breeds who can be psychologically destroyed by harsh training.

Personality and temperament are what really count in choosing a compatible dog. But when considering appearance, look at the whole package. Do you want a graceful "racehorse" like a Greyhound or Whippet, or a playful rascal like a Norwich Terrier, a regal "king" of a Pekinese or German Shepherd, a dignified "gentleman" (Boston Bull Terrier, Scottie)?

DON'T JUMP TO CONCLUSIONS ABOUT SIZE

Size is a factor in making your choice, but not in the ways you may think. Despite all the people who moan, "how cruel to keep such a huge dog in the city," the great giants are often very well suited to urban lives because they're quiet and lethargic as adults, mostly lying around like furry rugs. Consider the following nine reality checks:

1. **The Social Factor.** People run from big dogs. Small dogs are new-friend magnets. People literally crossed the streets to avoid my peaceful German Shepherd. But my Beagle and Sheltie brought me dozens of friends including many nameless dog-owners. Although we all knew the names of each other's dogs, we became close without ever introducing ourselves.

2. **The Safety Provision.** Out on the streets or at your open door, a big dog is an automatic security guard who deters any threat. But usually the "dog security alarm" is the

sound behind a closed door. Lots of sound from a small yippy dog stops intruders because they fear attracting attention. Deep, "big-dog" barks sound life-threatening and frighten off everyone, but they need not come from large bodies — Scotties, for one, have very "big dog" barks.

3. **The Portability Obstacle.** Tiny dogs can be smuggled into forbidden places in purses and pockets. They can legally travel in airplane cabins and trains. Taxis rarely avoid stopping for a small dog the way they do for larger models. Large dogs cannot be hidden. They bring out dog phobias in nice people and are often barred from establishments where small dogs go freely. Friends don't always welcome their visits. Frequent travelers are probably better off with a small dog.

4. **The Walking Preference.** Toy breeds never need a walk. They can be litter-box trained. Big dogs always have to go outdoors to relieve themselves although, as you'll see later, that doesn't require marathon walks on every outing.

5. **The Economic Crunch.** Big dogs cost significantly more to keep than small dogs. They cost more to feed, more to kennel, more to transport. They take bigger doses of medicines. Even their big toys and treats are more expensive.

6. **The Floor Space Requirement.** Giant dogs are the size of a full-grown human living horizontally. They need space to lie down full length and room to wag their tails without knocking all the knick-knacks off your end tables. Your apartment should be uncluttered and somewhat sparsely furnished if you're going to share with a giant.

7. **The Fitness Focus.** Very small dogs get plenty of exercise simply by tearing around your apartment during "crazy hour" and most giant-sized adult dogs need very little exercise.

But ALL young dogs require regular exercise when they're growing (two years for larger dogs) so their muscles and bones develop properly. Many medium and medium-large dogs also need regular exercise throughout their lives.

Consider your special requirements in selecting your dog. Chelsea (Sheltie) Skelly is an excellent jogger's dog.

For most of the dogs recommended in this book, regular exercise consists of three, thirty-to-sixty-minute, brisk walks a week plus an active, running, weekend play session of an hour or two — playing fetch or frisbee is perfect. Terriers need this in addition to their in-house workouts. If you can't provide this, you'll have to pay others to do so.

8. The Health Consideration. The bigger the dog, the more fragile his health. Since the huge breeds' very size is a strain, they're often subject to heart trouble, joint problems and other complications. All large dogs are prone to hip dysplasia, a congenital hip deformity which can cripple and shorten lives (and can't be accurately diagnosed in a puppy).

Medically, all large dogs are classified as "old" at the age of ten — they don't live as long as their smaller cousins who can be with you for thirteen, fifteen and even twenty years. Newfoundlands, the gentle giants, rarely live past age eight.

9. The Relationship Difference. Size can have a big impact on your relationship with your dog. Large dogs are companions who are usually patted and stroked. They can never be rocked in your arms or held in your lap. Because of their size, they must be very well trained, but at the same time, they give you a sense of security.

Small dogs are babies or small children who look to you for security. They're cuddled, tickled and snuggled. They're treated like spoiled babies (and expect to be) and training is often very lax.

Of course, all these differences primarily apply to the extremes. Dogs weighing between fifteen and forty pounds often give you the advantages and disadvantages of both large and small.

IGNORE THE MYTHS

When choosing your dog, separate real issues from the old wives' sayings that others will tell you.

Small dogs aren't as smart as large dogs. Nonsense! Some individual breeds have been created as our working partners and therefore are very quick to recognize and respond to our wishes — they seem smarter than others. But size is never a factor. Truth is, small dogs get away with murder because they're so little and cute — and they're smart enough to take full advantage.

By the way, city dogs as a whole seem smarter than country dogs simply because they live in closer proximity with their humans, are a more integral part of people's daily lives and are talked to more often. Just like human children, they blossom when we pay attention.

A dog who's alone a lot should have company. No! I've had solo dogs, two dogs and even three. So have several friends who join me in saying that when they had only one dog, the dog seemed happier! Trainers agree. Dogs aren't cats who *do* find real companionship in each other. YOU are the center of your dog's life. When you leave two dogs home, they merely lie down and wait for you. Sure, they enjoy each other, but they'll also compete for your attention and even punish you if they think you're favoring one over the other. The best thing two dogs in a household do is teach each other bad habits — two dogs are double trouble and not worth the effort.

Small dogs are yappier than large dogs. Again, it's not the size but the breed. Terriers, Toys and Herding Dogs are notoriously yappy (or "mouthy" as real dog people say) and of the three groups, the Toys are probably the quietest.

IDENTIFY YOUR SPECIAL REQUIREMENTS NOW

There are a number of significant, real issues that impact your choice of dog:

How do you feel about cropping and docking? Some breeds have their tails cut off (docked) on their third day of life. Some breeds have their ears cropped — part of the ear is cut off and the balance is set into an upright position with a heavy cast. This usually begins at about six weeks.

The British consider this so barbaric that they've stopped it, even in show dogs; but in this country, if you don't want your dog cropped or docked, you have two choices — tell your breeder BEFORE the pups are born and plan to live with a dog that looks rather strange, or choose a breed where this isn't done. By the way, you can see what Boxers, Poodles and others look like when left "au natural" in British breed books, available in most book stores.

What's your position on hair? In addition to long-haired dogs, all double-coated short-hairs leave a constant trail of hair behind them. And city dogs tend to shed continuously. If you choose a big shedder, hair is fact of life. You'll stop wearing dark colors, invest in an expensive vacuum and accept the constant existence of large, hair dust bunnies. Or you'll choose a Poodle, Schnauzer, Bichon or single-coated short-hair. (By the way, when they're nervous or frightened, dogs throw off hair by the bushel. Stress shedding stops the moment the dog calms down.)

Do you have allergies? Poodles and Bichon Frises have wool rather than hair, do not shed and rarely cause allergic reactions — they're hypoallergenic. Schnauzers, Greyhounds and other very short-haired, single-coated dogs may not spark an allergy. But be very careful if you're had allergic reactions to dogs (cats don't count). In an urban environment, you live in tightly closed, restricted atmospheres where dander is trapped inside with you. My cat allergy wasn't a problem when we lived in the country; but when we moved to town, it became so serious that my cat had to move in with friends. Test your reactions by visiting friends BEFORE you get a dog — and avoid heartache.

How much time are you willing to put into grooming your dog? Obviously dogs with long, lush coats require constant, lengthy grooming, but surprisingly many other dogs who don't look like they need much care actually do. The Dog Selection Chart (page 36) tells you about the grooming requirements for each breed. Be honest with yourself about what you're willing to do week after week, year after year. Dogs who don't get the grooming they need can develop health problems.

You can reduce the amount of work required on some breeds like Cockers and Shih Tzus by cutting their long hair short, but you may have to take special care when the temperature is very high or low, since their natural coats provide insulation.

Dogs with very fuzzy back ends have a further nasty requirement. You have to clean them every time they relieve themselves, even if you clip the hair out of the way.

Poodles, Bichons, many of the Toys and almost all Terriers also need periodic trips to a professional groomer, which isn't cheap.

By the way, before you get too deep into dreaming of your beautiful Bichon, let me reveal that none of those gloriously fuzzy breeds will ever look like they do in the show ring or in pictures of champions. A dog in full show coat has a complete sub-zero winter coat, obtained by spending several months in very cold air conditioning (think "refrigerator"). Before his show or portrait, he is bathed, blow dried and teased. If he's light-colored, talcum powder is worked into his fur to add volume. And his haircut is masterful — judges feel a dog down to the skin because, as handlers say, you can "cut a great dog out of the fur."

What about your family size now and in the near future? There are dogs who accept lovers and new significant others, and dogs who resent them with ferocious jealousy. There are dogs who welcome children and others who are much better with singles or couples. Toys, for instance, have been spoiled, pampered babies for so long that they usually fiercely resent "competition" in the form of children.

Even dogs who are "good" with children react differently to children at different ages. Their "goodness" can range from indifference, to hiding from them, becoming cohorts in mischief-making, patient endurance or raising the kids. If lovers and/or children are or will be part of your life, plan your choice accordingly. Also plan to teach your children how to interact with dogs. Without instruction, children can be unbelievably cruel and bring hostility upon themselves.

How comfortable are you with barking? Is a mouthy dog going to make you uncomfortable, constantly worried about your neighbors? Or do you have neighbors with super-sensitive hearing who are apt to be bitter complainers? Remember, you can stop SOME of a mouthy dog's barking but never all.

Not all dogs are good for children at all ages. Chelsea (Sheltie) Skelly adores "her" older children.

Is a high-pitched yip comfortable or does it irritate you like chalk on a blackboard? That can affect the dog you choose. If you're leaning towards a dog who doesn't bark very much, check the chart in Chapter 3 to be sure they're also quiet. Beagles and Bassets bay a deep sound designed for long-distance hearing, Huskies sing, and the famous no-barker Basenji yodels. There are more sounds than "woof."

Are you strong or do you have physical limitations? Even though you're going to train your dog not to drag you down the street, you do have to be strong enough to control your dog if he ever gets in a panic or wants to fight.

If you have trouble with your legs, back and/or shoulders, consider a smaller, lighter-weight dog. The same is true if you're of an age where you're more fragile than you used to be. Not only could your dog become hurt if you can't control him, he could hurt you!

Do you want an exercise partner, an athletic competitor or something special from your dog? A power-walker, runner or jogger canine companion is a small-to medium-size dog with high energy and long legs. Terriers and many others will flourish as your exercise partner. Large dogs are not so good. Their strides are longer than yours and you may just warm them up. Greyhounds, for example, can hit speeds of 45 mph.

What's your preference on sensuality? I'm talking about the tactile pleasures of touch. Part of the delight of a dog is petting him. So what do you like to touch? Some dogs feel like Brillo, others have velvet-like furs, then there are the silky coats, the soft brushy coats, the coats you must pet only in one direction lest you mat the fur, and the ones you can scrunch your fingers into. You're going to be touching your dog a lot, so this isn't a frivolous point!

Do you really, really want a puppy? Yes, they're wonderful, but babies also cause damage, use up great amounts of your energy and require a lot of time and attention. If you have a demanding job that leaves you exhausted at day's end, an adult or half-grown dog is a better choice.

Older dogs will love you just as much as a puppy. They will behave just as well as the puppy you train from scratch if you choose wisely. (In fact, they may be better trained than you could achieve on your own.) And fine, well-trained, purebred adult dogs are often available free or at a fraction of their puppy costs. I know all this from personal experience — I've raised puppies and taken in a ten-month-old, an abused three-year-old, an ill ten-year-old and many others. All have left me with precious memories of a wonderful time of sharing and loving.

Adult dogs adapt to new rules just fine, accept new names without problems, train well (more easily since they're old enough to work with you). And you'll be saving a life. Every day all over the country, wonderful adult dogs are euthanized because there are too many of them looking for homes and too few people willing to adopt them.

Male or female? Since most people have an automatic preference for one gender or the other, my advice is to go with your instinctive choice. There isn't that much of a difference, despite the myth that females are more affectionate. That's a matter of breed and individual, not gender.

DOG CHOICE WORKSHEET

1. Rate yourself on a scale of 1 to 5 for the following temperament characteristics:

1 on the scale		*5 on the scale*
Excitable, high-strung	_____	Easy-going
High energy, always saying "come on, we can't stop now"	_____	Often first to slow down
High vitality, don't need as much sleep as many others	_____	Need your Z's, love to nap
High-speed, move at half-run, do 10 things at once	_____	Low-speed, others pull you along, need to focus on what you're doing
Quick reactions, often take people by surprise	_____	React with deliberation, people sometimes say "hurry up"
Emotional	_____	Analytical
Demonstrative	_____	Aloof

This all adds up to a dog who is:______________________________

2. Rate yourself on a scale of 1 to 5 for the following personality qualities:

1 on the scale		*5 on the scale*
You like the drama of life, tend to overreact	____	You're low-key, underplay, people say they can't "read" you
You like a loud house (yelling, discussing, living at high volume with TV on in the background)	____	You like things quiet
You're outgoing, social, have many friends, love to give big parties where anything happens	____	You're a bit shy, a bit of a loner, with few but very close friends, you like smaller gatherings
You're a bit manipulative, certainly charming	____	You're straight-forward, even blunt
Your moods are apparent to all, you're mostly happy	____	Some call you moody or brooding
You're touchy-feely, love to touch people, hug, cuddle,	____	You're standoffish, don't like a lot of indiscriminate touching
You like confrontations, like to get it all out, explode and then forget it	____	You're a peace-lover, very uncomfortable with confrontation, wait to see if it goes away
You like power and challenge	____	You prefer collaboration and teamwork

This all adds up to a dog who is:________________________________

3. What are your requirements regarding looks? (check as many as apply)

❑ I like neatness ❑ I think big hair is pretty ❑ I think scruffy is cute
❑ I'd like a dignified dog ❑ I'd like a rascal and scamp ❑ I'd like a pretty charmer
❑ I'd like a regal dog ❑ I don't like exaggerated body features (long body, short legs)

4. What have you decided about size?

Small	Large
❑ I want a social magnet	❑ I want a guard
❑ I want security indoors	❑ I want security outdoors
❑ I want to travel freely with my dog	❑ I don't care about travel problems
❑ I want to litter-box train my dog	❑ I'll do the walks
❑ Cost is a factor in having a dog	❑ I don't care about cost in keeping my big dog
❑ I have a crowded apartment	❑ I have a big, bare apartment
❑ I really don't want to do all that exercising	❑ I look forward to all that exercising
❑ I want a baby to cuddle	❑ I want a companion

Naturally, there's a middle ground between the extremes into which a medium-sized dog fits perfectly. But if you have more checks on one side than the other, you should be leaning towards that size.

My dog should be:______________________

5. How do you feel about cropping and docking?

❑ OK by me ❑ Not OK ❑ Not OK, but I can live with a weird-looking dog

6. How much grooming are you eager to do?

❑ I don't mind spending up to an hour a day brushing and grooming — it's restful

❑ I don't mind spending fifteen to thirty minutes a day

❑ I'd rather brush only once or twice a week

7. Your health

❑ I have allergies and need a hypoallergenic dog

❑ I'm very strong ❑ I have limitations; need a not-too-powerful dog

8. How do you feel about fur?

❑ I really don't want fur drifting all over my house

❑ I can live with fur

❑ I like furry dogs, but would like to avoid the real fur factories

9. Family plans

❑ I have a significant other or am a nondating single, my dog is coming into a settled household

❑ I'm dating, my dog will have to accept others who may come for good, may come and go

❑ I do hope to have children within the next dozen years

❑ I have a child or children (how many____; what ages______________)

❑ No kids, never

10. I want my dog to serve special purposes:

❑ Exercise with me ❑ I want a therapy dog ❑ I want a star

❑ I want a dog to participate in athletic competitions ❑ Other:________________

Chapter 3

YOU AND YOUR BUDDY —THERE'S A BREED FOR YOU

Now you have a basic list of what you want in your dog. It's time to start narrowing the field to a single animal. How do you match personality, temperament, city suitability and special needs with a wriggling bundle of fur who shows little evidence of what he'll become as an adult? Or even an adult uneasy with strange-person-you and not very revealing of what your lives together will be like? The dog world makes it possible for you to do this with a fairly good degree of accuracy.

Dogs are far more predictable than humans because humans have been creating dogs for centuries. Humans have played with canine gene pools like masters to enhance certain characteristics and eliminate others. Once upon a time, Great Danes were so ferocious that when they started competing in show rings, they started deadly dog wars in every show they entered. The show supervisors banned Danes and in ONE generation, the breeders had removed all ferocity from the breed! Danes today are one of the gentlest breeds. Breeds allow you to predict your dog's character with remarkable accuracy.

Of course, every dog is also an individual and there are always exceptions, but even they fall within certain limits. You can change behavior, but you cannot make a dog betray his entire nature. You can temper a Terrier's tendency to bark constantly, but you'll never silence him. Never choose a breed with traits you don't want, planning to change the dog — you know that doesn't work with humans; it won't happen with dogs either.

BREED GROUPS

As the organization that sanctions dog show competitions, the American Kennel Club is the registry for all purebred dogs in this country. The AKC maintains the proof that a dog is a specific breed, compiles the judging standards (the distinct "conformation" ideal against which all representatives of the breed are judged), supervises the judges and shows, and records the championship points awarded to winning dogs. To be registered as a purebred, a puppy's parents must be registered purebreds and, of course, the parents had to have registered purebred parents, too. Show dogs have family trees (called pedigrees) going back many generations, and all purebred pups that qualify for AKC registration are sold with four-to five-generation family trees.

All this attention to breeding purity has resulted in breeds with definite, fairly dependable personalities, temperaments and other characteristics. Indeed, some of the standards for individual breeds call for specific qualities over and above appearance.

Zeroing in on a breed begins with zeroing in on the best group because the AKC has divided their 140 accepted breeds into seven groups or categories, all but one of which define the basic function for which all the breeds in the group were originally developed and continuously refined. In shows, dogs compete in breed first, then the best of each breed compete in group and finally the best of each group compete for best in show.

Of course, each group includes a few misfits who, over time, have moved into performing other functions and today really belong in other groups. Cocker Spaniels, for instance, are officially sporting dogs, but have been household companions for so long that many of the qualities of sporting dogs no longer apply. My Dog Selector Chart gives you these specifics.

Breeds also split over time. There are now English Cockers and Cocker Spaniels — they are quite different dogs. There are different coats on Dachshunds as well as different sizes (one has really become a Toy). Labrador and Golden Retrievers remain champions in field trials (hunting competitions), but have also become outstanding, versatile working dogs and house pets. Clearly, the bloodlines are diverging. For your companion, look for a dog with a family containing pets, disability dogs, obedience and agility competitors, rescue dogs, etc. You don't want a pure retriever.

For the most part, however, knowing something about a group can give you a lot of information about a breed. So let's begin with the groups.

Group 1. Sporting Dogs

Examples: Cocker Spaniel, Golden Retriever and Labrador Retriever.

These are the hunting dogs — retrievers, pointers and spaniels, most of whom work birds. They scent the quarry, locate it for the hunter, sometimes flush the game into the line of fire, then retrieve from land, water or both without damaging a feather. Some of these breeds are four-hundred years old. They are born to their work and little training is required. They are birding machines who take great joy at being outdoors, doing what their instincts demand, working across the fields and swamps on their own as the hunter's partner.

Because of what they are, Sporting dogs tend to be very independent, hard to train for the intricacies of city life and aloof — many are not very affectionate. Most aren't happy indoors and only truly come to life when given the freedom to use their beautiful, ground-eating gaits. It's been said an Irish Setter needs a mile to turn around. They cannot ever be let of-leash in town and can turn very destructive if not exercised enough. They simply aren't appropriate city companions — except for the few who've been turned into companion dogs over time.

Group 2. Hounds

Examples: Afghan Hound, Basset Hound, Beagle, Borzoi, Dachshund, Greyhound and Whippet.

Another gang of hunters, Hounds specialize in tracking and holding everything from rabbits to wolves, elk, caribou, foxes and human beings. Most are scent hunters who live by their noses. Judging from their behavior, Hounds turn off all other senses when they find an interesting smell — they certainly don't hear people screaming, "NO, STOP, COME BACK HERE, I MEAN IT."

Tenacity helps Hounds stay on the trail no matter what happens. This means a Hound will do what a Hound wants to do, regardless of how hard to you try to teach him otherwise.

In fact, several Hounds make excellent city dogs because they adapt well to the environment, tolerate confined living well and don't bark much. BUT having loved a Beagle for nearly fifteen years and through her, having met many other Hound owners, I warn you that Hounds are, above all, OBSTINATE. They're difficult to train and require forceful correction. You can let a Hound off-leash only close to you and under your constant eye because he'll wander off following a scent, never hear your calls and get himself lost. Many Hounds are compulsive eaters and difficult to keep trim. And on top of all this, Hounds are friendly and funny, but not overly loving and definitely not protective.

All the above applies to the *scent* Hounds like Beagles and Bassets, but not to a separate group of very ancient *sight* Hounds that includes the Borzoi and the Afghan. These dogs aren't overly loving, but they're not as obstinate as the scent hounds.

Greyhounds and Whippets have been used for other purposes for so long that they aren't hunters any more. Both can be very affectionate and warm, extremely gentle and quiet...good city dogs.

Group 3. Working Dogs

Examples: Akita, Boxer, Great Dane, Newfoundland, Rottweiler and Saint Bernard.

Here are the dogs of fable, the hero rescuers and humanity's working partners who have been performing an astonishing array of tasks for centuries. They work alone or at mankind's side, solve problems, apply what they know to new situations and are genuinely eager to know what you want of them. Quick to learn and eager to please, they often seem the brightest of dogs. Most have great discrimination, a rare ability to recognize if a threat is real or not.

The jobs they've done are astonishing. Rottweilers (Rotties) carried baggage for Roman troops and when abandoned in the Swiss mountains, turned into farm dogs and guard dogs. Newfoundlands (Newfies) went to sea with fisherman and dove into raging waters to pull boats to shore and rescue sailors swept overboard. Some dogs pulled carts to market so farmers could sell their crops. Saints rescued mountain travelers caught in avalanches. In one European region, Working dogs were even smugglers — carrying packs of contraband, they journeyed over mountain passes to the neighboring country.

Today, Working dogs also serve as sentries, message carriers and mine spotters in the military, contraband sniffers for customs agents, partners for police officers, members of search-and-rescue teams, guide dogs for the blind and deaf, mobile aids for those in wheelchairs and much more.

Working dogs are extremely honest — you get what you see. There's no trickery, manipulation or duplicity. They're also steady, calm, never hyper.

Although a few breeds are a little too quick about being protective (and not recommended here for that reason), Working dogs are wonderful companions whose discretion, judgment, empathy and efforts to understand you make them almost human at times. They're very affectionate and even cuddly. They're so devoted that they have a tendency to become one-man dogs. And despite their power and size, most are wonderful with children of all ages.

Because Working dogs have been protectors for so long, they tend to be highly suspicious of strangers. They're slow to warm up to new people and tend to make friends on their own terms, backing off or even growling at over-eager approaches. They're not social dogs. They make up their own minds about the people they like. You'll notice distinct differences in how they relate to each of your friends.

Most Working dogs are territorial; and because urban areas are everyone's territory, they aren't always as self-assured on city streets as they are in more rural area. Other than this minor detail, they fit into city life perfectly.

Most Working dogs want a reason for their existence. Tell yours that his job is to protect you and your property, then order him to PROTECT! when you leave him at home or alone in the car. That solves the problem.

One note of warning — in the breeds noted for protection, unscrupulous breeders have deliberately created bloodlines of ferocious, very untrustworthy guard dogs who don't belong in a home. These dogs tend to be oversized.

Group 4. Terriers

Examples: Airedale, Bedlington, Cairn, Fox Terrier, Miniature Schnauzer, Norwich, Scottish, Silky, Soft-Coated Wheaten and West Highland.

These perky, playful dogs often look like they have springs in their legs. Every single one of the scruffy, scrappy scamps in this large group is a perfect city dog because they were bred to live in small homes with their creators. I've only limited my selections because some are rare in the U.S. However, if you want to go afield here, please do — Terriers are remarkably consistent, so what I say applies to all the others.

Terriers are alert, curious, merry, very social, very clever, quick to learn and lots of fun for the strong-willed person who enjoys a constant challenge and respects those who will never, ever quit.

They have enormous stores of energy and high exercise needs. They're great exercise companions, even those with short, little legs. Many are very good jumpers and good at climbing out of enclosures. They don't like being ignored. And because of all that energy, they don't settle down for long periods, expect to be asked to "play with me" quite frequently. If you won't play, they may just go find some mischief...at any age.

Terriers are known as "the poor man's hunting dog" because they were created when the "common folk" in England became envious of the nobles' retrievers and foxhounds. Their creators required dogs who would go after vermin, badgers and other game that live in borrows in the ground. Terriers were bred to go into those burrow homes and bring out the prey. Can you imagine the tenacity and courage required for such an action? If so, you understand why Terriers don't know the meaning of the word "fear." They can't be cowed. I doubt many could be broken. Their feisty, scrappy spirit is so important that judges at shows will ask handlers to "set them against each other," looking for eager, instant aggression. Another thing you'll notice in show rings is that Terriers frequently bark their way around it. They have big mouths at often a piercingly high pitch.

If you have a vision of a brief training struggle with your dog followed by a peaceful, serene lifetime — don't get a Terrier. If the perfect evening for you is quietly reading a good book — don't get a Terrier. They don't suit the elderly or the peace-lover. They're also not good with small children — they're too energetic and too quick to snap if irritated.

They also have hard, bristly coats like scrubbing pads. That rough fur seems to make at least some Terriers prone to skin conditions which can require life-long treatments with prescribed baths, lotions and creams. The coats require regular trips to a groomer for "plucking." I've heard from several sources, however, that if you cut a Terrier's coat, it will become soft and silky.

Soft-Coated Wheatens are the exception — they have lovely, soft coats and a gentler, quieter, more biddable nature than the average Terrier. They aren't as energetic, and they aren't barkers. Some people say Westies (West Highland Terriers) are also not quite as spirited as the average Terrier, but the three I've known well were quite strong-willed, needing more effort and force than I'm comfortable with on a constant basis.

Because Terriers are naturally on the hyper side, it's possible to get one who goes over the edge into a kind of constant, manic hysteria.

Group 5. Toys

Examples: Chihuahua, Italian Greyhound, Maltese, Miniature Pinscher, Papillon, Pekingese, Pomeranian, (Toy) Poodle, Pug, Shih Tzu and Yorkshire Terrier.

For centuries, many of these minis of the dog world have been the pampered baby darlings of the wealthy. In China, disrespect to one of the emperor's Pekinese was punishable by death. In Tibet, the high lama's most honored gifts were Shih Tzus, all of whom were his private property. In the West, ladies of the Court carried their tiny Spaniels and Greyhounds everywhere.

Ricky (Chihuahua) Tojiero shows that even the tiniest dog can be perfectly at ease on a very busy city street.

For as long as two thousand years, Toys have been spoiled, pampered, treated like royalty or babies — and they know it. They demand it and there's no such word as "enough." Groom a Toy for eight hours and he'll wonder why you're stopping so soon. Dress your Toy in a dog tuxedo, sit him on a velvet cushion and feed him caviar out of a crystal bowl at the dining table, and he'll consider it only his due.

Make no mistake — most Toys are very smart. They get away with murder because they're tiny and know exactly how to use their charms. They're great manipulators.

Toys are very social, especially if they are the center of attention, but on the other hand, they don't like to be left alone and can be quite destructive if they are, which may be why so many people bring their Toys to work with them. Sometimes impatient, demanding, and unreliable, they can be viciously jealous of new lovers, children and other pets. Few can be trusted with small children at all. Although most Toys are very hardy and sturdier than they look, unsupervised children can hurt them very badly.

Many have big mouths with high-pitched, piercing barks. They're good watch dogs. In fact, many are so aggressive, they challenge huge dogs without fear — then hide behind you when the larger dog attacks.

Toys are very active, but can get all the exercise they need running around your townhouse or apartment. Most require a lot of grooming, usually with regular trips to a professional groomer. The short-legged, squashed-face breeds are also prone to breathing problems (they snore when asleep, snort when awake) and a genetically abnormal kneecap condition called *patella luxation* which is correctable by surgery.

Group 6. Non-Sporting Dogs

Examples: American Eskimo, Bichon Frise, Boston Terrier, Bulldog, Keeshond, Lhasa Apso and Schipperke.

This the AKC's name for a hodgepodge of dogs, many newly admitted to the AKC Stud Registry (and the right to show). At present, this group includes a couple of Terriers, a couple of Toys, several Working dogs and others not quite as easy to place. No generalities can be drawn about this group.

Group 7. Herding Dogs

Examples: Collie, German Shepherd, Shetland Sheepdog and Welsh Corgi (Cardigan and Pembroke).

At one time, all of these dogs were part of the Working dog group, but it became so large the AKC separated the dogs who were created to herd cattle, sheep and reindeer from the dogs who have always done a variety of jobs in addition to herding. The split is not accurate today, however. All the dogs I recommend in this group are really Working dogs, and everything I say about Working dogs applies to them.

Herding dogs are different from Working dogs in a few areas. They will herd you, nipping at your heels to drive you toward whatever they want. Several have big mouths, since barking helps control animals. And many are great jumpers and climbers — great in Agility competitions, but hard to keep fenced in, as they'll climb over a fence.

Miscellaneous

The AKC's Miscellaneous Class is composed of breeds that are being prepared for acceptance to the AKC Stud Book. Only the Jack Russell Terrier is popular enough to be covered in this book. The others, like the Italian Spinoni, are still extremely rare.

THE BEST DOGS FOR AN URBAN LIFE

By comparing your checklist to the group descriptions, I'm sure you've now spotted one or more groups that are most likely to contain the dog you want.

Now it's time to look at individual breeds. On the following pages, you'll find a detailed, alphabetically arranged analysis of the purebreds I believe are readily available and best suited for city life. Remember to supplement this information with what you've just learned about the dog's group.

The dogs I believe are inappropriate for an urban lifestyle with "working parents" are unsuited in a variety of ways — some are too aggressive. Others are happier outdoors, need a huge amount of exercise, are too high strung for an urban environment, can't be left alone (and are bigger than Toys) or are bred to live in packs. The final cut was based on availability. I eliminated breeds that are so rare in this country that it's very difficult to find a good selection.

MIXED BREEDS

The beauty of purebreds is that you can know a great deal about the dog you select. But purebreds are also quite expensive; and in their search to produce the perfect dog or meet the demands for a very popular dog, breeds have been almost destroyed — crazy Collies were everywhere a few decades ago. Cockers were so popular for so long that the breed is still filled with terrible bloodlines carrying everything from spinal degeneration to excessive shyness and uncontrollable aggression.

You can avoid all this by selecting a mutt, also called a mongrel, a cur, a mixed breed, a Heinz 59. Frequently, mutts are wonderful pets, often calmer, steadier, more intelligent and more loyal than their pedigreed relatives! And most are free or very cheap.

But how can you tell how a mutt puppy is going to turn out? I've seen cases where people were assured that both parents were small dogs only to see the supposed child grow into a Saint Bernard. There are others who chose a short-hair, only to end up with mattresses full of long, silky fur. You can look at feet, or more properly the first leg joint, to get a rough idea of size, but this is only a broad guideline. You can also look at the mother, and sometimes, the dog who is supposed to be the father, but the bottom line is that you can't be sure what a mutt puppy will become. The solution is to adopt a six-month-old or adult.

Another option is to take a cross-breed, the deliberate combination of two purebreds of different breeds. For example, the Cocker Spaniel/Poodle or Cockapoo, is on the verge of becoming an accepted new breed. A breeder who is creating a specific crossbreed over and over knows exactly what the new breed is like — which parent the dog looks like, whose temperament and personality dominates, etc. Accidental crossbreedings are as unpredictable as mutts. There are a million ways those genes can combine.

Dog Selection Chart

BREED/ GROUP	SIZE	ORIGINS	PERSONALITY	PEOPLE SKILLS	TEMPERAMENT	TOUCH	CARE	UNIQUE QUALITIES	TRAINING	ALERTS
AFGHAN HOUND Hound Called Afghan.	Large Ht 25-27" 56-60 lbs	Goes back to 4000 BC, hunted wolves, gazelles. A sight hound who also worked with falcons.	Very intelligent, lordly, gentle, calm, patient, comical only with family. Loyal, cooly affectionate.	Wary of strangers, tolerates your friends but not friendly; not very good with children, protectiveness varies — from over-brave to shy.	Lightening fast, needs exercise or will get bored and cause damage. Not noisy.	Silky soft.	Lots of grooming vital as can develop absesses and other serious problems if left messy. Some say weekly baths.	Pups born smooth-coated, Afghan fur develops after 1 yr. Very high prey drive — cannot ever let off-leash. Gets drippy nose or goes to sleep when anxious. A thief. Extremely touch sensitive — groom with care. See Anesthesia note.	THIS DOG IS NOT FOR THE MEEK or anyone who wants a cuddler. Hard to train. If you're harsh, he'll refuse to EVER do what you ask. Can be creative to get out of doing what you want, selectively deaf. Make him think it was his idea and lavish praise on him.	Rare: Hip dysplasia, juvenile cataracts, hyperthyroidism, enzyme deficiencies.
AIREDALE Terrier Also called King of the Terriers.	Large Ht. 21-23" 40-55 lbs	Great game hunters and one of first police dogs. More Working dog than Terrier.	Intelligent, calm for a Terrier, happy but not silly, loves to play, a sense of humor, honest. Loyal and affectionate.	Very social, friendly, not very good with children. Alert, fearless protector.	Quick moving, fast reactions, very active, needs exercise. Big barker with deep voice.	Wiry, rough (scouring pad)	Docked tail. Needs groomer for clipping. DOES NOT SHED, needs weekly brushing to remove dead hair.	Puppy coat is not the final color. Good swimmer. can be finicky eater. Digger.	Train early and firmly or will become impossible to control. Don't bore him with overtraining. Being firm does not mean being harsh.	Itchy skin quite common — usually can be remedied by change of diet; rarely, hyperthyroid problem.

Height is measured from shoulder to ground. Male and female dogs usually differ in height and weight; ranges given in chart extend from smallest female to largest male (and are AKC specifications). All toys and Terriers are good city dogs; the ones not listed here are eliminated because they are rare in the U.S. and hard to find. When I say "very dangerous" bloodlines, I mean that some irresponsible breeders are deliberately creating unpredictably aggressive dogs who can attack you.
NOTE: All sight hounds and Soft-Coated Wheaten Terrier are extremely sensitive to anesthesia and pain killers. They cannot tolerate some of the medications commonly used, need special dosages. Not all vets are aware of this.

BREED/ GROUP	SIZE	ORIGINS	PERSONALITY	PEOPLE SKILLS	TEMPERAMENT	TOUCH	CARE	UNIQUE QUALITIES	TRAINING	ALERTS
AKITA Working	Large Ht 20-27" 90-100 lbs	From Japan, 300 yrs old, used for hunting boar and bear, also pet.	Intelligent, calm, dignified, very loyal (can be a one-man dog) and a cuddler.	Suspicious of strangers, not good with children, outstanding protector but can overreact.	Moderate speed, doesn't need a lot of exercise as an adult. Deep bark, not noisy.	Slightly coarse top coat but dense, soft under-coat.	Very full, double coat. Prick ears.	Fans says they adapt to small apartment living with tremendous ease.	Very responsive and easy to train.	Shop with care: Some very dangerous bloodlines. Also genetic blindness and hip dysplasia.
AMERICAN ESKIMO Non-sporting Also called Spitz, Esky Miniature Samoyed.	Medium Ht 10-20" 9-25 lbs (great variation)	Not known. Has sled dog origins, is NOT a miniaturized Samoyed.	Intelligent, dignified but can also be clowns at home, Very proud, confident, self-assured. Very loyal (can be one-man), a cuddler.	Suspicious of strangers, not all are good with children, outstanding protector but can overreact	Very quick mover, fast reactions, very energetic (exercise can calm a bit). Barker, shrill sound.	Very soft and silky.	White, full double coat needs lots of continuous care. Prick ears.	Light-footed graceful — many are fabulous jumpers. Good runners.	THIS DOG IS NOT FOR THE MEEK. Defiant and strong-willed. Start young and be firm.	Many can be aggressive to all strangers, including children.
BASSET HOUND (Scent) Hound Called Basset.	Medium Ht 10-15" 25-40 lbs	Royals used for trailing rabbits; has been a companion almost as long as a hunter.	Smart, gentle; a happy dog (despite looks), very loyal (can be one-man) and affectionate.	Tolerates an active social life, excellent with children, too mild-mannered to be a good protector.	Very slow in everything (like slow motion). Big, deep, baying bark. Usually not noisy.	Smooth but a little hard on top, soft under.	Short-haired, double coat, easy-care. Long flap ears.	Nose is second only to bloodhounds; can be picky eaters; not for fast-movers.	NOT FOR IMPATIENT OR THOSE WHO DON'T LIKE TO MAKE STRONG DEMANDS. Very obstinate. Can be difficult to housebreak. Needs lots of praise, spirit can be broken by too much harshness.	None known.

Height is measured from shoulder to ground. Male and female dogs usually differ in height and weight; ranges given in chart extend from smallest female to largest male (and are AKC specifications). All toys and Terriers are good city dogs; the ones not listed here are eliminated because they are rare in the U.S. and hard to find. When I say "very dangerous" bloodlines, I mean that some irresponsible breeders are deliberately creating unpredictably aggressive dogs who can attack you.

NOTE: All sight hounds and Soft-Coated Wheaten Terrier are extremely sensitive to anesthesia and pain killers. They cannot tolerate some of the medications commonly used, need special dosages. Not all vets are aware of this.

Beagle — Bichon Frise

Dog Selection Chart

BREED/ GROUP	SIZE	ORIGINS	PERSONALITY	PEOPLE SKILLS	TEMPERAMENT	TOUCH	CARE	UNIQUE QUALITIES	TRAINING	ALERTS
BEAGLE (Scent) Hound	Medium 13-15" 20-35 lbs	Since 500 AD, has been specialist in rabbit hunting.	Smart, merry scamp, friendly but not especially devoted, affectionate.	Very social (life of the party), tolerates children, too friendly to be protective	Moderate speed, doesn't need lots of exercise, very adaptable and easy-going. Deep, baying bark. Not a barker but can be noisy.	Smooth, soft.	Short-haired, double coat, easy-care. Long flap ears.	Cannot be trusted off-leash, a wanderer. Most don't like lots of running. Overeater.	NOT FOR THOSE WHO DON'T LIKE TO MAKE STRONG DEMANDS. Very obstinate. Needs firmness, absolute consistency. May never be fully trained.	None known.
BEDLINGTON TERRIER Terrier Also known as Gypsy Dog (because he was often used for poaching).	Medium Ht. 15-17.5" 17-23 lbs	Bred to hunt vermin and game, probably has Whippet in lineage -- doesn't have all Terrier qualities.	Smart, graceful, inquisitive, opinionated, clowns a bit. Loyal and very affectionate, some may be cuddlers.	Social, good with older kids, but tends to be jealous. Slow to rouse, then is fearless, a good protector.	Quick mover, fast reactor, energetic, likes a fair amount of exercise. Not as much of a barker as most Terriers..	Soft, somewhat like a Poodle.	Easy to keep but needs regular clipping (not stripping). DOES NOT SHED.	Pups are born dark.	Easy to train although he does need firmness and consistency.	Be sure he's certified free of a genetic disorder called copper toxicosis (CT).
BICHON FRISE Non-sporting Pronounced Beeshone free-zay Called Bichon.	Small Ht 8.5-11.5"	Originated in ancient Rome; after 400 years as noblewomen's pampered pets, popularity waned and became an organ grinders' and circus dog.	Very smart, merry little scamp, very self-assured and confident. Loyal and a cuddler.	Very social, good with children, good with cats and other animals, too friendly to be a good protector.	Fast movers, energetic but adapts to your schedule well. Barks to sound alarm, not too shrill.	Very soft and silky.	Groomers may charge extra for cut, needs constant care to avoid mats. Hair does fluff out naturally but not as puffy as in shows.	Can walk for long distances on hind legs and wave front legs around, jump many times their height. Love to play in dirt.	Sensitive — don't be harsh. Eager to please, training should go quite easily.	None known.

Height is measured from shoulder to ground. Male and female dogs usually differ in height and weight; ranges given in chart extend from smallest female to largest male (and are AKC specifications). All toys and Terriers are good city dogs; the ones not listed here are eliminated because they are rare in the U.S. and hard to find. When I say "very dangerous" bloodlines, I mean that some irresponsible breeders are deliberately creating unpredictably aggressive dogs who can attack you.
NOTE: All sight hounds and Soft-Coated Wheaten Terrier are extremely sensitive to anesthesia and pain killers. They cannot tolerate some of the medications commonly used, need special dosages. Not all vets are aware of this.

BREED/ GROUP	SIZE	ORIGINS	PERSONALITY	PEOPLE SKILLS	TEMPERAMENT	TOUCH	CARE	UNIQUE QUALITIES	TRAINING	ALERTS
BORZOI Non-sporting Once called Russian Wolfhound	Large Ht 29-33" 75-104 lbs	Nobleman's dog in Russia for wolf hunting. Really a sight hound.	Intelligent, aristocratic, graceful, very careful not to break things, dignified. Affectionate.	Suspicious of strangers, reserved yet social, OK with children if raised with them. Not very protective.	Can be beautifully fast at full run, needs exercise but calm and even-tempered at home. Not noisy.	Silky.	An easy keeper. Double coated, bred for cold (watch for heat intolerance).	Eats only as much as a medium-sized dog. They never forget ill treatment. See anesthesia note.	Will not tolerate harshness.	Rarely, gastric dilation and volvulus syndrome (tummy problems), occasional dysplasia.
BOSTON TERRIER Non-sporting Also called The American Gentleman; Buster Brown's dog, Tuxedo Dog.	Small 15-25 lbs	Originally pit fighter (all ferocity has been bred out); one of few American breeds. Not a typical Terrier.	Intelligent, perky but dignified, gentle, self-assured. Loyal and very affectionate.	Enjoys social life, excellent with children. Alert, good protector.	Quick moving, fast reactions, enjoys exercise but doesn't need lots. Bit of a barker.	Sleek, smooth, like satin.	Ears may be cropped. Easy keeper.	Fewer breathing problems than most short-muzzled dogs but not good for smokers, very smoggy cities. Good for joggers, power walkers.	A bit strong-willed but biddable, yet very sensitive — be firm but not harsh, lots of praise. May be hard to housebreak. Easy enough that he's popular with active elderly.	Tends to have birthing problems because of narrow pelvis, Caesarians are common.
BOXER Working	Large Ht 21-24" 50-70 lbs	Ancestors used in bull baiting and fighting boars. Has some Terrier traits.	Intelligent with good common sense, dignified but merry at home. Honest. Very loyal and affectionate, even cuddly.	Suspicious of strangers, social in small groups; excellent with children. Outstanding protector with good judgment.	Fast mover and high jumper but as adult is sedate. Deep bark, not noisy.	Sleek, smooth, like satin. Brushy if rubbed in reverse.	Tail docked, ears may need cropping. Dewclaws usually removed. Short, crisp coat needs little care.	A big drooler. Boxes with front paws. Some breathing difficulties (not for smokers or in smoggy cities). A good runner's dog.	Stubborn but once he learns, very reliable. Be firm but not harsh.	A rare bloodline can produce a really vicious and highly nervous dog.

Height is measured from shoulder to ground. Male and female dogs usually differ in height and weight; ranges given in chart extend from smallest female to largest male (and are AKC specifications). All toys and Terriers are good city dogs; the ones not listed here are eliminated because they are rare in the U.S. and hard to find. When I say "very dangerous" bloodlines, I mean that some irresponsible breeders are deliberately creating unpredictably aggressive dogs who can attack you.
NOTE: All sight hounds and Soft-Coated Wheaten Terrier are extremely sensitive to anesthesia and pain killers. They cannot tolerate some of the medications commonly used, need special dosages. Not all vets are aware of this.

Dog Selection Chart

BREED/ GROUP	SIZE	ORIGINS	PERSONALITY	PEOPLE SKILLS	TEMPERAMENT	TOUCH	CARE	UNIQUE QUALITIES	TRAINING	ALERTS
BULLDOG Non-sporting Known as Winston Churchill's dog although he never had one.	Medium 40-50 lbs	May go back to 1500's, used for bull baiting and boar hunting (all ferocity has been bred out).	Smart, very sweet and dignified, extremely calm but fun-loving. Honest. Loyal and very affectionate.	Quite social, wonderful and playful with children. Totally non-aggressive, not a protector.	Slow moving and lethargic, not active. Deep bark almost never used.	Very sleek, smooth, like satin.	Flat single coat is easy-care. Short, flap ears.	Big drooler. Sloppy eater. Can have serious breathing difficulties.	Most gentle of dogs, can be destroyed by harshness but so powerful, needs firmness. Start young, go slow, never be harsh, give tons of praise.	Very difficult to breed, sterility is common, Caesarian is usual. Prone to elbow dislocation.
CAIRN TERRIER Terrier Toto in *Wizard of Oz.*	Small Ht 9.5-10" 12-14 lbs	Hunter of rats, badgers, also a house pet.	Intelligent, charming, infectiously bright personality, merry. Very loyal and a cuddler.	Aloof with strangers, not uncomfortable in groups. Good with older children. Great courage, good protector.	Moderately quick mover, fast reactions, needs little exercise but is very active. A barker, on the shrill side.	Very coarse, scrub brush.	Shaggy double coat needs groomer for plucking. Prick ears.	Adapts well to varied lifestyles. Usually likes water. Legs are too short for runner but good for walkers.	Needs firm hand, steady consistency.	Prone to skin conditions.
CHIHUAHUA Toy The Taco Bell dog.	Tiny 1-6 lbs	Lap dog. Some say was raised as food (like cows).	Smart, can be dependent and babyish if you let him; high strung. Very loyal (to only one or two people), a cuddler.	Does not like dogs or people outside family (not social), not good with children, tries to be protective.	Fast and energetic like a Terrier, a bit hyper. A barker, very shrill sound.	Soft and sleek. (There is a long-haired variety with silky fur, more care.)	Very short, smooth coat may be double; easy care.	Tiny, very delicate, does not travel well when shipped as baggage. Can be foolishly aggressive, provoking fights then hiding behind you.	Treat like a dog or will be a spoiled brat who cowers at the sound of a fly. Some say hard to train.	Health is somewhat fragile; needs coat in least chill.

Height is measured from shoulder to ground. Male and female dogs usually differ in height and weight; ranges given in chart extend from smallest female to largest male (and are AKC specifications). All toys and Terriers are good city dogs; the ones not listed here are eliminated because they are rare in the U.S. and hard to find. When I say "very dangerous" bloodlines, I mean that some irresponsible breeders are deliberately creating unpredictably aggressive dogs who can attack you.
NOTE: All sight hounds and Soft-Coated Wheaten Terrier are extremely sensitive to anesthesia and pain killers. They cannot tolerate some of the medications commonly used, need special dosages. Not all vets are aware of this.

BREED/ GROUP	SIZE	ORIGINS	PERSONALITY	PEOPLE SKILLS	TEMPERAMENT	TOUCH	CARE	UNIQUE QUALITIES	TRAINING	ALERTS
COCKER SPANIEL Sporting Called a Cocker.	Medium Ht 14-16" 20-28 lbs	Exceptional bird dog but has been house pet for very long time. Today's pet Cocker isn't a Sporting Dog any more.	Intelligent, merry, charming, sedate but with a mischievous streak. Very loyal, a cuddler.	Very social, enjoys children. Alert, fairly good protector.	Quick mover, likes but doesn't need a lot of exercise. Not usually a barker.	Soft, silky, curly fur.	Tail docked. Double coat grows to floor (most have groomer clip), needs care. Long flap ears.	English Cocker is NOT same dog. Most love water. Good for power walkers, joggers.	Needs firm hand but never harsh (some can turn/others are broken). Master at breaking out of enclosures.	Shop with care: Many bad lines with genetic problems: Shy, nasty, crippling spinal disease, spreading foot.
DACHSHUND Hound Also called Sausage Dog, Wiener Dog, Dach'l. Comes in Smooth Coat, Rough/Wire and Long Hair.	Tiny version weighs less than 9 lbs; Small is 9-15 lbs	Badger hunter but always house pet, too. Modern dog from Germany but may go back to ancient Egypt. More Terrier than Hound.	Smart, clever, merry but also tough and determined. Even-tempered. Very loyal (can be one-man/one-family dog), a cuddler.	Friendly but only truly loving with his family, very good with children. Courageous and even over-protective.	Lively and active, but slow mover (little legs). Moderate exercise needs, Big-dog, deep baying bark rarely used.	Smooth coat is short and bristly. Wire hair is hard, coarse.. Long hair is silky.	Flop ears. Wire needs plucking by groomer. Long needs lots of care.	Keeps self groomed like a cat, almost no odor. Can be a prankster. Quite long lived. Can't get up on furniture. Not good for runners.	Obstinate. Start early, be very firm and consistent.	None known.
FOX TERRIER Terrier (Asta in *The Thin Man*) Comes in Wired-Haired and Smooth Coated.	Medium Ht 12-18" 13-16 lbs	Vermin hunting, later fox, but also house pet.	Very intelligent, perky, good sense of humor. Very self-assured. Extremely courageous, very loyal and a cuddler.	Sociable but not with mobs, OK with older children. Fearless, aggressive protectors, quick on trigger.	Very rapid reactions, fast movers, quick to snap. Very active, enjoys long walks. Big barker on shrill side.	Wire hair is coarse, wiry scrub-brush; smooth is still a bit coarse.	Wire-hair tail is docked. Flip over ears. Needs plucking by groomer.	Walks with springy feet, great jumper, very sturdy and healthy. Good runners' dog.	A true terrier — start early, be firm and consistent.	Some bloodlines turn this naturally hyper dog to a nervous wreck or fight starter.

Height is measured from shoulder to ground. Male and female dogs usually differ in height and weight; ranges given in chart extend from smallest female to largest male (and are AKC specifications). All toys and Terriers are good city dogs; the ones not listed here are eliminated because they are rare in the U.S. and hard to find. When I say "very dangerous" bloodlines, I mean that some irresponsible breeders are deliberately creating unpredictably aggressive dogs who can attack you.

NOTE: All sight hounds and Soft-Coated Wheaten Terrier are extremely sensitive to anesthesia and pain killers. They cannot tolerate some of the medications commonly used, need special dosages. Not all vets are aware of this.

German Shepard — Great Dane

Dog Selection Chart

BREED/ GROUP	SIZE	ORIGINS	PERSONALITY	PEOPLE SKILLS	TEMPERAMENT	TOUCH	CARE	UNIQUE QUALITIES	TRAINING	ALERTS
GERMAN SHEPARD Herding Called Alsatian in England; also Police Dog. Rin Tin Tin was most famous.	Large Ht 23-25" 60-85 lbs	Not an ancient dog, created to herd and help farmers; has done more jobs than any other dog. Really a Working dog.	Very intelligent, regal bearing, great dignity but can be playful and happy. Very honest. Very loyal (can be on-man). A cuddler.	Suspicious of strangers not very social, extraordinary with children (all ages), great protector with good judgment.	Can be fast but is usually moderate in actions and activity. Needs trotting exercise when growing. Deep bark, not noisy.	A bit coarse top coat, soft wool under.	Dense double or triple coat (amazing shedder), requires little care. Prick ears.	Intense desire to please. Likes to have a job. Too fast a gait for runners.	Learns fast so be sure you know what you want before teaching. Responds to voice tone without any harsher training.	Special breeders are producing very large, incredibly aggressive, vicious and dangerous dogs. Hip dysplasia is epidemic.
GOLDEN RETRIEVER Sporting Called Golden.	Large Ht 22-24" 65-75 lbs	Originally a bird dog with a lot of spaniel traits. Now really a Working Dog.	Very intelligent, gentle, usually calm but can be very merry, even a clown at times. Naturally happy. Very loyal, a cuddler.	Very social, wonderful with children (all ages). A good protector.	Reacts and moves with moderate speed, likes and needs exercise. Deep bark, can be a bit barky.	Silky soft coat that glows gold in sunlight.	Coat may be double, is water-repellant. Often has webbed feet (clean out ice in winter).	Loves water. May carry toy in mouth. Nose may get pink in cold weather. Some use front paws like hands.	Great desire to please, can become overly nervous and timid if you're too harsh. Train with gentleness, lots of praise.	Shop with care: Irresponsible breeding around. Avoid field trial sporting bloodlines. Hip dysplasia common.
GREAT DANE Working Called the Dane.	Giant Ht 28-36" Up to 160 lbs	Originally boar hunters with terrible fierce temper (totally bred out now).	Intelligent, very elegant, sedate, amiable. Dignified but can be playful especially when young. Honest. Loyal and affectionate.	Suspicious with strangers but social. Great with children (may prefer to adults). Moderately protective.	Lethargic as adults but can move quickly if they want. Low exercise needs for adults. Very deep bark, not noisy.	Sleek, a bit coarse, very brushy when petted backward.	Cropped ears. Can have double coat. Very easy keeper.	Leaners (they lean on you all the time). Like company — not good if you travel a lot. Expose to traffic and outdoors when young or can become fearful.	Start training at 4 mos. They learn very fast. Very sensitive so handle gently, don't be harsh, give lots of praise.	Tendency to swelling and/or soreness around knees, bone disorders, severe calluses and hip dysplasia.

Height is measured from shoulder to ground. Male and female dogs usually differ in height and weight; ranges given in chart extend from smallest female to largest male (and are AKC specifications). All toys and Terriers are good city dogs; the ones not listed here are eliminated because they are rare in the U.S. and hard to find. When I say "very dangerous" bloodlines, I mean that some irresponsible breeders are deliberately creating unpredictably aggressive dogs who can attack you.

NOTE: All sight hounds and Soft-Coated Wheaten Terrier are extremely sensitive to anesthesia and pain killers. They cannot tolerate some of the medications commonly used, need special dosages. Not all vets are aware of this.

BREED/ GROUP	SIZE	ORIGINS	PERSONALITY	PEOPLE SKILLS	TEMPERAMENT	TOUCH	CARE	UNIQUE QUALITIES	TRAINING	ALERTS
GREYHOUND Hound Also known as The Racing Dog, the Grey.	Large Ht 26-30" 60-70 lbs Track dogs slightly smaller.	In ancient Egypt, they were mummified with their owners. In 11-14th centuries, only nobility could own a Grey. A sight hound.	Very smart, gentle, graceful, looks delicate, playful at home. Loyal and very affectionate, even a cuddler.	Aloof with strangers, tolerates children, not aggressive, not a protector.	Speed is a dash, not a lot of endurance. Not active, calm, easy-going, needs little exercise. Not noisy.	Softest velvet.	They keep themselves quite clean. An easy keeper.	Strong prey drive — can't be let off-leash, may kill cats (if you have a cat, get prospects tested). Many can swim. Metabolize toxins very slowly. See anesthesia note.	Quick learners, sensitive and docile.	Susceptible to bloat. Prone to elbow problems and hypothyroidism. Some say prone to cancer.
ITALIAN GREYHOUND Toy	Tiny 5-10 lbs	2,000 year old lap dog, not a miniaturized Greyhound. Not at all like other Hounds.	Smart, exquisitely dainty and graceful. Dignified, proud, self-assured. Loyal and very affectionate.	Not good with large crowds but sociable with small groups, not good with children, not very protective.	Fast mover, very active. Deep bark for its size. Not noisy.	Very soft, velvety coat.	Thin, glossy coat. DOES NOT SHED. Almost never needs bath. Flip over ears.	Very fragile — do not allow on furniture as could break leg getting off. Not a typical Toy. Good ruuner's dog.	Be very gentle as dog is very delicate. Don't use a slip collar of any kind.	Needs coat in cold.
JACK RUSSELL TERRIER Misc. Called the Jack. Eddie on *Frazier.*	Small Ht 12-14" 13-17 lbs	Developed in south of England in late 1800's to work fox above and below ground. Also bolted fox for The Hunts. Definitely a Terrier.	Smart, bold, clever, tenacious, playful, exuberant. Self-assured, demands attention. Very loyal and affectionate.	Friendly, social, not good with children. Very protective, fearless.	Fast, quick, energetic, constantly in motion. Needs lots of exercise. Can be a barker.	Quite coarse. Comes in Smooth coat, Broken and Rough (Eddie is Rough).	Docked tail. Flat, hard, dense doublecoat, needs plucking.	Closest to hunting roots of all Terriers — strong prey drive, some kill cats. Digger. Can jump, climb and dig under fences. Can also be aggressive with other dogs.	Needs great firmness and consistency. NOT FOR THE MILD-MANNERED.	None known.

Height is measured from shoulder to ground. Male and female dogs usually differ in height and weight; ranges given in chart extend from smallest female to largest male (and are AKC specifications). All toys and Terriers are good city dogs; the ones not listed here are eliminated because they are rare in the U.S. and hard to find. When I say "very dangerous" bloodlines, I mean that some irresponsible breeders are deliberately creating unpredictably aggressive dogs who can attack you.
NOTE: All sight hounds and Soft-Coated Wheaten Terrier are extremely sensitive to anesthesia and pain killers. They cannot tolerate some of the medications commonly used, need special dosages. Not all vets are aware of this.

Dog Selection Chart

BREED/ GROUP	SIZE	ORIGINS	PERSONALITY	PEOPLE SKILLS	TEMPERAMENT	TOUCH	CARE	UNIQUE QUALITIES	TRAINING	ALERTS
KEESHOND Non-sporting Pronounced case-hound. Also called Kees (Case), Dutch barge dog. The Dutchman.	Medium Ht 17-18"	Guarded Dutch canal barges on which families lived. Really a Working Dog. May have arrived in Holland on a Viking ship.	Intelligent, proud, self-assured. Great dignity but fun-loving at home. Honest dog. Very loyal and very affectionate (even a cuddler).	Suspicious of strangers but social. Very good with children (all ages), excellent protector with fine judgment.	Quick reactions and moderately active. Adjusts very well to cities, not big exercise needs. Not noisy.	Top coat a bit stiff, soft under-neath.	Very dense, double coat with lion mane. Coat is waterproof, does not mat, needs little care. Prick ears.	Looks like he's wearing spectacles. Very sure-footed. Good for runners. Expose to traffic and outdoors when young or can become fearful.	Quite sensitive, don't be harsh. Easy to train although occasionally resistant to doing what he doesn't want to. Persist with patience,	None known.
LABRADOR RETRIEVER Sporting Also called the Lab or Labby.	Large Ht 21-24" 55-75 lbs	Probably started as a ship dog-guard, later become an outstanding duck dog. More like a Working Dog.	Smart, sedate, solid, calm but fun-loving. Very honest. Loyal and very affectionate.	People-oriented, very social, very good with children, not a very good protector.	Easy-going, moderate mover, can become bored if left alone too much (will bark or destroy), needs lots of exercise. Very active when young.	Very soft, brushy coat that feels slightly oily.	Double coat. Easy keeper.	Doesn't mature til age 3. Nose can turn pink in cold. Has an otter tail (thick at base), web feet, loves to swim. May bring you gifts. May learn to open doors or latches. A roamer.	Easy to train but has the ability to disobey knowingly (needed in rescue dogs who must not obey orders they know take them into danger). A good rescue AND therapy dog.	Get show or pet dog, not field. Labs' temperament is bred in, so home breds are riskier than with other dogs. Rarely, hip or elbow dysplasia, eye problems.
LHASA APSO Non-sporting Also called Tibetan temple dog. Lion Dog of Lhasa.	Small Ht 9-11"	At least 800 years old, was indoor guard of Tibetan temples. More like a Toy.	Intelligent, regal attitude with occasional spurts of merry playfulness. Quite honest. Very loyal (can be one-man), a cuddler.	Suspicious of strangers and warm only to family, not social, OK with older children but can snap if teased. Aggressive protector with good judgment.	Fast reactions, fast mover for size, frisky. Deep bark sound, a bit of a barker.	Long shaggy coat is somewhat coarse; if kept short, silky curls.	Long coat needs constant attention and professional grooming. Long flop ears.	Ideal city dog. Very hardy and sturdy, not easily hurt. But skin is extremely sensitive — groom gently. From a cold country so watch out for heat sensitivity.	Trains best when started young, give lots of praise. If you're too harsh, dog can turn on you.	None known. If kept in short coat, watch for reactions to temperature extremes (could need coat and/or air conditioner.)

Height is measured from shoulder to ground. Male and female dogs usually differ in height and weight; ranges given in chart extend from smallest female to largest male (and are AKC specifications). All toys and Terriers are good city dogs; the ones not listed here are eliminated because they are rare in the U.S. and hard to find. When I say "very dangerous" bloodlines, I mean that some irresponsible breeders are deliberately creating unpredictably aggressive dogs who can attack you.

NOTE: All sight hounds and Soft-Coated Wheaten Terrier are extremely sensitive to anesthesia and pain killers. They cannot tolerate some of the medications commonly used, need special dosages. Not all vets are aware of this.

Dog Selection Chart

BREED/ GROUP	SIZE	ORIGINS	PERSONALITY	PEOPLE SKILLS	TEMPERAMENT	TOUCH	CARE	UNIQUE QUALITIES	TRAINING	ALERTS
MALTESE Toy	Tiny 2-7 lbs	Lap dog for centuries, some say 3,000 years old. Appeared in paintings in 1760's.	Smartest of Toys very gentle and sweet with eager, trusting nature, gay and playful. Loyal and very cuddly.	Sociable (likes to be center of attention), good with older children if not teased. Fearless protector.	Fast reactions, very fast mover. Highly energetic. Can be a barker, shrill sound.	Silky soft.	White, straight hair to floor needs enormous care, trips to groomer. Single coat. Flap ears.	Sturdy, healthy, great stamina and hearty appetite.	Treat as a dog. Train gently but firmly, lots of praise.	If kept short, watch out for temperature variations. Some Maltese have non-straight, wooly fur (AKC flaw).
MINIATURE PINSCHER Toy Also called Min Pin.	Tiny Ht 10-12" 6-10 lbs	Bred as lap dog, NOT descended from Dobermans (pre-date them by centuries).	Smart, perky, self-assured. Independent and a bit stubborn (not for the meek). Very loyal (can be one-man) and affectionate.	Aloof with strangers, not social, OK with older children. Alert, bold protector.	Fast reactions, very active, tends on hyper side. Barker with shrill sound.	Coarse.	Ears cropped, tail docked. Smooth single coats needs little work, easy keeper.	Has high-stepping "hackney" gait. Very muscular dog.	Be firm and consistent but not too harsh (can turn nasty if you come on too tough).	SHOP WITH CARE: Some bloodlines are producing hysterical, lethargic, shy or vicious dogs.
NEWFOUND-LAND Working Also called Newfie. Nana in *Pter Pan*. Black & white is called Landseer.	Giant Ht 26-28" 110-150 lbs or more	Life saver and assistant on boats (extraordinary life-saving instincts remain).	Very intelligent, stately air, calm, ever serene. Very loyal (can be one-man). Very affectionate, even a cuddler.	Slow to warm up to strangers, not comfortable in big groups. Magnificent with children, even infants. Protective but slow to rouse.	Extremely even-tempered, slow mover who can be fast when rescuing. Doesn't want lots of exercise. Great deep bark rarely used.	Very soft and silky but slightly oily.	Dense, shaggy coat sheds water, needs little care. Webbed feet (clean ice balls in winter), small flap ears.	Loves water (phenomenal endurance in water). Likes to have a job. Average life expectancy 8 yrs.	Easy to train, wants to please. Be very very gentle, praise highly. Harshness is totally unnecessary.	Prone to weak heart and hip dysplasia.

Height is measured from shoulder to ground. Male and female dogs usually differ in height and weight; ranges given in chart extend from smallest female to largest male (and are AKC specifications). All toys and Terriers are good city dogs; the ones not listed here are eliminated because they are rare in the U.S. and hard to find. When I say "very dangerous" bloodlines, I mean that some irresponsible breeders are deliberately creating unpredictably aggressive dogs who can attack you.

NOTE: All sight hounds and Soft-Coated Wheaten Terrier are extremely sensitive to anesthesia and pain killers. They cannot tolerate some of the medications commonly used, need special dosages. Not all vets are aware of this.

Dog Selection Chart

BREED/ GROUP	SIZE	ORIGINS	PERSONALITY	PEOPLE SKILLS	TEMPERAMENT	TOUCH	CARE	UNIQUE QUALITIES	TRAINING	ALERTS
NORWICH TERRIER Terrier	Small Ht 10" or less, 10-12 lbs	Not recognized in England until 1936; in 1979, separated into Norwich and Norfolk (only difference is ears).	Smart, spirited, no-nonsense. Self-assured, confident. Very devoted, craves affection, cuddly.	Friendly but not very good with children. Good protector.	Lively, vivacious, needs regular exercise to take edge off his energy. Can be barky.	Harsh, bristly coat.	Docked tail. Needs great deal of work (daily stripping) to maintain scruffy look.	Needs human companionship, not good for frequent traveler, can tolerate other animals better than most terriers.	Housebreaking may be difficult and take time. Be very firm and consistent but not harsh.	Be sure parents are free of epilepsy and collapsed trachea.
PAPILLON Toy Also called Butterfly Dog, Squirrel Dog.	Tiny Ht 8-11"	Started as a ratter but has been lap dog since 1500's. Featured in many Old Master paintings.	Smart, dainty, elegant, graceful. Very proud and self-assured. Strong-willed. A charmer. Loyal and very affectionate.	Sociable (likes to be center of attention), not good with children. Very aggressive, good protector.	Fast reactions, quick movements, very active and lively. A bit hyper. Can be a barker, with shrill sound.	Very soft and silky.	Full, long, single coat needs lots of care. Butterfly-like prick ears.	Healthy, can be good for power walkers and joggers.	Be firm and consistent — has a mind of his own.	Ears don't always go up (hard to predict); some dogs are too hyper, even in an otherwise good litter (test carefully).
PEKINGESE Toy Also called Peke, Lion Dog.	Tiny 6-14 lbs	2,000 years old, Chinese emperor's palace guards; nobles had to bow to them.	Intelligent, haughty and regal, not an ounce of servility, totally self-assured. Very loyal, affectionate but not warm.	Not fond of an active social life; aloof to strangers, jealous and intolerant of children. A brave and fearless protector.	Fast reactions, lively, active but short legs restrict movement. A barker with a shrill voice.	Coarse on top, wooly underneath.	Washes self like a cat but long, thick, double coat needs constant grooming and professional sessions. Long, flap ears.	Front legs shorter than back. Pushed in muzzle causes breathing difficulties (not for smokers or smoggy cities).	NOT FOR THE MEEK. If you're not firm, Pekes will take over. Stubborn, will test you but sensitive—don't be harsh.	None known.

Height is measured from shoulder to ground. Male and female dogs usually differ in height and weight; ranges given in chart extend from smallest female to largest male (and are AKC specifications). All toys and Terriers are good city dogs; the ones not listed here are eliminated because they are rare in the U.S. and hard to find. When I say "very dangerous" bloodlines, I mean that some irresponsible breeders are deliberately creating unpredictably aggressive dogs who can attack you.

NOTE: All sight hounds and Soft-Coated Wheaten Terrier are extremely sensitive to anesthesia and pain killers. They cannot tolerate some of the medications commonly used, need special dosages. Not all vets are aware of this.

Dog Selection Chart

BREED/ GROUP	SIZE	ORIGINS	PERSONALITY	PEOPLE SKILLS	TEMPERAMENT	TOUCH	CARE	UNIQUE QUALITIES	TRAINING	ALERTS
POMERANIAN Toy Also called Pom.	Tiny 3-7 lbs	Originally a larger sled dog and reindeer herder; a lap dog for centuries but they still think they're big.	Smart, full of pride, a charmer with occasional spurts of infectious merriment, self-assured, assertive. Loyal and affectionate	Only fair in large groups, good in small; not reliable with children. Protective, a bit quick to react.	Fast reactions, very lively and active (on the hyper side). A barker with a shrill voice.	Very soft and wooly.	Huge double coat needs lots of care all the time plus trips to groomer. Prick ears.	Fox face; very alert to everything that's going on around him. Good power walker or jogger dog.	Be firm and consistent. NOT FOR THE MILD-MANNERED.	Test pups carefully to eliminate any who are snappy.
POODLE Non-sporting Toy Standard size is not a good city dog.	Small Ht 10-15" Tiny Ht under 10"	A very old retriever with spaniel roots. Smaller versions have been companions and lap dogs for ages.	Very intelligent, assertive, very self-assured. A charmer and prankster, happy. Very loyal, a cuddler.	Very social (life of parties), not totally trustworthy with children. Fairly good protector.	Fast reactions, very active. Can be a barker if babied and the smaller the dog, the shriller the bark.	Soft and wooly.	Docked tail. Dense, curly coat needs regular trimming by groomer but DOES NOT SHED. Little to no odor.	Does not like being alone, can become destructive. Easily bored. Miniatures are excellent runner and jogger dogs.	Don't let him charm you out of lessons; be firm.	SHOP WITH CARE: Quite a few overly hyper, nervy poodles are being produced.
PUG Toy Also called Dutch Pug.	Tiny 14-18 lbs	From China, not The Netherlands. Came to Europe in 17 century. Always a lap dog.	Smart, placid but happy. A busybody who always wants to know what's going on. Demanding and self-assured. Loyal and affectionate.	Very social, OK with older children, not a very good protector.	Very easy-going, not very active. Has a deep bark for size but not noisy.	Coarse and rather brushy.	Short, dense coat needs little care. An easy keeper.	Breathing problems (not for smoggy areas or smokers). Snores wonderfully well. Otherwise very robust, sturdy and healthy. Sensitive to cold (use coat in winter).	Never use slip collars (easy to suffocate). Avoid distractions while training.	None known.

Height is measured from shoulder to ground. Male and female dogs usually differ in height and weight; ranges given in chart extend from smallest female to largest male (and are AKC specifications). All toys and Terriers are good city dogs; the ones not listed here are eliminated because they are rare in the U.S. and hard to find. When I say "very dangerous" bloodlines, I mean that some irresponsible breeders are deliberately creating unpredictably aggressive dogs who can attack you.

NOTE: All sight hounds and Soft-Coated Wheaten Terrier are extremely sensitive to anesthesia and pain killers. They cannot tolerate some of the medications commonly used, need special dosages. Not all vets are aware of this.

Dog Selection Chart

BREED/ GROUP	SIZE	ORIGINS	PERSONALITY	PEOPLE SKILLS	TEMPERAMENT	TOUCH	CARE	UNIQUE QUALITIES	TRAINING	ALERTS
SAINT BERNARD Working Also called Saint, Avalanche Dog, Keg Dog.	Giant Ht 25-28" up to 175lbs	Life saver in cool mountain regions, especially used in Switzerland to find people lost in avalanches and blizzards.	Smart, placid, dignified but can be very fun-loving. An honest dog. Very loyal and very affectionate.	Easy-going and social, excellent with children of all ages. Very good protector with good judgment.	Passive, slow, very lethargic and inactive as an adult. Not noisy.	Slightly coarse outer coat, soft under-neath.	Short and long hair varieties, both with dense double coat. Sheds profusely. Flap ears.	Drools profusely (slobbers) but keeps self clean. May not tolerate heat well. Not long-lived.	Train very young. Cannot be treated harshly (will turn excessively fearful or worse). Generally, learns well and easily.	Choose most outgoing, energetic pup in litter (quietest will be almost comatose as adult).
SCHIPPERKE Non-sporting Pronounced sheep-er-kee. Also called Skippy, Little Captain.	Small Up to 18 lbs More like a Working dog.	Guard dog on Flemish barges, which were often family homes.	Smart, bright but serious air, can be merry at times. Very loyal and affectionate.	Suspicious of strangers, not good with large groups. Tolerates chil-dren well. Very protec-tive	Fast reactions, active and alert; bred to live on a boat so city life is perfect. Doesn't bark without cause.	Somewhat coarse to pet.	Docked tail. Has full lion mane that needs regu-lar groom-ing; hair short every-where else and keeps easily.	Curious about everything. Exceptionally long lived (20+ years). Good for joggers.	Generally learns well and trains easily.	None known.
SCHNAUZER Terrier (Standard size is not a good city dog.)	Medium Ht 12-14" 12-15 lbs	Ratter and all-purpose dog, also companion for horses.	Very intelligent, merry but with great self-possession and assurance. Strong willed, assertive. Very loyal, a cud-dler.	Social with smaller groups, not large; not good with small or teasing children (can snap). Alert, fearless protector, a bit fast to react.	Very fast reactions, very active, a bit hyper. A barker though not as bad as most Terriers.	Coarse to touch; when plucked and groomed, short hair is sleek.	Cropped ears, docked tail. Short, wiry, double coat needs plucking by a groomer.	Doesn't mind being left alone, very robust, very adaptable. Good runner's dog.	NOT FOR THE MEEK. Can be obsti-nate. Be firm but not harsh, provide lots of praise and never give an inch.	SHOP WITH CARE: Some lines can be excessively shy, fear biters; others are vicious.

Height is measured from shoulder to ground. Male and female dogs usually differ in height and weight; ranges given in chart extend from smallest female to largest male (and are AKC specifications). All toys and Terriers are good city dogs; the ones not listed here are eliminated because they are rare in the U.S. and hard to find. When I say "very dangerous" bloodlines, I mean that some irresponsible breeders are deliberately creating unpredictably aggressive dogs who can attack you.

NOTE: All sight hounds and Soft-Coated Wheaten Terrier are extremely sensitive to anesthesia and pain killers. They cannot tolerate some of the medications commonly used, need special dosages. Not all vets are aware of this.

BREED/ GROUP	SIZE	ORIGINS	PERSONALITY	PEOPLE SKILLS	TEMPERAMENT	TOUCH	CARE	UNIQUE QUALITIES	TRAINING	ALERTS
SCOTTISH TERRIER Terrier Also called Scottie.	Small Ht about 10" 18-22 lbs	Hunter of vermin and ground game in the wilds of Scotland.	Intelligent, has an air of great dignity and wisdom, but at home, can be merry.. Honest. A tough-minded spirit. Very loyal and very affectionate.	Sociable, even amiable, good with older children. Good protector.	Moderate reaction speed, only moderately active for a terrier. Not a big barker for a terrier, has a very deep, big-dog bark.	Very coarse and stiff coat, like a scrub brush.	Docked tail. Wiry, dense double coat needs little care but should be plucked by a groomer.	Doesn't like being alone for long periods. Very short legs limits speed. Bred for a cool climate, watch in great heat	NOT FOR GENTLE PEACE LOVER. Hard to housebreak. Be firm, give lots of praise, persevere.	Rare lines produce shy, fear-biting or timid dogs.
SHETLAND SHEEPDOG Herding Also called Sheltie.	Medium Ht 13-16" Up to 20 lbs	Sheep herders and farm dogs (not miniaturized Collies). Big winners in herding, agility and obedience competition — very versatile.	Very intelligent, dainty and elegant. Dignified with spurts of great merriment. Self-assured, proud. Very loyal (can be one-man), cuddlers.	Reserved with strangers but sociable, not reliable with children (can get irritated and snap). Alert, good protectors.	Fast reactions, moderately active, good stamina, tend to be nervy. Big barker with rather sharp tone.	Very soft, guard hairs on top a bit stiffer.	Long, dense double coat that mats, needs constant care, occasional groomer visits. Flip-over prick ears.	Prefers peace and quiet in environment rather than lots of noise. May herd you around. Good for power walkers and joggers.	Very sensitive, handle gently, give lots of praise. Learns well and quickly.	Expose to street and strangers when young or can become excessively fearful. Poor breeding can produce snappy, shy, extra-nervous dogs.
SHIH TZU Toy Also called Tibetan lion dog.	Tiny Ht 8-11" 9-18 lbs	Exotic gift dog of Tibet's Dalai Lama, lap dog and pet for centuries.	Smart, merry, with great self-possession. A bit of a regal air. Loyal and a cuddler.	Reserved with strangers but comfortable with crowds. Not reliable with children. Alert protector.	Moderately fast reactions, can be active but rather calm-tempered for a Toy. Can be a barker if not curbed young.	Silky top coat and wooly underneath. If you keep in short cut, silky curls.	Long, dense double coat mats, needs lots of attention, occasional groomer visits. Flap ears.	Short legs prevent fast movement. If you keep in a short cut, watch out for temperature extremes	Hard to housebreak. Needs a commanding, firm, consistent attitude.	A rare few are too hyper and snappy.

Height is measured from shoulder to ground. Male and female dogs usually differ in height and weight; ranges given in chart extend from smallest female to largest male (and are AKC specifications). All toys and Terriers are good city dogs; the ones not listed here are eliminated because they are rare in the U.S. and hard to find. When I say "very dangerous" bloodlines, I mean that some irresponsible breeders are deliberately creating unpredictably aggressive dogs who can attack you.
NOTE: All sight hounds and Soft-Coated Wheaten Terrier are extremely sensitive to anesthesia and pain killers. They cannot tolerate some of the medications commonly used, need special dosages. Not all vets are aware of this.

Dog Selection Chart

BREED/ GROUP	SIZE	ORIGINS	PERSONALITY	PEOPLE SKILLS	TEMPERAMENT	TOUCH	CARE	UNIQUE QUALITIES	TRAINING	ALERTS
SILKY TERRIER Toy Also called Sidney Silky or Australian Silky.	Tiny Ht 9-10" 8-10 lbs	Hunted vermin and snakes, also used as a house companion. One of few breeds from Australia.	Smart, bright and alert attitude. Merry, fun-loving but self-assured and confident. Loyal and affectionate.	Sociable and friendly, does not tolerate children well. Keenly alert and protective.	Quick reactions, very lively and active, a bit on the hyper side. A barker with a shrill tone.	Very silky, soft fur.	Docked tail. Straight, 5-6" coat needs groomer and your constant attention. Prick ears.	Tiny but very much a terrier in personality. You might be able to keep in a short cut.	Needs a frim hand.	Expose to street life when young. Watch out for excessively nervy or shy dogs.
SOFT-COATED WEATON TERRIER Terrier Also called Wheaton.	Medium Ht 17-19" 30-40 lbs	Irish farm dog, around for about 200 years. Served all needs including hunting vermin, guarding and herding. Not a typical Terrier.	Intelligent, great joy of life, a bit puppyish and very playful but great courage. Very loyal and very affectionate.	Social, good with older children. Protective but never picks a fight.	Fast reactor and mover, very active, destructive if not exercised regularly. Not noisy.	Silky soft.	Docked tail. Single coat, does not shed, needs groomer 4-6 times/yr (do not pluck), does mat if not brushed often.	Mature at 2 years, long lived. Pups dark colored, all adults are blonds. Can be picky eater. Heat sensitive. Whirls when happy. Good runner's dog. See anesthesia note.	Eager to please, not nearly as tough or strong-willed as other Terriers. Very good competitive dogs — obedience, agility and flyball.	Some dysplasia and eye problems.
WEST HIGHLAND TERRIER Terrier Also called Westie.	Small Ht 10-11" Up to 20 lbs	Hunted ground animals, also a house companion.	Very intelligent, great self-esteem but light-hearted and merry. Very determined. Loyal, a cuddler.	Very sociable, good with older children who don't tease. Very protective, good judgment.	Quick reactions, high activity level but calm and steady. Does not like being ignored. A bit barky, high pitch.	Coarse if plucked, soft if cut.	Flat, dense, double coat is easy care but needs plucking. No dog odor. Prick ears.	Called "best of Terriers" — good city dog. Very hardy. Ones I've known all watched TV!	Must be firm and consistent, use lots of praise, not as stubborn as most terriers.	
YORKSHIRE TERRIER Toy Also called Yorky.	Tiny Ht up to 7" 3-7 lbs	Created as a lap dog from working terriers and retains much of the terrier spirit.	Intelligent, merry, very self-possessed. Determined. Loyal, a cuddler.	Very social, tolerates older children. Alert protector who doesn't always take his size into account.	Fast reactions, very active but quiets down as he ages. Can be a barker, with high shrill tone, but usually only for cause.	Silky to pet.	Docked tail. Long hair to floor, lots of grooming, professional visits. Prick ears.	Born black. Very sturdy. Ask groomer if can be kept in short cut (watch temperatures).	Housebreaking may be a bit difficult. Be firm and start training when young.	Avoid pups that seem too nervy.

Height is measured from shoulder to ground. Male and female dogs usually differ in height and weight; ranges given in chart extend from smallest female to largest male (and are AKC specifications). All toys and Terriers are good city dogs; the ones not listed here are eliminated because they are rare in the U.S. and hard to find. When I say "very dangerous" bloodlines, I mean that some irresponsible breeders are deliberately creating unpredictably aggressive dogs who can attack you.

NOTE: All sight hounds and Soft-Coated Wheaten Terrier are extremely sensitive to anesthesia and pain killers. They cannot tolerate some of the medications commonly used, need special dosages. Not all vets are aware of this.

Chapter 4

LOOK FOR LOVE IN ALL THE RIGHT PLACES

Now that you know what kind of dog you want, where do you find him or her? We tend to blame the humans when pets are a headache, but truthfully some people spend a great deal of money acquiring and trying to train a pet who was an insolvable problem before the person ever saw the dog. You can avoid a great deal of heartache and the unimaginable aggravation of a highly neurotic, outright crazy or perpetually sick dog by shopping in the right place and knowing what you're doing.

THE LINGO OF DOG SELLING

Before you start shopping, learn the "magic words" used in selling dogs that mean a great deal less than you may believe.

"AKC" does not guarantee quality. All Sunday newspapers contain dozens of classified ads offering you "AKC-registered" purebreds as if those three letters were proof of the finest quality. Not so! AKC only means the pups and/or parents are registered in the Stud Book and the dog is eligible to enter AKC shows. The AKC has no system for checking quality. An AKC dog could be so inbred that he's cross-eyed, three-legged and utterly lacking a brain or internal organs.

Don't be dazzled by "show dogs." To produce a show dog, all that you need to do is show your AKC certificate and pay an entry fee. When you walk him around the ring, the judges might boo or laugh, but he's still a show dog.

"Champion" can also be senseless. Champion of what? In which shows? Against how many competitors? Taking what prize? The Best of Show at a large show with maybe a thousand dogs is indeed a champion although of only one show. The dog who takes third prize in breed in a show that had only three dogs in that breed is also a show winner.

In the show world, a dog is not entitled to put "Champion" before his name until he has won a great deal more than one prize. He must accumulate a specific number of points at a number of officially sanctioned shows — the number of points given for each win depends on the size of the show and the prize won. Even this may not be that impressive — that three-legged no-brainer could become a champion by competing in a hundred shows, taking third prizes whenever only three dogs were shown. The more popular the breed, the harder it is for inferior specimens to become champions — "Ch. Troll von Richthaven" is a very good German Shepherd, but don't blindly accept his title as proof of that. If, like Troll, the dog also has ROM or SOM after his name, he's produced champion children, and Int. Ch. means he's "finished" his championship in at least two countries. He's very, very good. A German Shepherd with Sch. I, II or III accompanying his name is also a German champion in both obedience and beauty.

"Certified free of hip dysplasia" has limited meaning since dysplasia and other disabling genetic flaws are not always evident in small pups. I had a German Shepherd certified-free who had Grade IV (the worst) by age two. Do check before you buy, but don't count yourself as home free. Anyone who assures you the problem will never crop up is either lying or seriously ignorant — don't buy from such a person.

Lifetime guarantees are just promotional devices. There's no way any breeder can guarantee any dog for life, so he's betting that few people will ever return a dog. After all, a dog isn't a coffee pot — there's too much emotion involved.

DO YOUR HOMEWORK

The more you know about your breed, the smarter you'll be as a shopper and an owner, and the more you'll enjoy your pet.

It isn't difficult to learn more about the breed or breeds you're considering. Every pet store has books on individual breeds, and there are many people eager to educate you. Every breed has a national club, with regional divisions right in your area. Most have regular meetings, some have training programs, newsletters and more. The American Kennel Club and other groups have competitions all over the country. There are sure to be some nearby where you can see your breed in action.

The two leading dog magazines, *Dog Fancy* and *Dog World*, cover a different breed in every issue — a trip to the library to check back issues will provide you with in-depth, fact-filled articles, pictures and data on where to get even more information.

Among other things, a little research will help you avoid looking like a fool. I once sat, very bored, while a breeder walked me through a six-generation pedigree of my new pup, pointing out eight international champions, four sires of merit and scores of champions. I thought, "Yeah, well, I'm buying a dog from a show breeder. That's what you get when you do that."

Two weeks letter I bought a book on the breed and found that the pedigree printed in the book, which traced lineage back to the very first champion in that breed, was MY DOG's pedigree! I hadn't bought a show dog — I'd acquired The Crown Princess of Show Dogs!

LOOK FOR A HIGH-QUALITY DOG

Unless you plan to show your dog, you don't want a state-of-the art, top-of-the-line example of your breed. You want a good companion who has been given every opportunity to be healthy, psychologically sound, steady, stable and long-lived. This is what dog people call "a high-quality dog."

Egg-queena Murphy is a friendly Pug. These sturdy Toys are usually great at snoring.

A high-quality dog has no recognizable genetic flaws. His parents are healthy. He has been meticulously cared for, even before he was created. Most importantly he has been fully socialized to human beings — which means people have handled him and cuddled him frequently from the time his eyes opened. This is an absolutely vital step in creating a dog who will relate well to human beings. You cannot make up for the lack of socialization at this stage of a dog's development since in a way, he's "imprinted" toward people.

How is a high-quality pup created? There's a vast difference between the way responsible breeders raise pups and how ignorant or money-hungry people do. One of the great dangers in dog shopping is the "puppy mill," a fast-buck operation concerned with churning out AKC pups as cheaply and rapidly as possible for maximum profits. Puppy-mill dogs are genetically poor, unhealthy, overstressed, unsocialized, badly bred and more. Puppy-mill dogs are a recipe for heartbreak.

Despite the high prices for good, purebred dogs these days, reputable breeders are not out to get rich on puppies but to produce more great champions. In the process, however, they make many puppies who aren't quite good enough to be the very best. These "pet quality" pups are ideal companions, because they've been given the best of everything. Often they are deemed "pet quality" because of flaws that ban them from the show ring but mean little or nothing to you. For instance, some Maltese are born with wooly coats instead of the long, straight fur required for show ring. Some dogs are the wrong color. And dogs who have prick ears with flipped-over tips often have problems with the "flip." A totally prick-eared Sheltie, for example, is not allowed in the show ring, but as you can see from the photos in this book and on the cover, they are still beautiful dogs. None of the home remedies for flipping the tips of the

WHAT A GOOD BREEDER DOES	*WHAT A **BAD** BREEDER DOES*
Parents are carefully selected to enhance the strengths of each and exclude the weaknesses, utilizing detailed records on many generations.	*A single AKC "stud" is used constantly because he's owned by the breeder, so there's no breeding fee.*
Inbreeding of any relatives is rare and done with exceptional care.	*Inbreeding is rampant; the father dog is almost constantly bred with daughters.*
Bitches aren't bred until at least a year old and are given "vacations" between litters.	*Bitches are started with the first heat (six months) and bred as often as possible.*
Before breeding, the mother is put on a richer diet and given vitamin/mineral supplements. She's also examined by a vet. She may be given her annual shots so she will pass on better immunities to her pups.	*The mother is fed the cheapest food available, with no supplements; no vet check, no shot. In fact, there may be no records of when mother had her last shot.*

WHAT A GOOD BREEDER DOES

After breeding, the vet often checks the pregnant dog again to be sure everything is OK. Pregnant dogs live in sheltered kennels, with an indoor section for cold, wet days and all nights.

Throughout her pregnancy and while nursing, the mother dog gets a special diet with vitamin/mineral supplements.

The pregnant mother is also given exercise to be sure she stays fit.

At whelping time, the mother is moved to a special warm, very clean box near the breeder (often inside the house); she's checked constantly.

At birth, the breeder is watching, ready to help, and the vet is notified and on call. Immediately after birthing, the box is cleaned and pups are carefully examined.

Pups are examined by a vet fairly soon after birth, shots begin on schedule, the mother is also examined after birth and watched closely while she's nursing.

Caring people socialize pups regularly at the right time. Their personalities and litter rankings are known.

Pups are started on solid food supplements early, with carefully chosen, nutritious puppy food.

Pups stay with mother and litter until weaning and often a few weeks afterwards; they live in a large, very clean, warm pen where they have room to play.

WHAT A __BAD__ BREEDER DOES

No vet, no change of kennel. Her home is often an outdoor run that's dirty, drafty, exposed to the elements and even in dangerously poor repair.

All dogs are given the same food, generally the cheapest dry mix available, which may not even be properly stored. Nothing else.

The dogs never come out of their kennels.

The mother is neither moved nor checked.

The mother is lucky if someone notices she's had her pups the same day; dead or deformed pups may not be removed for a day or two. Exam is cursory and delayed. No vet.

Pups may not even get shots until shipping day. If the mother has a nursing problem that endangers her life or the lives of her pups, no one may notice until it's too late.

Pups get no special attention or the human handling vital to creating good pets. No one knows the pups.

Pups may nibble a bit of mother's food, but they rarely get anything for themselves since mother's milk is free.

Pups are often "pulled off" mother at four weeks to be shipped away in crowded boxes. Until then, they stay in mother's dirty, exposed kennel.

ears, such as chewing gum, work. Even with these flaws, "pet quality" pups aren't cheap; however, you'll pay the highest price possible on the breed.

In fact, if you find a breeder offering pups for substantially less than the average going price, be very, very careful.

Alexandra (Zandy) Bell is a tiny Toy Poodle with a merry, mischievous personality and tons of charm.

Understanding how puppy mills and show breeders produce their puppies will help you no matter how you shop, so look at the specifics.

HOW A WONDERFUL DOG IS CREATED

If you're soft-hearted, you may be saying that you'll take one of the bad breeder's pups and "make up for his awful infancy." GET THIS THOUGHT OUT OF YOUR HEAD RIGHT NOW. You will NOT take a puppy mill dog. You will NOT take a dog that has spent six months in a pet shop. You will not take the smallest, thinnest, weakest pup in a litter. You will not do this because you can NEVER make up for a dog's bad beginning. Dogs are not people — you cannot compensate for the failure to socialize. You cannot make up for a foundation of bad nutrition (such pups will be sick all their lives or live very short lives). You cannot compensate for irresponsible inbreeding or bad genetics that could have dreadful medical consequences for the rest of the dog's life. You CAN help an animal heal from abuse, torture or neglect AS AN ADULT. If you have a soft heart, this is how you can help dogs.

WHERE TO FIND YOUR QUALITY COMPANION

There are five places to find your dog:

1. Pet shops are NOT a good place to buy a dog. Puppy-mill dogs supply the "inventory" of pet shops, where the puppies' disadvantages are usually compounded. Just imagine a human baby in the conditions you see in pet shops. Stuck in a cage in a wall of cages with a constant parade of strangers bothering you. Walking on wire mesh. Surrounded by other dogs you can smell, but not really see or play with. No exercise. Very little actual contact with people. Lots of stress. Great risk of contagious illness. Is this the way to let a baby discover the world, grow strong and healthy, start learning his lessons or anything else? Yet this is how petshop dogs live, often for a month or more at a critical age.

I told a dog expert I knew someone who bought a ten-month-old Husky in a pet shop. "What illness?" she shot at me. "Seizure disorder," I replied. "Trainable?" "No." "Affectionate?" "Hostile." "Ending?" "She had to be kept in the garage. Then she started killing the neighbors' dogs whenever she escaped. Put down."

The expert nodded. "Predictable."

There are a very few shops that don't sell puppy-mill dogs but instead, act as agents for local breeders — they advertise this, have only a couple of dogs at a time which are not kept in a wall of cages. Unless you happen on a shop like this, NO PET-SHOP PUPPY.

2. Good breeders. As I've already made clear, professional breeders are a good way to get a great pet.

3. Amateur home-breds. It's possible to get a great pup who is wonderfully socialized and even started on his training from a dog-lover who bred his pet and advertises the puppies in your local papers and on the supermarket bulletin board. Be alert, smart and careful, however, because best intentions aren't always enough. Don't take a pup unless you have the opportunity to examine at least one parent to be sure he/she is healthy, well formed, not too young or old. If you have any inner reservations, even if you can't put them into words, pass.

Molly Patterson was adopted from a shelter when over a year old. She looks like Benji, is bright, very loveable and adores her "mother."

4. Humane societies, sanctuaries and shelters. There are many kinds of shelters today where you can find wonderful pets including purebreds, puppies and even purebred puppies.

Shelters estimate that twenty to thirty percent of their animals are purebreds, although few come with their "papers" (AKC registry). If you're looking for a specific breed, don't rely on shelter waiting lists — "breeds" are adopted so quickly lists are often never accessed. Keep calling. If you want a pup, they're plentiful, especially in late spring and right after Christmas.

There are different kinds of shelters. The ones run by the "dog catcher" (usually called Animal Control these days) are sometimes horrific places run by elected officials with no love of animals and a much-too-small budget. They frequently have strays (no history so you really don't know what you're getting) and even "feral" dogs who have never known a home or a human (and will never make good pets). Animals may not be vet-checked so you could be adopting disease or illness. The lack of concern and proper care are immediately apparent the moment you walk in the door.

On the other hand, every urban area has at least one welfare society with a fine shelter staffed by concerned, devoted people. Their only fault is that in their eagerness to give as many dogs good homes as possible, they could possibly minimize a dog's problems or embellish what they know of the dog's background. So stay alert and confirm what you're being told with your own observations.

In addition to shelters, there may be a sanctuary near you, a place that specialize in providing life care (on a no-kill basis). Sanctuaries often take senior dogs and dogs with disabilities or treatable chronic illness, the dogs most likely to be euthanized in public shelters. Don't overlook these animals. They can be absolutely fabulous, often well-trained, serene companions who somehow understand that you're one in a million and love you accordingly.

A quick note on euthanizing: Shelters that euthanize are not doing so because they're heartless or cruel, and no-kill shelters are not automatically better. Euthanasia for dogs is a terrible fact of life caused by the huge overpopulation of animals. There is simply no way to find homes for over ten million dogs a year in this country, and the moment we bring overpopulation under control through spay/neuter, animal people everywhere will weep with relief at being able to stop the euthanizing.

Shelters ask for a small donation, in part because paying something for your dog is a small insurance policy that you'll take good care of him. Most shelters spay or neuter all dogs before they're put up for adoption, as an effort to stem the overpopulation problems. Other shelters ask you to promise you'll take care of this. Do it!

If you shop wisely and don't let your heart run away with you, getting your new companion from a shelter does much more than provide someone with income — you are really saving a life.

5. Breed rescue. The newest source of outstanding purebred pets are the breed rescue operations springing up all over the country. Breed rescue became popular when people discovered the fatal ending of most racing Greyhounds, but now EVERY breed has a rescue organization and there is surely a nearby local group helping surrendered and abandoned dogs of your breed.

Tasha Langevin is a Keeshond, a perfect, medium-small city dog with a full coat that does not need a great deal of grooming.

Breed rescue grew because breeders and breed clubs couldn't stand the idea of their beloved dogs going to bad homes or the euthanasia rooms at big shelters. They stepped in and said, "We'll take them" and take them they have; from shelters, from dogcatchers, from the dogs' former owners. Whenever possible, they take the papers, too, so you can get a fully registered dog. They also ask a host of questions so they can provide you with detailed information on the dog.

What's even better, most breed rescue operations are

based on fostering dogs in private homes; few operations have kennels. That means the dogs have not experienced the trauma of being left in kennels and, more important, you can get absolutely current information on your prospect directly from someone who is living with him.

Chelsea Skelly is a loyal, smart, gorgeous Shetland Sheepdog, pet-quality because her ears never tipped over.

What's best of all, you don't pay what you'd pay for a breed from a breeder — just a token adoption fee!

Breed rescue groups are perhaps the toughest when it comes to evaluating YOU as a prospective owner. At all good shelters, you can expect to be asked to fill out a detailed questionnaire, after which you'll be interviewed. Only then will you be shown dogs and you'll be observed while you examine the dogs. Every animal welfare organization wants their dogs to go only to GOOD homes with loving parents. Bring along all adult family members because the shelter demands to know they all agree to the adoption. They'll also want a photo ID and proof of residence (a phone or electric bill). They'll demand you have a phone and call at least one of your personal references. Breed rescue organizations may insist on a home visit before finalizing the adoption — they want to see where "their" dog will live.

Chapter 5

CHIN-LICKING IS NOT A RELIABLE CRITERION

Now that you know what you want and where to go, how do you select your dog from a crowd of lovable prospects? Whether you're seeking an infant or a senior citizen, steel your heart to ignore any soulful meeting of the eyes or gentle licks of your chin. These are not the signs an intelligent person uses to choose a roommate for the next ten to twenty years!

Resurrect your Worksheet to remind you of what you're looking for and make a stringent effort to keep the thinking part of your brain dominant. Do this, and you can choose the companion who will make you happy forever after.

HOW TO SHOP SMART

No matter where you go to find your companion, stay alert and don't hesitate to ask questions. Be suspicious and vigilant. Never accept everything you're told at face value. Consider the source of your information and what other agendas those sources might have. Compare what you're told with what you already know and what you see. Remember, for example, that well-meaning people may truly believe their Golden Retriever was "caught" by the neighbor's Labrador, but if you've done your homework, you know these are two heavy-boned dogs with big, blocky heads and the fine-boned, delicate little beauty before you could not possibly have those two parents.

Look smart. Are you seeking a professional breeder? Breeder lists are available from the AKC and breed clubs, both on-line and directly. The pros also advertise their show-dog breeding activities in professional journals like *Dog World*, not the daily newspapers. (They don't promote their "pet quality" pups.) Small, local breeders who do advertise locally, are usually on the fringe, one step up from dog-owner,s and may not be as knowledgeable as they think they are. I once helped a friend buy a Sheltie from such a place and the dog developed a genetic eye problem, probably caused by too much inbreeding with too little genetic knowledge. This lovely dog spent her life with her red, hairless eyes, and there were a lot of extra vet bills.

Your safest bet in searching for a breeder is the one whose name keeps coming up. By the way, don't worry about dealing with a breeder long distance if there's no one nearby.

Dogs offered in your local papers and shoppers and on public bulletin boards are dogs in private homes and nearby shelters. Although both are excellent sources of wonderful dogs, vigilant questioning and suspicious observation should be part of shopping.

Sellers can have hidden agendas. Overcrowding at your local shelter could cause adoption counselors to oversell to obvious good prospects like you. Private individuals can also have hidden agendas that color the truth — maybe they're guilty about giving away their dog or operating under a tight deadline imposed by a landlord or an upcoming move. Perhaps their spouse said, "That dog is out of here by Friday or I am."

Listen smart. From your first contact with your prospect's caretaker, encourage long conversation. No matter who you're dealing with, you want to hear a deep love of dogs and a strong desire to place this dog in a good, loving home. If your contact is cautious and hesitant about immediately offering you the dog, GREAT! Unless they have some sort of miraculous ESP, what do they know about you at this point that guarantees you're not a dog torturer?

You don't want to talk to a reluctant person for a long time. If you've caught the person at a bad time, he or she should make arrangements for another call, not cut you off with, "Well, come and see the dog" or "Are you taking the dog?" In fact, when I volunteered at The ASPCA, I was taught to go through a lengthy questionnaire with people, engaging them in conversation in order to give myself time and information so I could make solid judgements about the prospects. I was also taught that if my instincts ever went on alert, no matter how vague my feelings, I was to listen to them and turn the people down. I say the same to you.

Professional breeders should be proud and delighted to tell you more than you want to know about the pup's lineage, the family's show history, details of conformation and more. Private owners who love their dogs should sound sad about giving them up and be eager to tell you about the animal's antics.

No one should be willing to release a pup before eight weeks of age, and don't be surprised if a professional breeder wants to hold the litter for twelve and even fourteen weeks in order to make more reliable judgments about which pups have real promise for showing. I've also known breeders who wanted to hold pups headed for cities longer, so the pup can get his second shot and be better immunized against contagion.

Pups released at six weeks are newly weaned and still quite infantile, and no training is possible for weeks yet. They're somewhat more likely to have transition problems such as crying at night, and a lot of vets agree that it's better for them to stay with Mom until eight weeks at the very least. At my vet's encouraging, I've even paid for two extra weeks of "board." I've only taken one very, very young pup and that was because I felt the home environment was so unhealthy I wanted to get the pup out.

The object of your first call should be an appointment to see the dog or, if he's too far away, the offer to send you photos and other information about the dog. Anyone who offers you a dog after one short conversation is dumping a dog. IF you proceed, proceed with extreme care. Don't say "yes" to the offer. People who buy "sight unseen" after one brief conversation often get exactly what they deserve.

Private owners, of course, have the dogs available when you find out about them, but professionals usually do not have pups "in stock" and ready to ship out. Instead, you'll be told about a litter that's due fairly soon and, if the breeder is favorably impressed, he or she may offer to put you "on the list." Since the breeder doesn't know how many pups are coming and how many will be available as pet quality, he or she is not making any commitment to you. What they often do is compile a list, then match individual pups to the prospects — if there's no pup suited to your personality, temperament and other needs, you won't be offered anyone out of that litter. You aren't expected to commit, either, until you've met the pup.

What should you say? For all dogs: This is what I'm looking for in terms of personality and temperament, and this is how my dog will live. Would you say your dog will be happy with me? If yes, why?

For adults: Why are you giving this dog up? Most people will give the easy answer that makes them look good; few will admit that they failed to train the dog or haven't been keeping up with the grooming so you must probe and read between the lines. How much training has the dog had? How did he get the training: Formal obedience classes, private at-home trainer, self-trained by owner? Would the owner call the dog well-trained or have they spoiled him? Make it sound casual and friendly, not judgmental. Was he crate-raised? Do you work? Does the dog stay home all day? If yes, are there ever any problems with that? You'll probably get a "no" even if there are, so again, probe. Do you have a yard? Is the dog outside a great deal? If so, adjusting to your way of life might be difficult.

For pups: How big is the litter? How many litters has mom had? When did she have her last litter? Are the pups still nursing? If they're under 6 weeks, the answer should be "yes" even if they're eating a little solid food. If the answer is no, ask why.

For shelter dogs: How did you get the dog? If he was picked upon the street, did he have ID or a collar? Was he found in an area where people abandon pets? If the answers are no, be careful; this could be a feral dog. What sort of training do you think he's had? Have you seen any behavior problems? What do you know about his medical history? Did the dog have any medical problems when he came in? What do you think caused them? Has the dog had a vet examination, and how thorough? Any signs of phobias, excessive shyness or aggression or other problems?

See smart. Wherever you go to see your prospect, go prepared to look at everything with a cautious and careful eye. If you're the type who tends to focus on the people speaking to you, bring a friend who can look around corners while you're chatting.

Start with a sniff. Whether shelter, kennel or private house, a good dog home does not smell, except for maybe a little antiseptic. A smelly home is a dirty one and a sign of inferior care.

Look at where the dog is living. I once saw a litter living on a thin cotton sheet on a November-cold, stone floor — not a good start for a healthy life. In contrast, at every professional breeder I've ever visited, the pups were in a "whelping box," a big "playpen" filled with shredded paper, IN THE KITCHEN or a specially heated room in the kennel or a special area of the house. They were warm, had room to play and were isolated from the other dogs. They could be watched but weren't in a high traffic area where they might be overstressed. Some breeders even bar visitors from areas containing young, unweaned litters in order to avoid stress and contagion.

Take a careful look at Mother Dog. She's probably thin and her coat may be a bit ragged and dull, because nursing pulls a bitch "down" a bit, but she shouldn't look sick and her eyes should be bright. She should never show fear or nervousness around the owner/breeder, although it's natural if she's a bit wary of you. Poppa Dog should have a shiny, full coat, bright eyes and all the signs of very good health.

If there are children in the house, how are they around the puppies? If they're permitted to grab puppies and carry them all over like inanimate toys, this household doesn't understand dogs well and isn't treating the pups properly. The pups can also be getting the message that humans are hurting, unpredictable and unpleasant.

Older dogs should be comfortable in the house, not acting as if they've never been inside before. They should have some toys scattered about or in an accessible "toy box." Water should be available.

CHOOSING A PUP

If you're buying your puppy via long-distance, you must rely on the breeder to select the right pup for you. Be very specific about what you want in terms of temperament and personality, then trust the breeder's reputation and good judgment. Several friends have purchased this way with full satisfaction. Don't worry about shipping a puppy, either. These breeders ship highly valuable show dogs all the time, so they know how to do it safely.

Chances are, however, that you will find a prospect nearby and will be able to visit him before making your decision. Try to arrange more than one visit. If you're fortunate to locate a young litter, arrange your first visit when the pups are four to five weeks old. The best time to see the litter is right after a nap when the pups are at their most lively. Owners who don't know their pups' schedule should raise your suspicions. If you do arrive when the pups are napping, wait — sleeping dogs tell you nothing.

Agenda for your first visit: Your first visit is for observation and research. You want to ask the rest of those questions. You also want to review the pedigree if you're buying a purebred, look at the puppies' home, the mother and father (if available), and the home/kennel in general.

Now sit down and WATCH the puppies. Do they look fluffy, bright-eyed, alert, curious, playful, roly-poly, healthy? Are their baby teeth strong, white needles? Are they supplementing their milk with solid food? Staying exclusively with mother's milk at this age is a way to cut costs.

By four weeks of age, every litter has a rigidly established hierarchy starting with the boss puppy, called the Alpha dog, and going right down to the lowest-ranking dog, who is not always the smallest although he's probably the thinnest, since he gets food last. Alpha pup is often the fattest and biggest. He could be a "she" because in the dog world, males usually submit to females. In any case, he'll be the bully of the litter who gets first choice of food and toys and the best sleeping site, often on top of everyone else. When the puppies are tussling, he's the one on top and almost never on his back with his belly sticking up. He'll probably show the most interest in you since he's the most aggressive and outgoing — he may be curious or protective, depending on his breed. He'll also wander the farthest away from the litter while exploring. Pick out the Alpha and try to remember him.

Now look for the low man. He's most apt to be the crawl-in-your-lap chin-licker because he seeks security from humans. In his litter, he'll always be the underdog, the one at the bottom of the pile of sleeping pups, the one pushed away from the food, the one without a toy. If he finds one, someone will take it away. In any tussle, he'll be the bitten not the biter, on the bottom, rolled over with belly showing, freezing in that position, licking the other pups' faces to show submission. He'll probably be the shyest, the last to go toward anything and the first to run away. Remember this one, too.

It's very important to identify these two pups because you don't want either of them. Alpha has been boss since birth and will be a handful all his life. He's adventurous, tends to have a strong mind of his own, is difficult to train and apt to be aggressive. I went against my own advice with my Golden, reasoning that Goldens are rather meek and I wanted a dog with "spirit." I got spirit all right — basic training was a nightmare. A friend's American Eskimo was an Alpha. At age ten, she threatened to attack me because I issued an order she didn't like; me, who had bottle fed her as an infant! Alphas aren't a fun challenge. They're a lifetime of battles over who's the boss.

By the same token, bottom-rankers aren't gentle souls who need lots of your love. They're likely to become excessively fearful and hyper-sensitive. These are the dogs who get the shakes if you yell at a telemarketer on the telephone. They develop phobias more often than other dogs, don't like to be left alone and can eat your house to calm themselves. Many forget about housebreaking when frightened even by a pot dropped in the kitchen or a gunshot on the TV. Bottom-ranking dogs also have a reputation for turning into fear biters, which are dogs who easily become so frightened that they attack — in totally harmless situations, often while signaling fear rather than aggression. Very dangerous!

If you want a dog who's confident and protective with a strong personality, take Beta, the second dog in the ranking — Betas become Alphas when Alpha is removed, but they're not such great bullies and are more tractable. If you prefer a more docile dog, take a middle-rank pup. To identify Beta, remove Alpha and Beta will take charge. Most breeders know the ranking in their litter; many private owners also know but don't understand what they've seen, so ask questions. Then double-check with your own observations.

One way to confirm your judgment of the litter is to bring a fuzzy cat toy or soft plastic squeaky toy and toss it into the litter. The bottom-ranker will probably run away from it, while Alpha pup will pounce on it, bite and shake it. The second dog to get the toy will be Beta.

Your second visit agenda: Schedule your second visit for at least a week later. Ideally, you should go at weaning time (six weeks), but if the pups are being chosen before, go early enough to give you a selection of pups (try to get first pick).

Once again, arrive after a nap and start by observing. By now, the pups are starting to undergo the enormous physical transformation from fluff balls that don't look like any particular kind of dog, into the beginnings of their adult form. At this point, they look a bit funny and are definitely clumsy because different parts grow at differing speed, but you should see the beginnings of smooth gaits, strong musculature and powerful bones. If any pup is markedly more awkward in movement than the others, eliminate him.

Testing your puppy. The final part of your second visit is to test the pups you've tentatively chosen to see which has the personality and temperament you want.

Prepare for this by enlisting a friend to accompany you and scheduling time for a pre-visit rehearsal. Pack a bottle of bright nail polish, a squeaky toy and an empty soda can with a couple of coins inside. Before the tests, position two straight chairs side-by-side near the litter for you and your friend.

In evaluating these tests, remember that the breed will affect the outcome. All Terriers will be more alert, less fearful and more aggressive than, for instance, a Basset Hound. When in doubt, test the top and bottom ranking dogs for comparisons.

Don't rush from one test to the next. After every test, cuddle the pup until he's completely relaxed before proceeding to the next. The way he reacts to you is also a test. If he grows more comfortable and affectionate as the time passes, he is starting to bond to you, a very good sign. If the pup shows signs of growing tired or unnerved by all the unusual happenings, by struggling to get back to his litter well into the testing, or losing his concentration, he needs a rest break. Put him back with his litter-mates for a while.

Do these tests in order since the dog's reactions also depend on the building relationship between you.

1. The Swoop. Very quickly and suddenly, swoop down to pick up the puppy you've tentatively chosen and sit down with him on your lap and start cuddling him. He should be momentarily startled but not aggressive or seriously frightened. He could yip, Terriers might turn to try to bite your hand FOR A SECOND OR TWO.

He might struggle for a few seconds to return to his litter, but should almost instantly quiet down. He might sniff you to see who you are, look up at you or look around in interest at seeing the world from a new view. All good signs that he is even-tempered, alert, curious, not too nervous or fearful. You don't want a dog who is completely still (cowering, in other words), shaking or very passive. Nor do you want one who bites you.

2. The Big NO. Ask the caretaker if the dog has been taught NO!

If the pup does not know the word, this test will give you good indications of his intelligence and willingness to obey your commands as well as more of the pup's personality and temperament.

While he's sitting in your lap, offer your pup the squeaky toy. Most pups will reach for it, but if he doesn't immediately pay attention to it, squeak it a couple of times. Any pup that reacts to the squeak with aggression (other than a bark from a barking breed) or fear is a problem dog. As he reaches for it, drop it in front of him as if you're giving it to him, then say NO in a loud, stern, rather harsh voice. A too-aggressive, hard-to-train pup will hesitate fractionally, if at all, and grab the toy. A too-timid, hard-to-train pup will look at you in horror, avoid the toy entirely, even cringe away or start to shake. The ideal is the pup who is momentarily started, maybe looks at you in puzzlement, then within no more than a minute, goes for the toy.

A pup who knows what NO! means should NOT go for the toy. It has been forbidden to him. A good pup in this case is one who looks puzzled, frustrated or sulky. Failure to respond properly could, of course, be the fault of the caretaker's training techniques. Look at the caretaker's adult dog to see if he or she obeys well.

Now pick up the toy and play with it in front of the pup, encouraging him to take it with a soft, warm, happy voice saying, "It's okay, here, look at this toy." After a little hesitation and maybe some glances up at you, the pup should take the toy and play with it. A pup who gives any sort of, "Oh, no, I'm not touching that thing" response is a little too meek and may require great gentleness in training.

3. Upside Down. A dog on his back is fully exposed for a quick kill — when a subordinate is threatened by a dominant animal, all canines signal absolute surrender by rolling over and opening their bodies to the superior. In dog language, it means "you can kill me if you wish." That's why this simple test is very valuable. You force extreme vulnerability on the dog.

After your pup is calm, start to play gently with him, with a little rough petting and a soft, playful voice. Still playing, bend down with him and place him on the floor ON HIS BACK. Without stopping your play, tickle his tummy, rock him from side to side, make it all a game, but continue holding him securely in this position. Then suddenly remove both hands and stop playing. A very dominant and hard-to-handle pup won't stay in this very submissive posture. He might fight you even when you're playing and the moment you release him, he'll roll over, may even growl or show aggression to you. Terriers, American Eskimos, Pekingese and Schnauzers will probably all show aggression. Yorkies and Dachshunds may also be aggressive. This is their nature.

A too-submissive, might-be-fearful pup freezes for several moments. The ideal pup will pause briefly, then turn over. He accepts your authority, but has a solid ego of his own.

4. The Drop. Take a long time after The Upside Down to get your pup completely calm and past any emotional aftereffects. Then start playing again and this time, during play hold the pup up in the air above your lap, then suddenly drop him and catch him again after a fall of a couple of inches.

Rolling eyes, the shakes or even losing bladder control are signs of too much fear. Growling, snapping or showing teeth are too much aggression, except in the breeds mentioned above. The best pup is momentarily startled, somewhat alarmed, then quickly reassured. It shows you he's alert, even-tempered, not an over-reactor, and able to accept changes without a big fuss.

5. The Big Noise. Now your friend goes to work. While you're cuddling, he moves behind you and suddenly rattles the noisemaker can.

Your pup should swing immediately to the direction of the noise to show you his hearing is good and his first reaction is to spot the source of this new thing. His eyes should open very wide and he might bark, a reaction that demonstrates he is startled, alert and vigilant. Even if he does growl, raise his fur or show his teeth, however, it's still acceptable in this case. He should not cringe, cower, try to crawl inside your clothing or ignore the noise.

6. The Snatch. By this time, your pup should have begun to attach himself to you. Give him five more minutes of devoted, loving attention, then your friend, who is sitting beside you, should quietly reach over and firmly take the puppy away from you. Your friend should hold the pup in his or her lap but pay no attention. Does the pup look back to you? If so, he has begun to identify you as someone to be trusted and loved. This is excellent.

Does the pup look to the caretaker. This is also good. He trusts his caretaker; that can be transferred to you.

Does he simply snuggle up in the new lap? He's a bit too friendly, may never be deeply loving, probably won't be protective.

Does he struggle to get to you or the caretaker? He could become a one-man dog. Is he hostile? Watch out. This one may react to all change with aggression which could be dangerous to live with in a city.

CHOOSING AN ADULT DOG

It's unlikely that you'll have the opportunity for two visits to choose your adult dog. Therefore, you need to go prepared to accomplish everything in your first visit and probably return home with your choice if all goes well.

A breed rescue operation and some of the private shelters may not let you take the dog home at once — they could ask for a "home visit" to see what the dog's environment will be. Don't be alarmed. There are so many horror stories that these people have started to use more and more of the requirements for human adoption. This tells you that your dog has been extremely well cared for, dearly loved and the information you're given is highly reliable.

If you're shopping at a shelter, you'll probably be taken into an area where there are many dogs. How do you make your preliminary selection? First, zero in on the size, gender and breed mixture that most appeals to you. Once you've narrowed the field, turn to the adoption counselor for help and read the records on each dog. If you have a lot of choices, skip the strays. You know surrendered dogs have lived with humans, but strays could be feral, although many shelters never offer ferals since they make such poor pets.

Look for signs of abuse or serious neglect — extreme thinness, scars, great fear. These dogs can become wonderfully devoted, loving pets, but they do require a great deal of therapeutic care, with much extra loving and very gentle training. You might have to rebuild trust by providing a very rigid structure (feeding at x hour, walk at x hour, cuddle time at x and x), which is difficult if you work full-time. In most cases, dogs with this kind of damage really need an experienced dog person with a deep understanding of dog needs and behaviors.

Of the remaining dogs, don't arbitrarily head for the dogs who jump up and down happily, shouting "Take me, take me." Some dogs are very aggressive in their kennels because they somehow know the next step is death — it's their last stand. Dogs like this turn into pussycats when they're taken out of the kennel and shown some affection. Most shelters don't offer truly aggressive dogs for adoption. Other dogs are totally passive and unresponsive, may even lie in their kennels with their backs to you — they're heartbroken. They are most likely to come from a loving home. With extra TLC and a little time, they'll love you more than any dog in the world because they know what they've lost.

Once you get a dog out and on a leash, he's probably going to be hyper. The shelter environment is stressful and the possibility that you're going to take him home over-excites the dog. You need to calm the dog down in order to evaluate him properly. Get him out of the adoption room, away from the other dogs. If he still doesn't settle, ask if you can take him out for a short walk.

When he's calm and you've gotten acquainted, it's testing time. Start with what he knows. Try the Big NO! test. NO is the first command a puppy learns. If this dog doesn't know it, he knows nothing. He may have lived in a yard, a cellar or whatever, but he has not lived with people, has not been loved by people and is not housebroken. Reject him.

If he knows NO, try SIT in a firm command voice. If he doesn't react, start the teaching movement of pulling his head up with the leash and bending to push his rear down. Iif he's just forgotten momentarily, he should sit before you apply pressure. Since SIT is the second thing people teach, dogs who don't know SIT have minimal training. He's had some contact with people, but it's impossible to tell how much. He may be housebroken, but it probably isn't thorough.

If the dog knows SIT, move on up through the basic commands to see what else he's learned. The more the dog knows, the better he is as a candidate for your home because you know he's had good care.

You cannot test to see if a dog has been housebroken. The adoption counselor may know, however, from the way the dog has behaved since coming into the kennel.

What else can you learn? You can give all dogs the complete Big NO and Big Noise tests. With small dogs, you can also use The Swoop, The Snatch and The Drop. Results actually give you a much clearer picture of temperaments and personalities than with puppies. Don't do Upside Down with adults — some dogs could become dangerous.

Additional points: A dog that ducks your hand or cringes away is called "hand shy." This means that the dog's previous owners swiped at him a lot, trying to hit but missing, or hit the head a lot. In itself it's simply a sign of a very poor training technique which can, over time, be overcome. However, it could point to abuse that has caused fearfulness, so look at the dog very carefully and watch his reactions to other stimulations.

Selection is easier in a private home but also more limited. Ask the caretaker to "show what your dog does." A dog who cowers when his owner works him may have been mistreated or too harshly trained and can therefore be neurotic or overly fearful. This sort of dog is difficult to train because he becomes overanxious.

A dog who's casual about obeying, who does some things well and doesn't do others at all, is a dog who has been given sporadic, overly permissive and inconsistent training. Such a dog may well have a host of bad habits, and will likely require a lot of firmness to convince him that you really mean business. Most dogs enjoy the opportunity to show off what they know and will work willingly, happily and even exceptionally well in front of audiences.

Finally, look for signs of bad habits: Is anything chewed? Are things placed in odd locations out of the dog's reach? Leave a purse or bag on the floor — does the dog do anything about it?

FINALIZING YOUR ACQUISITION

As soon as you've selected the puppy or dog you want, negotiate the final purchase. If you're buying a pup who's not ready to go home, use your nail polish to mark a nail on your choice so there will be no mistakes on pick-up day and leave a deposit, with the exact details of the purchase agreement written on the check.

Ask what your pup or dog has been eating: specific brands, specific amounts, specific feeding times. You will want to duplicate this at least for the first week or so to help your dog settle in. If you're taking the dog with you and haven't got that food at home, ask for a one-day supply so you don't have to abandon your dog in his new home during that first day.

Shelters have their own procedures but in other cases, you have the following rights as a buyer:

If you're buying a purebred AKC dog, you should receive the AKC registration certificate or all the data and forms required to register your dog: litter registry, registration numbers of parents, names of parents, etc. You should also receive a formal pedigree for your dog of no less than three generations, preferably five.

If you're buying a breed known for congenital defects, you should receive a statement from a vet certifying that the pup is free from those defects at the time of your purchase. Remember, this doesn't guarantee problems will never emerge in the future. If one is not provided, ask the owner to pay for the cost of x-rays during your vet visit. This isn't standard and he/she may not agree.

You should receive a written list of the puppy's shots — which ones, when and where. Find out when the mother had her last shots, too, as this can affect when your pup gets his. If your pup has had NO shots, reconsider buying this animal as the owner has not provided the most rudimentary care. If you want to proceed, call your vet BEFORE you bring in the pup for any special instructions — without any immunities, even the vet's waiting room can be dangerous.

Ask about worming. Most litters are wormed just before selling, but you need to know if the pups were actually tested and given specific veterinary medication or an over-the-counter general purpose product. You also need to know precisely what brand was given and when, plus whether any follow-up testing was done. Many pups need more than one treatment, in any event, but a responsible vet doesn't want to administer wormings too close together.

As a buyer, you have a right to get your new pet examined by your own vet within 24-48 hours. If found to be ill or defective, the dog can be returned for full refund. GET THIS IN WRITING, THEN DO IT!

YOUR DOG'S FIRST VET VISIT

Although Chapter 19 provides details about good vet care, this first visit is a vital part of purchasing your companion so I cover it separately here. This is your last chance to identify a problem pet before it's too late. Make this appointment before you pick up your dog.

While at the vet's office, cover the following:

1. Explain that you have the right to return the dog so you want a thorough exam. Be sure the vet tests vision and hearing, examines heart and lungs, feels abdomen, looks at mouth and examines "bite." In older dogs, he should check for tarter and tooth decay, examine weight and musculature.

2. Spending a few dollars now can save you a fortune and heartache over the life of a sick pet. If the breeder failed to x-ray for known congenital defects or the vet has any suspicions of problems at all, get the x-rays done now. If the vet suggests any tests, go for them, reminding the vet of your 24-hour deadline.

3. Have a stool sample tested and discuss further worming. An adult dog should be blood-tested for heartworm.

4. Provide the vet with the pup's inoculation schedule and his mother's, then schedule his shots. Puppies receive four multipurpose shots against a host of ailments, usually scheduled four to five weeks apart starting when the pup is six weeks. A recently inoculated mother can delay the shots until the dog is eight weeks. On his final visit, the pup will also get a rabies shot which he should receive even if it is no longer legally required in your area.

If you don't know for sure that your new adult has had his annual shots or his rabies booster, get them again. It won't hurt him even if they're duplicated.

5. Review the dog's current feeding program with your vet to see if he or she agrees with the type of food, brand, amount and frequency. If he recommends any changes, discuss a program to gradually switch the dog over from the current routine.

6. With older dogs, ask the vet to specifically check for signs of distemper or other past ailments which can cause serious problems throughout a dog's life. Ask him or her to try to verify the dog's age as well.

Chapter 6

A DOG IS NOT A THING

At this point, I'd like to "preach" for a moment about something I feel is very important. I have seen enough tragedy to understand that many people do not view animals the same way I do, and I can only assume they don't realize the great pain they cause. You see, I worked as an adoption counselor volunteer in a large, big-city shelter until I "burned out." A better description would be that my heart was broken by seeing, week after week, scores of wonderful pets for whom we could not find new homes.

Ebby Verna is a combination of Labrador Retriever and German short-haired Pointer. She's enough Lab to be a good city dog.

The adoption office was open twelve hours a day and more, kept files of special requests, and ferried animals back and forth between other shelters where they might have better chances for adoption. Purebreds were sent to breed rescue groups, an aggressive advertising program tried to increase adoptions, unweaned puppies and injured dogs were sent to volunteer foster homes until they were ready for adoption. No stone was left unturned in an almost frantic, continuous effort to find good homes for as many as possible.

Whenever I met an employee at the shelter, I was asked, "What do you have?" Everyone had animals, many animals. When their homes were full, they strong-armed friends into adopting, even paid one another to nurse sick dogs back to health so they could be adopted. Even today, as you walk through the halls, cats are running around the conference room, a sick dog is resting in someone's office, a litter is being hand-fed in another. That so many cared so deeply was wonderful to see.

Still, since at that time, the shelter where I worked was the city's dogcatcher, dogs arrived in numbers so great that nothing we did was enough. It was a flood we could not deal with — there was no way to find good homes for all. In the United States today, it's estimated that thirty to sixty percent of all animals brought into shelters are euthanized. Is that because the shelters are bad? NO! Staff at shelters that kill are heartbroken and wish with every cell in their bodies that they could stop doing this. The truth is that despite tens of thousands of adoptions every year, 10,000,000 American animals cannot find good homes and must be "put down." Ten million!

It doesn't take a genius to quickly recognize that no matter how much we did, most of the dogs I saw in the shelter each week would not go to loving owners but to "that room" at the end of the hall. There was a constant air of desperation as everyone worked to save as many as they could. Secretaries took dogs for walks on their lunch hours to try to make them calmer, better adoption prospects. Janitors washed down kennels while playing with a gang of frisky, free-for-a-few-moments dogs. No one went past the adoption rooms without stopping for a fast visit and a few quick pats.

Some of the animals were surrendered by loving owners faced with no other options. Many of these dogs were heart-broken. They gave up, and people didn't find them attractive adoption prospects. Other dogs ferociously protected their last home, and people felt they were "bad dogs." We tried so hard to convince people these were good pets. We rarely succeeded. We quickly learned to instantly recognize the dogs who had no real chances of being adopted. Every week when I came in, I'd walk through the kennel area familiarizing myself with the available dogs. I'd talk to them, give them quick pets and I'd know that most were going to die. There was no way that this one shelter could find several hundred homes in the next week. Even now, my eyes fill with tears.

Today, most shelters are deeply involved in spay/neuter programs and vets all over the country are performing these surgeries for minimal fees. In many shelters, all dogs are spayed or neutered before they are offered for adoption. *This is the only way to stem the tide* and the efforts of the animal welfare people are having results — the numbers are starting to drop but so very, very slowly.

How they came to the shelter was a book of horror stories. We once saw an extremely emaciated Great Dane come in with either mange or scarring so bad he had no hair. Although Danes are famous leaners, this boy leaned because he was too weak to stand for long. The woman turning him in, who claimed she was not the real owner, kept assuring him that he would get a nice new home — no chance! He went right to "that room." The adoption rooms were already overflowing and there was no space for a scarred bag of bones no one would take.

My Beagle, Penny, had a shattered pelvis when I found her. I adopted her because I knew she would have immediately gone to "that room." There are always too many healthy dogs up for adoption. What a wonderful spirit would have been lost! Why was she hurt? She had been tossed out of a moving car on a parkway like a candy wrapper.

Every fall, the shelters fill with "summer dogs." Many people actually acquire dogs to enjoy at their summer homes then leave them behind in the fall without a thought. The dirty little secret of summer communities is that hundreds of abandoned household-companion animals starve to death in the beautiful countryside every fall and winter.

Each spring, thousands of puppies are born because owners felt it would be nice for their dog to have a litter or wanted their children to experience the "wonder of birth." The babies are an unwanted side effect so they're dumped. If they're lucky, they're dropped off at the shelter; many are left in garbage cans, empty lots and dark alleys.

Shelters are always filled with dogs between six months and a year, too, as a result of people who don't train their dogs and then can't live with them.

I'm not talking about real torture or abuse here, just thoughtless people who never recognize that a dog is a living, loving creature with needs of its own.

Let's be very, very clear: You must understand that getting a dog is a commitment to another living being. A dog is not an object. If you grow bored, you cannot simply plan to cast off your acquisition — any more than you would have children with the idea you could dump them if you later decided it was too much work to be a parent.

When you buy a dog, you are undertaking a long-term parent/child-type relationship of as much as twenty years, through sickness and health, when it's tough and when it's a joy, a relationship that will extend into a possibly difficult old age. Sure, there are situations when you simply must get rid of a pet, but finding a happy home for an adult dog is not easy. And even when homes are found, not all pets will accept them. There are one-man dogs who do actually pine away.

Please do not go into ownership with an "easy out" in mind. And do recognize that you are incurring certain obligations for this creature. You are responsible for his happiness and well-being. You must provide companionship, structure, play, food, exercise and all the other things a living creature requires. Medical care could become expensive; at times, you must administer treatments that are very difficult for you. At the end, you might have to make that hardest decision of all...and no matter how the end comes, you will hurt agonizingly and grieve deeply while friends say, "I don't understand; it was just a dog."

When you first hold that wonderfully wriggly puppy or look into the eyes of that devoted adult, you're taking responsibility for a life. Accept and acknowledge it. You will reap rewards you cannot imagine. And if you can't do this whole-heartedly, please DO NOT GET A DOG.

Chapter 7

DECORATING THE NURSERY

Has anyone ever waited until the new baby came home from the hospital to begin thinking about where the baby would sleep? Of course not! Well, whether you're bringing home an adult or a baby, a little preparation and advance planning can make your pet's introduction to your life a lot easier, too.

TIMING CAN MAKE A BIG DIFFERENCE

When you adopt a puppy, you're suddenly removing a small baby from mother, brothers and sisters, the humans who cuddled him and the only home he's ever known. Adult dogs have been traumatized by losing their homes and people, and have the same needs.

Your new companion needs (1) his own place that he can see is safe, (2) time and the freedom to explore, (3) constant reassurance that everything is all right, and (4) the peace to nap. He does not need you to drop him off in a foreign place and then leave for work, nor does he need a welcome-home party with dozens of strangers fussing over him.

In fact, do NOT bring your dog home when...

You're about to change your address, with all that moving chaos, excitement and change.

You'll soon be off on a long business trip and he'll be in another new place with other new people.

Thanksgiving, Christmas and New Year's Eve are all just ahead, with absences, confusion, erratic schedules and riotous celebration.

You've just gotten a big promotion and will be working a lot of overtime OR it's the busiest season of your work year.

The perfect time to bring your dog home is at the beginning of a stay-at-home vacation in the early spring or fall (so you can housebreak during pleasant weather). If this isn't possible, bring your dog home Friday night after work and plan a quiet weekend together. Keep travel, parties and overtime to a bare minimum for at least a month in order to give your pet a chance to realize that you own him.

Timing from a puppy's point of view: I've already mentioned the health reasons for bringing home an older puppy. There's an additional issue to weigh against your desire to have your dog with you NOW — your life will be much more pleasant with a puppy at least ten weeks of age and ideally twelve weeks. Why? Very small pups cannot be trained at all because they don't care! A dog fits himself into your life because he wants to please you. Pups under ten weeks haven't got the least interest in pleasing you. And until twelve weeks, they have no ability to control their bodily functions and are too scatter-brained to absorb any lessons. Please think twice before taking a very young pup.

YOUR NEW COMPANION NEEDS HIS OWN SPACE

Unless you live in an empty house carpeted with newspaper, your dog will have to be confined when first brought home. This is true for adults as well as puppies — it's quite common for adult dogs to forget their housebreaking during the stress of changing homes.

Confinement isn't necessary just because of housebreaking. You cannot imagine the damage an unconfined dog can do. My Beagle, Penny, literally dug a hole in my sofa. When I tried to confine her in my bathroom, she ate my shower curtains, laundry hamper, scale, five towels and a full roll of toilet paper. While I was absorbed in a good book, my Sheltie chewed the fabric off the corners of my bed's box spring. Friends have reported destruction of Oriental rugs, wall-to-wall carpeting, baseboards and antique furniture. The wiring, stereo speakers, books on lower shelves, magazines in coffee tables and clothing you haven't hung out of reach are all frequent targets. Shoes, wallets, belts, slippers...need I continue?

You cannot dog-proof a house. You must house-proof the dog by providing him with a place where he lives whenever you aren't paying direct, focused attention to him until he's old enough or settled enough to be civilized.

In addition to your comfort and the safety of your possessions, your dog craves such a space. He wants a safe (to him, not you), den that's well ventilated but not drafty, private yet never "banishment distance" from you. He needs a place to be alone, to sleep deeply, to hide favorite toys and to escape from "dangers." Since they first came into the world, canines have grown up in dens like this, a small, tight-fitting hole in the earth or rocks with only one opening that can be easily watched for approaching danger (one opening insures that nothing can sneak up on a blind side). The need for a den is in every cell of a dog's body.

Where is this wonderful den? No room in your home is effective — even a windowless bathroom, laundry room or kitchen (all of which are very inconvenient bathroom/dog houses) have ceilings that are too high to resemble a dog den.

The perfect solution is the wonderful crate. A crate is a den, with the additional advantage of being portable so your dog can go where you go and still have his secure home! Of course, a crate looks exactly like a collapsible cage so dog neophytes always gasp in horror, They're forgetting that dogs don't always see the world the way we do — they honestly love crates and professionals, who certainly love dogs, swear by them. At any a dog show, hundreds of thousands of dollars worth of dog are stacked five crates high all over the backstage area and every champion is quietly resting in his "home."

Sandy (Bichon Frise) Fahringer is very content in his den.

The right crate is one made of metal bars, a tightly latching door and a sliding metal tray as a floor that can be removed for easy cleaning. Traveling crates with solid plastic sides perforated with a few breathing holes are NOT recommended as they can limit fresh air and trap too much heat in the summer — they're great for travel but not for raising your dog. The right crate is such a tight fit for an adult dog that it's astonishing to see dogs easily turn in them. Buy adult-size for your puppy so he can use part of the floor as a bathroom at first. When at home, drape a light blanket or sheet over the top and three sides to give your dog that one-entrance security he relishes. And once the crate stops serving bathroom duty, put an inexpensive, fuzzy bathroom rug on the metal tray to give him a nice bed.

The crate can make basic training a breeze for two reasons:

Dogs do not soil their dens unless they can't help themselves. When a pup gets control at about twelve weeks old, a major part of housebreaking is automatically complete if you rush him outside every time you open the crate door.

By putting your dog in his crate whenever you're out, sleeping or too busy to pay attention to him, your dog will never learn bad habits. Whenever his teeth head for a slipper or a chair leg, you're alert and able to stop him before he begins. There's nothing to unlearn.

In addition:

Your dog has a safe place to retreat to whenever he's frightened, overwhelmed or simply in need of a sound sleep. If you have a house full of guests, your dog may retire to his crate entirely on his own volition. During a move, my seven-year-old German Shepherd was so excited when the movers brought her collapsed crate into the new house that I set it up. Although she hadn't seen it in five years, she was inside the second it was up. She'd been a nervous wreck before, but for the rest of the move she contentedly observed from inside her den.

Throughout your dog's life, the crate can make travel and visiting easier. Your dog will feel more comfortable in strange surroundings, and your hosts will be happier when you all go out if your dog is confined.

Crates are readily available these days at all large pet supply stores.

SHOPPING LIST FOR YOUR NEW DOG

What else does your dog need in addition to his crate? On the following pages is a shopping guide for what you'll need during the life of your dog. I've indicated when you will need each item. This is basic equipment — I haven't included every possible toy and game or specialty training items.

DOG OWNERSHIP SHOPPING LIST

Item	When To Get	Specifications
Food:	Before arrival	*Start by feeding your dog what he has been eating so you don't cause an upset tummy. If you want to change foods, do it gradually by mixing the new food in with the old.*
Food Dish	Not before 6 mos	*Get dish with weighted bottom so dog doesn't lick all over room, choose one wide and shallow. Only dogs with long ears should have a high, narrow dish (to keep ears out of food). Permanent dish is too big for small pup.*
Water Dish:	Before arrival	*Get a big dish you only need to fill once a day even when your dog is thirsty. Forget those mats and trays — dogs don't usually leave a mess where they're placed.*
Bed	Before arrival	*Use soft, inexpensive bathroom rug. Puppy may eat his bed, don't invest now.*
	After teething	*You don't HAVE to get a fancy bed. Be sure your dog uses a bed and that he likes the type you've chosen before finalizing purchase.*
Collar	Before arrival	*Soft trainer—soft fabric slip collar with 2 rings. Slip collar through one ring to form and attach leash to other ring.* ***Do not leave on.***
	6 mos or when most growing is done	*Buckled collar—All collars should have about 2 fingers of slack. Attach ID, license and rabies tags to this collar.*
CHECK ALL COLLARS FREQUENTLY. While pup is growing, he will grow out of several collars. Do not get a body harness; these can hurt dogs under their legs and offer you no control over your dog.		*Smooth nylon, small chain link or large link training collar, type chosen to match size and fragility of dog. Use this collar for walks to insure good control. Collars with "teeth" should not be necessary if you've trained properly.*

Item	When To Get	Specifications
Leash	Before arrival	*Fabric or soft leather, 6′ long (at least 5′), not so heavy it pulls slip collar down. For small dogs, no wider than 1/2″. For giant dogs 5/8-3/4″, bolt-type, swivel snap clasp that opens by pushing hinged piece (dogs can open others). Make sure leash is comfortable for you to hold, some hurt hands. YOU MUST HAVE THIS TYPE OF LEASH. Retractables are options not to be used in many situations.*
Retractable Leash Do not use in crowded places or when you aren't paying close attention to your dog (they can cause bad accidents in cities). Not to be used in training except at very beginning and when teaching COME.	Any time, after arrival	*Leash that's 20′-30′ long and retracts into handle —get one where you can fix leash position.*
Brushes & Combs	Before arrival	*Start with very simple brush and comb, then add as you need; exactly what you need depends on your dog — a good pet supply store or a groomer can guide you. When in doubt, use a gentler model — you never want to scratch or hurt your dog, but you must get down through all fur to the skin.*
Nail Clipper	Before arrival	*I prefer the razor variety with a circular opening that you slip the nail into, then close handles to slide razor across opening; I find scissors tear nails but others disagree. Get the very best; saving money here may only hurt your dog and make clipping more difficult.*
Shampoo Never use people shampoo on your dog.	After arrival	*Any good brand shampoo for dogs., I prefer those containing lanolin for no very good reason.*

Item	When To Get	Specifications
Pooper Scooper	Before arrival	*Colored, small kitchen scrap bags work fine; some people use paper towels.*
Muzzle	After arrival	*New, molded, hard plastic, mesh-style muzzles don't bother dogs the way old ones did. Need for travel in Europe; good idea to have one handy just in case your dog is injured or you run into some other problem.*
Chew Toys	Before arrival	*Start with thin rawhide strips or small chips available in any supermarket; as your dog grows,add bones and other toys. These are vital to exercising gums and teeth, and removing tarter from teeth. Crucial during teething to give the dog something good to chew instead of your belongings. Some say the pure white untreated rawhides are easier on a dog's digestion. My dogs never had a problem with any variety.*
Other Toys	Before arrival	*Offer variety of soft and hard; shapes and colors really don't matter to dogs. Avoid brown lumpy toys — across the room on the floor, they look like "that." If your dog destroys them, get stronger toys and immediately remove the ripped up ones (they are not good eating).*
Tug-of-War Toy	4-6 months	*An old sock of yours is great, especially if you've worn it for an hour to give it your smell. The dog can learn this sock is his, all others are yours. While dog is teething, don't pull too hard. Dogs don't play this game or ball until they're at least four months and sometimes not until six months.*
Balls	4-6 months	*If you, like me, don't enjoy crawling around, reaching under furniture to retrieve rolled-away balls, don't get one.*

Make sure ball is big enough not to lodge in throat and choke dog (common emergency).

Item	When To Get	Specifications
Newspaper	Before arrival	*You need a lot more than you think you do. Glossy magazine paper doesn't absorb liquids.*
Seltzer water	Before arrival	*Use to clean up messes (removes scent), get a case. You'll also want lots of paper towels.*
Vitamins	Before arrival	*Get a good one-a-day multi-vitamin from your vet. Even vets agree this is a good idea while your dog is growing; optional when adult.*
Cod Liver Oil	Before arrival	*Mix a small amount into food several times a week (1 teaspoon for dog 20-25 lbs). Provides vitamins dogs get from sunlight; urban dogs don't get that much sun.*
Treats	Before arrival	*Milkbones — all dogs like these; all dogs are very, very fussy about anything else so experiment. Feed several a week to help clean teeth and keep tarter from building up.*

Chapter 8

HOW TO BE A GOOD TEACHER

Before we move into areas requiring you to train, let's pause to turn you into a great teacher — one who gets the desired results quickly, painlessly and accurately.

Ambra (Golden Mix) Farley is learning how to sit up during a play session on the roof of her city condo.

Dogs are taught in a combination of ways, but there are some fundamentals that apply no matter what you're teaching or how you're doing it. Let's start with four essential facts about dogs and training.

Fact 1: Dogs obey in order to please you. Humans have found dogs so helpful in so many ways throughout history because dogs don't work for rewards or to avoid discipline — they work simply to make you happy. Don't complicate this by giving rewards like food for proper behavior. Teach a dog to work for food and he'll become lax when food isn't always offered. It is in his genes to find your pat and warm, "Good boy!" sufficient.

Fact 2. If a dog decides on his own that he doesn't like doing something, he'll never do it again. Self-discovery is far more permanent than teaching him to obey you, so use this method of teaching whenever possible.

Fact 3. It's tremendously difficult and sometimes impossible to break bad habits. Better your dog never learns the habits in the first place.

Fact 4. The more your dog learns, the more he can learn. I firmly believe dogs can develop the habit of learning and continue throughout their lives. I once read an animal behaviorist's statement that dogs' brains have only room for fifty words and then are filled up. I made a list of what my German Shepherd knew — and stopped at a hundred words and phrases. I later added at least twenty more.

Take every opportunity to talk to your dog, stretch his experience and add to his reservoir of knowledge — it will become easier and easier; your companionship will become ever more rewarding. Deliberately expand his vocabulary by naming his toys, combining the things he knows in new ways. Soon he'll "go get" each of his toys at your request and impress all your friends with what a genius he is.

Now we add to these five rules for effective training:

Rule 1 - Be consistent. Dogs are extremely observant and quite able to make connections. If you bend the house rules a few times, your dog will quickly figure out you don't always mean what you say and test every order, every time.

Rule 2 - Never repeat. A dog will take every inch you give him. If you don't get an immediate response when training, correct the dog. Do not simply repeat your command or your dog will decide he can wait until you really mean it. My Beagle obeyed everything the fifth time I said it, by which point I was apoplectic. It was my fault — this is what I'd taught her.

Rule 3 - Keep your cool. Teaching a dog, like a child, is best done with a cool head and aloof emotions. A temper tantrum only confuses and frightens the animal, and risks the danger of abuse. Remember you're teaching a baby the right way to behave, not dealing with a malevolent, deliberately destructive incorrigible. Your dog isn't throwing your love back in your face by misbehaving. Administer corrections calmly and deliberately so you can completely control your tone of voice and the severity of the correction.

As with children, there are times that try men's souls. When you come home to find your garbage spread all over your house with tasty morsels decorating all your upholstered furniture, ignore your dog until you chill out. (If you use a crate, this will never happen.)

Rule 4 - Follow up with positive reinforcement. There may be times when you deliberately withhold affection and attention from your dog as a form of correction, but generally speaking, when shaping a dog's behavior, a "bait and switch" training is most effective. Example: When a puppy starts to chew your table leg, administer the negative (a loud NO!), then offer your pup one of his toys; when he takes it, give the positive (GOOD DOG!).

Rule 5 - Avoid excessive use of force. Your corrections should only be as strong as they need to be to get the desired action or reaction. What you must make clear is that you are displeased — with some dogs, the sound of displeasure in your voice is sufficient all by itself. My German Shepherd was shattered when I was displeased and NEVER repeated that action. Other dogs, particularly Terriers, require a more forceful communication of your displeasure to get the message. Start with the least force and escalate until your dog is listening to you. I'll tell you more about this later on.

For now, remember that excessive force can ruin a good dog. It can break his spirit, cause him to turn on you or convert him into a cringing, cowering ball of fear. Start with kindness and firmness. Don't approach training with preconceived notions about what you will or won't do.

THE VOICES OF A GOOD TEACHER

Your voice is the most important part of good training. Dogs are so highly skilled at "reading" tones of voice that your voice can have a greater impact than the words you say. It's so vital that a great trainer is really a master of the three voices.

Voice 1. Command. This is the voice in which you issue orders to your dog. You speak at a normal volume. This voice is neither angry nor hard but stern. It's like a military command, saying, "No nonsense now, obey this instant." It's clipped, never crooning or cajoling.

Voice 2. Correction. This is the "mad" voice. It's a bit louder, harsh and very abrupt. It says, "I don't like what you're doing one little bit and you WILL stop it this moment." The harsher you make this voice, the better training will go. You always use the correction voice when you say NO! and BAD DOG!

Voice 3. Praise. This is the baby-talk, filled-with-love voice that's overflowing with absolute delight at how wonderfully good your dog is. It's crooning, a bit higher than normal, soft, syrupy and intensely emotional. Men have a hard time using this voice well, but it's priceless for good teaching — this is the voice dogs will work for; to them, it's the biggest reward in the world. The praise voice always says GOOD DOG!

The more dramatic and exaggerated these voices are, the easier and more solid your training.

YOUR TRAINING ARSENAL

From the moment you bring your dog home, you need to begin teaching him a variety of behaviors. For the fastest and surest results, you'll use several different methods. Sometimes, you'll utilize a strict "lesson" format, but at other times, other methods may actually work better and be a lot more fun for both of you. Teaching should actually permeate your life with your dog and become a part of all interactions.

Formal instruction. Lessons are used to teach basic commands such as SIT, DOWN, HEEL and other behaviors you want to be able to induce. Lessons are also used to drill your dog on better performance of commands you've initiated with other methods — such as SPEAK, SHAKE HANDS or ROLL OVER.

Lesson commands are always issued in the command voice and the praise voice immediately rewards obedience. The correction voice is not used very much in formal instruction since you should assume your dog isn't obeying because he doesn't understand what you want of him. Instead, you "correct" your dog by reteaching him. The only exception to this is when you have a very obstinate dog who knows what you want but chooses not to obey (be certain this is the case). In such situations, a harsh correction voice can underscore that you're serious.

Formal instruction is always serious. This is not play time but learning time. Because lessons are intense, they shouldn't be longer than half an hour, even less with young dogs. Very little formal instruction can be done before the dog is six months old.

Correction. This is the way you shape your dog's behavior to suit your lifestyle. Correcting is how you teach the house rules. You want to make it clear these actions are forbidden now, in an hour, next week and forever. To communicate this message, use your correction voice to say NO! Speak so harshly that at first your dog is startled into stopping, then when he does, shift to your praise voice and tell him he's a GOOD DOG! for not doing what he was doing.

If your dog is oblivious to your tone of voice, a sharp slap across the bridge of the nose with your fingers underlines your command (it startles rather than hurts). Some dogs respond well to simply clapping your hands as you say NO!

Self-discovery. This is a wonderfully tricky form of teaching in which you do not seem to be involved in the learning process at all. Your dog simply finds that his actions have unpleasant consequences and decides to stop them. It's a way to avoid excessive use of your harsher voices and what dogs learn for themselves is a permanent lesson. This is the way I taught all my dogs not to destroy shoes. Every time they started chewing, the shoes had the most distressing tendency to slap into their faces. That quickly made chewing no fun at all. Of course, what was really happening was that I unobtrusively grabbed the end of the shoe and flipped it, but the dogs didn't notice that.

Self-discovery is also a wonderful way to teach your dog not to crisscross in front of you on the leash and trip you. Every time he crosses, walk into him; he'll quickly decide he doesn't like getting tripped and stomped and will never suspect you were deliberately involved.

Positive reinforcement. Here's another tricky one: Praise your dog for doing something he doesn't know he's doing until he figures out what it is and starts doing it deliberately in order to get your praise. You can use this method in three different ways:

1. *Supply a command when your dog is performing a function you like, then follow up with praise. This is the way to teach a dog to relieve himself on command. Soon the dog associates the word with the action and you'll then be able to start the action with the word.*

2. *Trick your dog into doing what you want then praise him for it. This is the ideal way to teach a dog to speak. Give the command SPEAK, trick the dog into making any kind of noise, then tell him he's "speaking" and this is wonderful. Once he understands that SPEAK means to make a noise, it's quite easy to refine the command until he's barking nicely. To stop the speaking, say STOP or SHUT UP in your correction voice — to startle the dog into silence, then praise.*

3. *Praise your dog for doing something good as a means of turning the action into a behavior you can command. This is a good way to create a protective dog — just praise him every time he acts the least bit protective (or even alert) and soon he'll behave that way more and more strongly and more often.*

This also can be used to show your dog you prefer one action instead of another. Suppose your dog is devouring everything in the house. One day you hear silence and go to see what he's destroying now, only to find that he's quietly chewing on his sock toy. "You've got your sock," you say in your most syrupy praise voice. GOOD BOY!

Play. While you never play during lesson time, teaching during play time can be a wonderful way to expand your dog's vocabulary, expose him to new experiences and give him important lessons about his own self-confidence and the world in general. It's not the way to teach specifics you want your dog to obey, however.

Example. The last way a dog can learn is by copying the actions of others. Because dog language is body language, dogs are incredibly observant. They watch you all the time and the proof is that eventually your dog will make a really weird-looking face at you with bared teeth and lips pulled way back. This is as close as he can get his face to your human smile! Dogs make this face only at people, never other animals. For some reason, mine only did this secretly, when I was deep in a book or absorbed in a television show. I'd glance over and there would be a dog resting quietly across the room grinning at me.

Use their powers of observation to enhance your communications with your dog. Obedience training will teach you hand signals which experts find improve dogs' responses. The best way to teach COME mimics dog body language. I found my dogs quickly read rather complex messages from my actions at home so, at times, I deliberately used those observations to communicate back to them. My dogs all quickly recognized that when I took my slippers off and put on outdoors shoes, I was going out. If I began putting on makeup and jewelry, they'd settle down and stare at me sulkily, clearly understanding that makeup and jewelry usually meant I was going out but they were staying home. If that wasn't true and they were coming along, I'd go get their leashes and put them by my purse — they understood immediately.

YOUR OPTIONS FOR CORRECTION

To me, the word "correction" is more appropriate than "punishment" because a dog does not commit crimes deserving punishment. They merely need correction or adjustment of their behavior. However, correction can only be effective if your dog understands that you are displeased. Sometimes it takes more than a "mad voice" to convey your unhappiness.

Correction must be done carefully, first by following these three rules:

1. **Never call a dog to you for correction.** Coming to you must always be associated with pleasure or you'll never have reliable, complete obedience to the vital COME command. If your dog has misbehaved and left the scene of the crime, go get him. Carry him back, if possible, drag him if necessary, but do not call him to you.

2. **Never swipe at a dog and miss.** This is what leads to hand shyness and, even worse, it will teach your dog that he can evade correction by running away — a very dangerous lesson.

3. **Never confuse your dog by using anything but your harsh correction voice when you're telling your dog his behavior is unacceptable.** Crooning "This hurts me more than it hurts you" may work with humans, but in dog lingo it means, "I'm bad and I'm good" at the same time.

The tone of your voice is EVERYTHING. If you don't believe me, try saying BAD DOG! in a praise voice to a well-trained dog and watch him wag his tail in pleasure.

When voice alone isn't enough, escalate. Use the least amount of corrective force necessary to make it clear to your dog that you are not happy. Some dogs are so sensitive that voice alone is enough. Many Bulldogs and several breeding lines of Cockers can be destroyed by excessive force. German Shepherds and some of the other working breeds have such inner dignity that they are offended and deeply upset at correction.

But alas, that's the exception. At least initially, you may be forced to do something more to establish clear communications with your dog. If yours pretends he's deaf, or gives you a brief look then continues, or bounces around the house merrily as if it's all a game, you need to do more. Try tapping him sharply on the snout with your fingers, snap your fingers, clap your hands or keep a soda can with a few pennies around to shake noisily. These are all devices to get his attention and once you have it, use your correction voice at its harshest.

If none of this produces a dog who's not happy that you're displeased, you have to get tougher. With Beagles, American Eskimos, Schnauzers and many other Terriers and Hounds, you've got to break through that powerful will and impose yours. Training books offer an intriguing array of ideas for more forceful corrections and as a person who hates spanking, I've tried them all — sometimes with horrendous results. One book said to throw that pennies-in-the-can rattle. When I did it with my Golden, I created a lifetime fear of falling and tossed objects. Other books suggested grabbing the dog by the neck and shaking him roughly — when I tried this on a Schnauzer, he came at me in full attack and a Sheltie crumbled into a pitiful shaking heap — it took weeks to get her back to normal. Only after that incident did I realize, in dog language, this is total, absolute domination — it's literally the way dogs kill. Now I say to use this only if everything else fails.

The fast hand. A very good friend of mine who had never been around dogs acquired a Rottweiler who grows into a very large, extremely powerful dog. Her form of training was to beg, "Oh, please don't," and needless to say, when I met the six-month-old dog, he was out of control. I was sitting at the kitchen table, chatting while my friend cooked, when the dog tried to get up onto a chair next to me. I smacked him smartly, saying, "NO! OFF!"

Next, the dog decided to take the butter off the table. Another smack across the snout that was already on the table and a "NO! BAD DOG!"

Ten seconds later, the dog decided sample the potato chips on the table. Smack again, with another harsh correction.

"Stop beating my dog!" my friend shouted. "Boy, do you have a fast hand."

Three fingers across the snout of a Rottweiler merely gets his attention; it does NOT hurt him. But it is true, I was not really aware that I use the smack so frequently until this episode. Although I don't smack dogs who listen to my voice and learn from it, a Rottie who's gotten away with murder for six months needs some reinforcement and so, alas, do a great many other dogs.

In correcting unacceptable behaviors, administered just as the behaviors start, as in the situations I just described, a smack can really speed the learning process. Even that Rottie wasn't trying to repeat any of his behaviors near me. I think a fast hand is a good thing to have, if it's used with discretion.

Coventry: A kind form of tough correction. One of the most effective forms of forceful correction is what I call "sending the dog to Coventry" — which means putting the dog in isolation. Since I use crates, I don't actually send the dog anywhere, although friends have effectively sent dogs into the bathroom, the tub or other places of banishment. Whether the dog stays or leaves, Coventry means that he ceases to exist for an hour or more. No one sees, hears, talks or touches him. This must include everyone in the house.

When he comes crawling to someone (which he will do repeatedly to everyone in the house), the person says harshly, "Is this the bad dog that did that bad thing? Get away — I don't want a bad dog here." Then the person turns away, with no touches or further interaction.

This must last for a considerable time after it has begun to bother your dog. If he settles down peacefully for a nap, you might have to go for many hours. Remember, that nap may be a "Well, you're not bothering me" defense. It's your will over his.

Remember, too, that if one member of your family creeps off to offer consolation, the battle is lost.

Spanking the right way. When Coventry doesn't work, spanking is the next step. And except for tiny hairless Toy breeds, spanking with your bare hands really does hurt you a great deal more than it hurts your dog. All that muscle and fur cushions any blow from a bare hand so effectively, it's probably felt like a strong pat. Unless you're a linebacker with the NFL or a prize fighter, you're going to need something more than your hand for any dog who weighs more than ten pounds or has very thick fur.

I know that for decades, people have said the right correction tool is a rolled-up newspaper or magazine, but this never worked for me. First, I couldn't find the paper or magazine when I needed it and had to delay while I rolled it — during which time my dogs got into their crates where I couldn't correct them. (Of course, just running to the crate means the dog got the message of my displeasure so it had some effect.) Second, I've seen dogs become shy of paper and others turn into habitual paper chewers as a result of using the rolls.

My favorite correction tool is a wooden spoon which has no other association to a dog. The spanking, of course, was always applied with totally controlled force and a cool head — I was always making my displeasure known, not trying to hurt.

Another advantage of using the spoon is that once I use it a few times, I can threaten with it and get my dog's immediate attention, with instant understanding that Mommy is not happy. I pick up the spoon, shake it and say, "Stop now or you'll get the spoon." Soon, I only need to mention the spoon, not show it — "Listen to me or you're going to get the spoon." The spoon has worked so well for me that with four different dogs, I only applied it ten times!

Jumping up to the top of the correction ladder. There are a few things dogs will try to do which must be absolutely, totally forbidden forever, either because they're so dangerous or so awful you cannot live with a dog that does them. Eating anything on a city street is extremely dangerous — the tasty scrap could be poisoned. The first time your dog reaches for anything like this, jerk the leash so hard, the dog is literally pulled off his feet — while you use your very harshest, loudest voice to shout, "NO! BAD DOG!" It must be totally clear to your dog that this is forbidden forevermore.

Relieving himself on your bed is completely taboo. Even if you've never used anything but your correction voice, a stronger method should make it clear to the dog that this is way beyond normal behavior adjustment.

LEARN "DOG"

Your entire life with your dog will be much richer and more enjoyable if you learn a little about your dog's language. No, I'm not suggesting you get your sense of smell enhanced. Dogs, like all canines, speak with their entire bodies. Tail position, ear position, body position, even mouth — all are parts of "dog language." When a dog bows with the front of his body, waves his tail high and opens his mouth (and even pants), he's saying, "Let's play" to another dog. Try bending over in a pouncing movement and opening your mouth — and you'll be stunned by the delighted reaction of strange dogs. There are excellent books available that tell you all about the language of dog (see Appendix).

Chapter 9

YOUR FIRST DAYS TOGETHER — PLEASURES & PAINS

The first weeks with your new dog — whether puppy or adult — are precious times you'll never forget. You'll spend hours simply watching your dog in fascination. You'll store up countless wonderful memories. Be sure you have a camera ready along with dozens of rolls of film to catch all the unforgettable moments. This time, when you and your pet are falling deeply in love with each other, is indescribably special.

But be warned: It isn't all marvelous. There will be days when you drag home in desperate need of peace only to be greeted by a dervish whirling around with so much extra energy he's nearly exploding. There will be days when you're still picking up the remains from one act of mischief when your sofa cushion flies past you with a pup underneath. You'll have moments when you look at your formerly neat house and wonder if you or the house will survive. You may also question whether or not your dog is retarded, insane or otherwise completely unmanageable. As the saying goes, this too shall pass. Eventually your pet will become calm. He'll learn and pay attention to you. Damage will diminish then disappear. Those most wonderful and most nerve-wracking of times will simply become a memory. So be prepared to treasure and endure your first days together.

UNDERSTAND YOUR PUPPY

Puppies are much like human children. They have enormous amounts of energy which they expend in tremendous bursts during which I honestly believe they're incapable of hearing you. Fortunately, the hyperactivity is dissipated quickly, after which, like toddlers, they drop instantly into sound sleep. After about the twelfth week, this nap-and-dervish cycle starts to dissipate.

You must allow your puppy to expend all his energy. If he's been confined all day, you may have to ignore your own exhaustion in order to give him an hour of vigorous play. Don't try to communicate or cuddle with him until he's calmed down. And if your home has little open space and a lot of knick-knacks on delicate tables, you might want to puppy-proof your place for the first few months.

By the way, even small-and medium-sized adult dogs can have what I call "crazy hour" after a long day of waiting for you. They charge around the house as if pursued by demons, spending their energy in an excellent workout. You or a visitor can also cause energy attacks in puppies and high-strung adult dogs by playing too hard for too long — just as with small children, you have to watch for signs that you're getting the dog overexcited. This is when bites often occur, and I don't think such bites are truly the dog's fault.

As you watch your puppy discover the world around him, remember infant bodies can't do all the things adults can. Don't urge your puppy to do what he's not ready for, such as jumping too high or on and off furniture before his bones and muscles are sufficiently developed. And don't be upset if you occasionally hear a sharp yelp during active play even if a limp follows. Muscles do get pulled and don't require emergency trips to the vet. Move the leg around to see if everything works normally, then wait to see if the limp is still there the next day.

Just because a dog has arrived in your home, don't turn into a storm-trooper. Slow and gentle is the rule with all forms of training during the early days. Puppy minds aren't fully developed. They cannot learn too much quickly. As with human children, their attention spans are short. Teach them what's necessary and be patient with backsliding.

UNDERSTAND YOUR ADULT DOG

When an adult dog enters your home for the first time, he needs a great deal of loving understanding. Like a puppy, your adult dog has lost his home, his neighborhood and the people he grew up with. Unlike a puppy, he doesn't have the innocence to greet this massive change with a sense of eager discovery. He feels abandoned, no matter what the conditions of the change. Insecure. Uncertain. Homesick. This is true even if he was abused or neglected in his last home. Dogs love unconditionally — it was home to him and he loved his people. If you've adopted from a shelter, your dog has also experienced an examination by a strange vet and life in a crowded kennel.

When he arrives, he'll be stressed, confused, perhaps frightened. "What's happening NOW?" he'll be wondering. "Where am I? Will I be staying here or will they change everything around again in an hour or a day? Who are these humans? What do they want of me?" When people feel like this, they call it traumatic shock.

He needs even more peace and quiet than a baby. He needs lots of love and reassurance. Don't spoil him. Do insist he follow the rules, but do it with gentle, loving firmness. And give him a great deal of affection.

Don't be surprised if he "reverts," forgetting his lessons and his housebreaking. He may even behave in an infantile manner. This is quite common in children as well as dogs who have suffered traumatic shock. Be loving and supportive, but gently insist that he remember what he knows.

If you work full time, leave on the television or soft music on the radio while you're gone for the first couple of weeks. The sound of human voices will reassure your dog that he hasn't been abandoned and will mute sounds outside of your home which could frighten him. Thirty percent of all "working parents" leave the radio or TV on whenever they leave their dogs behind.

Over-stressed dogs are very susceptible to illness; it's important to help him heal and watch him carefully for signs of sickness during his first couple of weeks with you.

When you say COME!, neglected or abused dogs may come on their bellies, with tail tucked beneath them. Call such dogs to you only to love them and gradually they'll come proudly and eagerly. They may also cringe away from your hand and flinch if you raise a hand suddenly — show them hands are for loving.

If you know your dog was lost, hold his leash tight enough to let him feel that he's attached to you when you go out. He needs reassurance that he can't get lost again.

IN THE BEGINNING: A NAME AND LOTS OF LOVE

To win your new dog's devotion, do what comes naturally — love him. Pet him, cuddle him, play with him and reassure him. Spend as much time as possible with your new dog during the first few days. And don't get lost in a book or a video. Interact and talk with him, cuddle him, watch him (that's fun anyway). Praise him highly for being good for the slightest of reasons.

While you're doing all this talking, teach your dog his first lesson — his name. Use the name constantly. Repeat it, say it, say it again and again in every context you can. Do exactly the same thing with adult dogs and puppies — and in less than a week, he should be responding to his name without hesitation.

GIVE YOUR DOG HIS NEW DEN

If a dog has not been confined in an unpleasant way, he will take to his crate without problems. Bring him to the crate and encourage him to enter — perhaps there's a toy inside or a treat. Any dog who has had positive or no experiences with crates before should go right in without pause. If he's uncertain, put him in, leaving the door open, and praise him. If he settles down inside, let him be. If he comes out, accept it and let him continue exploring. Later, put him back in again. And repeat. (If an older dog plants his feet and balks or runs away, there's a bad crate in his background — you can't overcome it. A crate is not for him.)

To make being locked in the crate pleasant, be sure there's water, a few treats, some rawhides and toys inside for your dog to enjoy. For a young puppy, he'll have to sleep on a pad of newspaper on top of the metal tray. Older dogs can have a nice fuzzy floor as a bed.

Keep the crate pleasant by following some basic crate rules:

1. **Never scold for anything your dog does inside his den** — if he wants to make it a bathroom, fine. If he chews his bed into fluff balls, it's his bed to do what he wants with it. (That's why I recommend cheap bathroom rugs.)

2. **Never pull or call a dog out for correction or scold him when he's inside.** His crate is sanctuary. You won't believe how quickly he'll figure that out.

3. **Never send him to the crate for correction.** It's not a bad place, it's a good one.

4. **Never lock him inside for correction.** Whenever you lock him in, be matter-of-fact — this is what we do at bedtime, this is what we do when your parents go to work, this is what we do when your parents want to watch a movie.

5. **Never take him out when he cries to come out or he will quickly be crying at you at three in the morning.** Say sternly, "No, I'm not ready for you yet." Then when he has settled down quietly, he can come out.

Eventually your dog will use the crate less and less on his own — sometime between six months and a year. If it's in your way, you can put it away at this point, but don't get rid of it. The crate will come in handy on many occasions throughout your dog's life.

SOCIALIZE YOUR DOG TO THE WORLD AROUND HIM

Experts talk about two forms of socialization. I've already told you about the imprinting done on very young pups. The other form is habituating dogs to all the different experiences of the bigger world, and it's just as vital as the first. A dog raised in a cocoon grows up terrified of noise, crowds and all the other things that surround him the moment he comes out of the cocoon.

Although you want your dog to settle into his new home quietly, you also need to begin to acquaint him with the wider world in which he's going to live. You do this by gradually but steadily exposing your dog to a variety of people, settings and experiences.

Start by taking your dog outside. If your pup doesn't have all his shots, don't let him sniff anything in the street or make any new friends. But get him outside! At first, take him on a short walk on quiet streets at a quiet time of day, but as soon as he's comfortable outdoors, expose him to more until he has experienced a full range of the urban life on the street. Take him to shopping malls with outside walkways. Take him INTO stores wherever you're allowed. Take him to parks and let him see skateboarders, inline skaters and runners. Let him see buses, trucks, bicycles, strollers, wheelchairs, everything you can find. Let him be close to a truck as it rumbles by. Allow him to hear police and ambulance sirens. Let him see that there are other dogs around in all sizes. If you live in a protected area where so much stimulation isn't normal, take your dog into the downtown — the more he sees at a young age, the easier it will be to take him anywhere without problems when he's grown.

Of course, while he's learning about this confusing, noisy, often chaotic world, you will be talking to him in a soothing voice, laughing about sudden noises or startling events, showing him you see no reason for alarm and expect him to be the same.

If you live in a high rise, let him run up and down the hall, exploring that. Take him into the stairwell and learn how to go up and down stairs.

If your dog is ever timid or nervous, speak encouragingly to him but don't pick him up or take him back inside. This can teach him things really are frightening or that acting scared gets attention from you.

At the same time as you're exploring the outdoors, invite friends over to meet your dog, one at a time at first, then two and three, so your dog becomes comfortable with people coming in and out of your home.

Adult dogs also need to become familiar with your neighborhood, the experiences they'll encounter. In fact, if they haven't been properly socialized, they may well be quite fearful and will need extra time on quiet streets and lots of reassurance from you. The only exception is very traumatized older dogs — they need quiet time with just you for about two weeks before you start socializing them. Take them out to do their business on a quiet street at quiet hours, then bring them right back inside.

HABITUATING YOUR DOG TO CARE

As soon as your pup or adult dog arrives home, you should begin getting him used to the things you're going to be doing TO him all of his life. If you skip this, you could be setting yourself up for a lifetime of battles that make you wish you were a wrestler and could even force you to spend a great deal more on professional care than is necessary.

Handle his food and water. You are the giver of food and water, and you have the right to remove it or change it at any time you wish. Not all dogs agree — and possessiveness about their food and water is the first step in a type of aggression that can end in biting.

During his first meal, pull his dish away. If he growls or shows any aggression, say NO! very sternly, hold the dish for 10 seconds, return it, then take it away again. Keep it up until he does not growl. Whether he growls or not, do this at least every other meal for at least a week. Do the same with his water when he's drinking from the dish.

Groom him. All dogs need grooming at least once a week — a good brushing, at the very least, to massage and stimulate the skin, remove dander and move the body oils up through the fur. All dogs should also be carefully and completely examined to spot any problems early.

To make grooming sessions a pleasure, dogs must understand that correct behavior does not include biting brushes, wriggling all over or trying to escape. A dog should be still, allow you to move him and his body parts without a struggle and hold positions. Teach him this behavior on his first day home. Make grooming pleasurable by crooning to him as you work and telling him repeatedly he's a good dog, and start out by being exceptionally gentle. But if he starts wriggling, he's a BAD DOG!

During your first several grooming sessions (at least three times a week for the first few weeks), touch every part of his body. Pick up his paws and separate the pads so you can check in between them. Open his mouth and run your finger over his gums.

At least simulate clipping his toe nails. He probably doesn't need a nail clipping yet, but during your "lesson grooming sessions," take your nail clipper and position it on each nail.

Teach him about eye and ear cleaning. Many lighter colored dogs have "weeping eyes," especially in city environments — some people think cigarette smoking and city pollution create or exacerbate the problem. Unless you want your dog to have long black streaks down his face, get him used to having his face cleaned regularly. Every day, I would hold my dog's head firmly and using a finger wrapped in a tissue, gently but firmly clean out the inner part of the eye area. If black streaks form or if you don't want to go so close to the eye, get him used to you literally washing his face every day with a face cloth. To cleanse, use a dot of dog shampoo (not people soap unless your vet approves a specific type) on a wet cloth, scrub away, then rinse with a clean, wet cloth.

Dogs with long, floppy ears also get very dirty ears (the big flap on the ear traps dirt inside) which need constant cleaning. You can swab out the visible ear with a cotton ball soaked in olive oil. For deep cleaning, get your vet to show you what to do. Again, simulate cleansing on your new dog as part of each grooming session.

ESTABLISH THE HOUSE RULES

Before your dog arrives, decide what you do and don't want your dog to do so that you can stop anything undesirable before it really gets started. It's very hard to break a bad habit, easy to prevent one from forming. And remember that what's cute in a puppy is not always appealing in a full-grown dog.

Establishing house rules isn't a matter of giving lessons — instead, it involves using your dog's first three phrases: GOOD DOG, BAD DOG and NO! If you use your voices correctly, your dog will instantly understand what these words mean.

House rules must be absolutes. You cannot say, "do it sometimes" — dogs understand Yes and No, not Maybe, not Sometimes, not Just This Once. All those equivocations merely indicate GO FOR IT! to a dog.

How do you teach these rules? Since you're watching your dog, the moment he begins to do something forbidden, you say NO! in a strong, loud voice. He's startled and stops. Immediately, you say GOOD DOG! in your warmest voice. When appropriate, offer an alternative — a toy instead of a table leg for chewing, for instance. And when he takes his toy, you say GOOD DOG! again in your warm voice. That's all there is to it!

Suggested House Rules. House rules are the basic behaviors which make the difference between enjoying your life with your dog and suffering or bending over backwards to change your own behaviors. Here are my rules — use them as a starting point for building your own list.

1. **Stay off the furniture.** Frankly, I didn't mind dogs on the sofa until I discovered that the weight and nails of a large dog will shred delicate upholstery fabric. If you don't want dogs on the chairs and sofas, PICK UP your puppy for a cuddle and put him back down. Hold him only on your lap, not beside you. Never let him learn he can jump up on the furniture — and if he tries, use a very strong NO, BAD DOG!

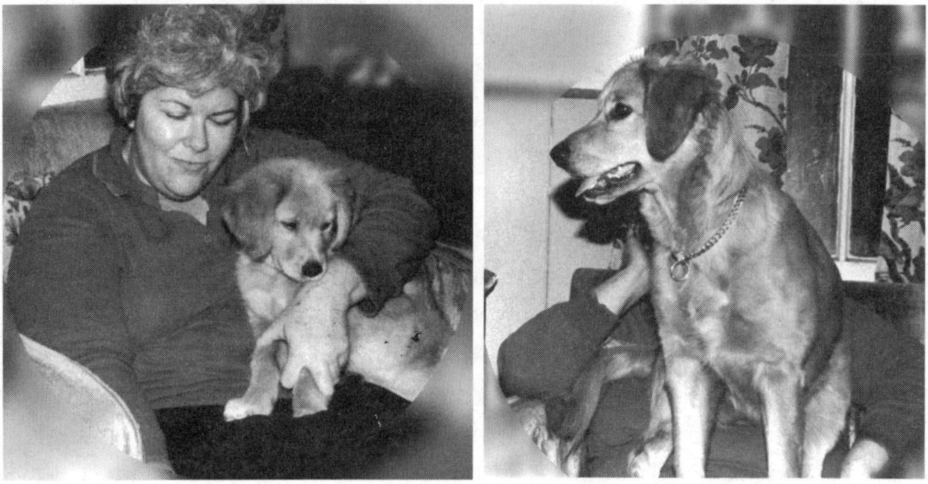

Remember that what's cute in a puppy isn't always so much fun in an adult. This is the author paying for her own mistake!

2. **Do not remove anything from a table, counter or other furniture surface.** Even if a tossed toy lands on a table, the dog should ask you to get it for him. Don't let him discover he can take anything off tables.

3. No begging. Dogs learn to beg at the speed of light. Do not ever permit yourself or anyone else to give your dog scraps from the table. If your dog starts giving you soulful looks, give him a sharp NO! then tell him he's good when he goes away and settles down.

I reward good non-beggars by letting them lick the dinner plates AFTER dinner ONCE IN A WHILE. If you do this too often, your dog will demand "his" plates before your guests have finished their coffee and conversation. Keep "plates" a rare treat, not a right. If your dog ever becomes insistent, tell him he's a BAD DOG and refuse plates until he makes no moves toward them at all.

4. No dogs in bed. Think about this carefully. Even if you're alone in that bed now, will this always be the case? If not, sudden banishment on "The Night" could be very difficult because your dog may already be jealous and insecure due to your focus on another.

6. No eating shoes or anything else made of leather. Dogs do graduate from shoes to belts, wallets, purses and even clothing.

6. No chewing clothing. I had one dog who loved to remove buttons and or run around the house waving underwear in front of guests. Yes, it happened.

7. No chewing furniture, upholstery or rugs. No throwing cushions or pillows around the house. The sole exception is the washable throw rug you give your dog for his bed — that's his to do with as he pleases; you gave it to him.

8. Do not remove anything from the lower shelves.

9. Do not eat the houseplants. Some houseplants are poisonous to animals. Making them forbidden could save your dog's life!

10. **Do not remove anything from closets or drawers.**

11. **No chewing paper, toilet paper or tissues.**

12. **Do not go into women's purses.** Or briefcases or pockets.

13. **It is forbidden to even sniff the garbage cans.**

14. **Do not throw your body against windows.** I only knew one dog who did this whenever she saw a dog outside and went through THREE picture windows! Never got a scratch.

15. **No chewing wooden furniture legs, baseboards, woodwork, paneling or electric cords.** Many puppies try all these.

Full-time workers also need to remember that whether you've adopted a pup or adult, training is going to go slower and take longer, simply because you aren't there to catch things and correct them for many hours of the day.

And never compare your dog's progress to other people's comments about how fast their dogs learned; their memories are more than likely flawed.

Chapter 10

GROWING PAINS: MORE PUPPY LESSONS & COMMON PROBLEMS

Unlike a country dog who can learn his lessons gradually, a city dog has a tremendous amount to absorb almost immediately. As a result, his first few months are spent in a world of NOs and BAD DOGs. Personally, I think this is an awful way for any creature to start life, and why I urge all new dog-owners to provide their pups with lots of love, crate confinement, positive reinforcement (saying GOOD DOG any time you can), using self-teaching tricks whenever possible, and doing everything else you can to minimize the NOs and make the dog's life more enjoyable.

HOUSEBREAKING — THE GREATEST BATTLE

Housebreaking starts the moment your dog arrives home. With puppies, the first thing is to learn your puppy's pattern so you can catch him BEFORE he goes and get him to the right place in time. You can't start with scolding when your dog first comes home. Puppies cannot control their elimination processes, but each does have a distinctive pattern — the faster you learn that, the fewer the in-house accidents and the easier the housebreaking. All dogs go right after you take them out of their crates. Small pups go every couple of hours, and almost always after sleeping, eating and playing. The trick is to figure out how long after sleeping, how long after eating and how long after playing the urge strikes your particular dog. And are there any other consistent occasions — does he stop fifteen minutes into play and go, for example? Every time you get him to the right place and he goes, you praise him effusively. At first, however, you don't scold at any other times. After a few right moves, some incredible dogs will start to tell you they need to go out — but you have very little time to read that message, which could be very subtle, before a puppy's urges are overpowering.

Older dogs are easier to housebreak because they take their time getting ready to go. They have elaborate sniffing and turning rituals which are easy to spot, and they can hold on while you rush them outside. Try to do this with your puppy as well, but don't expect miracles of yourself. Pups don't give obvious signals of their needs and the signals often last for about ten seconds. Pups are likely to just plunk down and go in one continuous motion.

As your dog approaches his fourth month, he'll start to have some control, but you can't expect complete housebreaking until the fifth or sixth month.

Unfortunately, this is also dog puberty, the time when most dogs challenge your authority by strongly resisting your efforts to tell them how to behave. I've known this to happen over basic house rules (suddenly, your dog starts shredding books or chewing rugs after weeks of being good), but usually the big challenge arises over the final steps of housebreaking when your dog knows where you want him to go and where you don't but hasn't completely stopped using the house. This is a rough time for all, when even the best trainers with the mildest dogs wonder about their abilities and despair of ever having a well-behaved companion. And if you've chosen a willful, independent, tough-minded breed, prepare yourself for a major battle.

Prepare to keep on to the end because this is not a battle about housebreaking. To your dog, it's a war over who's going to be the boss. If he wins, he runs the house and you'll never have a reliable dog. With a very strong-willed dog, you could have a dangerous dog who one day might decide to discipline you for trying to order him around. You must win.

The good news is that this is the only such battle; your dog will never challenge you again.

Start housebreaking by defining your goals. If you're using the crate properly, you aren't bothering with paper training — your dog is having "accidents" in the house or you are getting him to the place you want him to go, whether that's an in-house litter-box or the curb outside.

People who want to give their dog the option of using a papered area in the house OR the outdoors are fooling themselves. Dogs are black-and-white — it's here or there, not mostly there but sometimes here. Don't go there. All dogs occasionally have problems which end up with a mess in the house. A well-housebroken dog will generally choose a spot close to the door and will usually avoid carpeting. And they feel awful about it.

Once your dog has reasonable control and shows some understanding of where you prefer him to go, it's time to make it clear that it's not a preference but a requirement. You must begin to show him that it's not good to go inside and it's very good to go out. Every time he goes in a forbidden place, he has to understand this is unacceptable. Show him what he has done and tell him he's a BAD DOG. Show him even if it's hours later. That saying that dogs don't remember is balderdash. Don't they remember who you are, and to sit, come, and not to eat your rare books? Whenever he does things correctly, tell him he's good with lots of pats and a really syrupy voice.

It won't take long before he's going outside just fine, but still using the house as well. Unfortunately, this final stage is where that who's-the-boss battle begins. You must escalate your correction of his "accidents," making it ever clearer that this is totally unacceptable. Not allowed. A VERY BAD DOG thing. Put him in Coventry. Leave him in longer and longer. At the same time, praise him longer and even more lovingly when he's good and start rewarding his goodness with small treats, like a piece of cheese or small piece of meat. Make it more unpleasant to be bad, more pleasant to be good. Keep it up.

As you come out of the battle the victor, it's time to take the next step in training — to move from your dog's schedule to yours. When the time approaches for your dog's usual trip outdoors, delay a while, watching him to see if he really needs to go. Gradually shift over to the walk schedule you want to follow, and whenever accidents occur, back up a bit. Learning to follow your schedule is something that happens almost automatically.

Dealing with piddlers. Many young dogs become so excited by events like your arrival home from work that they "piddle" uncontrollably. You shouldn't punish this because they literally can't control it. You can avoid piddles by making events quieter and not indulging in elaborate greetings — rushing the dog into another activity to distract him, such as immediately hurrying him out for his walk, or picking the dog up.

In fact, picking the dog up is a great solution for other housebreaking problems. If your dog has a tendency to let loose en route to the street, in the hall, elevator or lobby, your neighbors will look much more kindly on your dog if you pick up your dog and carry him UPSIDE DOWN to the curb. Upside down keeps everything inside, right side up usually wets you.

Do not teach your dog to take long walks. Have you seen those poor dog-owners hiking for miles in the gutter, out for what seems like hours in even the worst weather? They've all been bamboozled by their dogs! The dogs have figured out, "The longer I hold it, the longer the walk!"

Wouldn't you like to be able to take your dog out for two minutes when you're in a rush or the weather's bad? If so, separate the walk from the "business." From the very first time you take your dog out, take him to "his place" and wait a few minutes. Nothing happens? Go back into the house. Wait a while and try again. For a while, you'll be going in and out rather often, but the result will be a lifetime of freedom! Now don't destroy this by always giving your dog a walk afterwards — the walk happens sometimes but not always. It is not linked to the "business" part.

Teach your dog to go on command. It's very helpful if your dog relieves himself on your command. The first time I took one of my city dogs to the country, she was bewildered — where was the curb, the asphalt? "Go potty," I ordered. She did. This is so easy to teach: Every time your dog begins to go, issue your order (whatever words you want to use), then say GOOD DOG! in your praise voice. Eventually, try ordering him to go before he begins. It's done!

Don't spend half your life taking the dog out. I keep hearing about people who take their dogs out every three hours when they're home. This is ridiculous. As adults, my city dogs thrived on two walks a day no more than fifteen hours apart. Most days, they went out at eight in the morning and eleven at night. Mornings were strictly business; evenings, if the weather was nice and I had time, included a tour of the neighborhood of up to an hour. They only got an after-work walk if I was planning a late evening.

Does this sound cruel? **One more time: DOGS ARE NOT PEOPLE.** None of my dogs ever developed kidney, bladder or colon problems so this is healthy. In addition, several of my dogs were trained to ask to go out if nature called and they never, ever asked for an extra walk unless they were ill — my Shepherd frequently got diarrhea and would wake me at night when she had it, but she never asked for an extra walk on a normal day.

I gather they managed to control themselves without discomfort because every single one of my dogs trained herself not to drink much water when I was away, even though it was always present. I have no idea how they figured this out.

You achieve long intervals of continence by gradually lengthening the time between walks as the dog matures. Until he is nine or ten months old, at least three walks a day are mandatory. It's easy to tell if you're stretching your dog beyond his abilities — he shows signs of discomfort or accidents start happening after housebreaking is complete.

Don't ever ask your dog if he wants to go out. I have never known a dog who said, 'No, I'm not in the mood." The opportunity for a walk at any time is too great a treat to pass up.

COLLARS AND LEASHES

Your new dog must learn about wearing a collar and a leash immediately. Most dogs take to them so easily that you wonder why anyone bothers to discuss the topic. A very few dogs have extreme reactions so it's best to be prepared. Problems are truly unusual. I've worked with scores of dogs and only encountered bad reactions three times. None of this, by the way, applies to those who adopt adult dogs — they all know collars and leashes.

Teach collar and leash in the house.

Start with the collar. Show it to your dog. Let him sniff it, but no chewing; collars and leashes are serious things, not toys. Then slide it over his head. Most pups will shake, then act as if nothing happened. But one Sheltie rolled all over the room and managed to get an end into her mouth, then raced around growling, pulling and choking herself. I didn't remove the collar until she settled down. This is important: Your dog must never conclude that acting crazy about the collar will get it removed, or you'll never be able to collar the dog.

With the Sheltie, this act continued for nearly a week, then suddenly, the collar was nothing worth paying any attention to at all!

Once your dog is at ease with his collar, introduce the leash. Again, show it to him, let him sniff but not play with it. NEVER LET YOUR DOG PLAY WITH HIS LEASH, no matter how much fun it seems. A leash is for training, for work, for paying attention. When it goes on, it's time to be serious not just for your dog's training, but for your dog's safety in an urban environment.

Although most dog books tell you to let your dog drag the leash around the house to get used to it, I am most vehemently against this for city dogs. City dogs should never know they can run away by dragging the leash!

I think it's much smarter to get the dog used to the leash by slowly, rather playfully getting the dog to understand the leash controls his movements. I hold it high so the dog gets accustomed to how it will be held normally. During our first session, I go where the puppy chooses, without allowing the leash to pull tight at all. Gradually I start directing the dog's movements with the leash by wriggling it and making lots of sounds to encourage the puppy to move where I want, without any pulling. So long as the puppy is relaxed, I continue to guide him a little more forcefully, bit by bit.

Eventually, however, there comes the moment of reckoning when the pup suddenly charges off in a new direction and the leash pulls taut. If you're lucky, he'll think, "Oh, guess I have to go where this thing is going" and that's it. You're also fortunate if he sits down abruptly, then bites the leash. You bend down, pull it out of his mouth with a "BAD DOG! NO CHEWING YOUR LEASH!" followed by "GOOD DOG!" when you've got it out of his mouth. Then go back to the same activity.

Leashes are NOT toys. Ebby (Lab/German Short-Haired Pointer) Verna is being a very BAD GIRL!

The worst reaction is a panic attack, which you'll recognize by the pup's total terror of the leash. Immediately walk closer to your dog to create slack and remove pressure, then bend over while you croon to your dog. When he's calm, remove the leash. Remember you don't want to teach him that a panic attack gets the leash off or you'll have panic attacks every time you want your dog to do ANYTHING. Start again the next day; he'll relax eventually.

The most common adverse reaction is a full-blown temper tantrum which could be passive resistence ("I'll sit here until it goes away") or back flips and other acrobatics which may be accompanied by barks and growls. The puppy must not win. He must learn that (1) to reduce the pressure around his neck, he must come to you, and (2) if he goes where you go, he stays comfortable. He must, therefore, come to you and stay with you.

Call him to you and pull on the leash. If he fights harder, literally drag him to you by the leash, then reach down to be sure the collar has loosened while you tell him he's now being a good dog. Then start walking again, encouraging him to follow you. As soon as he's taken two steps with you, this difficult lesson is over. The reaction may continue a few times more, or once will accomplish what you need.

Dogs very quickly learn that collars and leashes mean they're going OUT WITH YOU! Since this is just about the best thing in the world, they love leashes and collars and many dogs will fetch leashes and put their own heads into their collars.

TEACHING "COME"

Most training books don't get to COME! until they've told you how to teach a whole bunch of other things, but the truth is you're using the COME! command within five minutes of getting your dog home. There he is sniffing around in the corner saying to himself, "What is this interesting new place?" and you're so eager to cuddle him and love him that you call, "Buster, come to me!"

Therefore, if you want your dog to come correctly whenever you give the command, you've got to know about COME! before the dog comes home!

The problem with not teaching COME! early and correctly is easy to see all around you — just look at how many people in your nearby park are screaming "Come, come, come," often followed by expletives, at dogs who are merrily ignoring everything. Given the dangers to a loose dog in an urban area, it's clearly vital that your dog obeys you at once.

COME means your dog should come to you instantly at a run and stop right at your feet. Accept no approximation. Teach this to your dog the very first time you use the word so that he doesn't learn there are other ways to respond.

This is one of the few commands you teach with "bait" or food rewards. Assemble several delectable treats like small pieces of cheese or meat. Show the treats to your dog and let your dog see that you're holding them in your hand. If he's not too interested, give him one. Now let him wander away. This will take a while since he now knows you're holding. Just relax; eventually he'll find something else of interest.

When he's distracted, crouch down and spread out your arms lovingly (this says "let's play" in dog talk). Open your hand to show your tidbits and using a loving, slightly playful version of your command voice, say his name and "COME." He will invariably charge you, at which point you tell him he's a good dog, pat him and give him a tidbit.

Repeat this procedure three or four times twice a day. Strengthen your voice until you're using the full command mode. After a week, shift to commanding while you're standing. After he responds to that, don't always have a tidbit on hand.

Always insist that he come fast, immediately and directly to you; never let him get away with anything less. Do not use the command for any other reason; if you want to bring him to your vicinity, use some other word or phrase. I use "Here" when I feel my dog is wandering too far and merely want him back in my neighborhood.

Once your dog is responding to COME! properly, take him outside and start all over again with crouch and rewards. Pick a totally deserted area where it is completely safe to let him off leash (the roof of your building, for instance) or use a "long line," a leash with 6' of rope tied onto the handle so the dog can wander really far.

Sometimes dogs get sloppy, testing to see if you really are going to insist that he come like that. If this happens, use the leash to give him a tug, then reel him in properly by pulling him to you hand over hand. When he's back where he should be, tell him he's good. As this manner of returning isn't too pleasant, he'll prefer to obey.

TEACHING SIT

COME! and SIT! are the two most basic commands, the first things taught to a dog and with lazy owners, often the only thing dogs ever learn. They're important because they give you control over your dog's actions.

To teach SIT, pull up your dog's head while you push his rear down. As Molly (Mutt) Paterson discovers, she must sit.

SIT! is very easy: Put your dog on leash, loop most of the leash around your right hand so your puppy is on your left side with no slack in the leash (but it isn't pulling). Now you want to coordinate what you do: Say his name and SIT! in your command voice while simultaneously pulling the leash up with your right hand and bending so your left hand is pushing down on his rear back. In other words, you're pulling his head up and pushing his rear end down so he has no choice but to sit. Now praise him highly.

Do this five or six times, twice a day.

Within a few days at most, you'll notice your dog beginning to sit before you apply any pressure. The next time, just use your voice and pull the leash up. If he sits, praise him. If not, go back to the full treatment.

Once he's sitting without the push, try the command and wait about ten seconds before pulling the leash.

This usually takes about a week.

THE AGONIES OF PUPPYHOOD

All puppies go through some unpleasant phases. Here's how to deal with common difficulties:

Cries in the night. A lonely puppy can howl, sigh, moan, bark, yowl like a cat and more, all at very high volume. And a few pups can keep it up long enough to break you and your neighbors!

First of all, never put a puppy to bed right after a nap or just after you've returned home. He's wide awake, no matter how tired you are — and raring for play. He's got energy he needs to expend. In the beginning of your life together, you must go to bed when your puppy is tired out and ready for sleep.

When the noise first begins, wait it out. Puppies sometimes cry themselves to sleep within ten or fifteen minutes.

If it continues and he's just moved in, he probably wants his mama as well as the warmth and comfort of all his siblings. Try giving him a hot-water bottle wrapped securely in a terrycloth towel as a substitute for his litter mates and a loudly ticking clock somewhere in the room to replace the sound of their heartbeats. You'll probably only need this for a few nights.

If he's in a crate, bring the crate into your bedroom. That way, he'll have you but will still be confined and safe. He might try for more of you, figuring if he got into your room, maybe a little extra crying will get him into your bed. Unless he's extremely stubborn, your silence in your bed will make him give up within ten minutes or so.

If he's teething, he could be crying because his mouth hurts, especially if he starts later in the night. Give him a dish with small ice chips or a frozen teething ring (available in pet stores, you put it in the freezer for a while before using it). Both will numb his mouth and allow him to rest.

If none of these methods works, yell at him in a very angry voice. DO NOT EVER GO TO A CRYING PUPPY. That's just what he wants and an angry you is preferable to solitude. To him, his crying worked and he'll cry all the louder and longer when you leave. And the next night and the next. And when you leave him home alone.

Always be sure your puppy has food to munch, water and a few non-squeaky toys to keep him company when he wakes during the night because dogs do not ever sleep straight through the way we do.

If the crying begins some time after your dog has been living with you, something else is going on. If he's around six months, he may be ready to leave his crate. Provided he's fully housebroken, try leaving the door open to see if that's sufficient. If you've gotten a strong-minded, aggressive breed, he may be testing you to see who's boss. If he brings you out of bed and to him, he wins. Don't let him. If this is the situation, wait him out, occasionally shouting BAD DOG! QUIET!

If he's between three months and five months, he's probably teething.

Teething. Teething can start before three months and continue until he's six months old — different breeds teethe on different schedules. The entire process lasts about five months, first for the baby teeth and later, for the adult teeth. As I've mentioned, teething hurts. Ice chips and teething rings can give relief. The reason I've mentioned teething separately is because teething puppies use their new teeth on EVERYTHING. This is when they're apt to chew wires behind your chairs and outside. They're very prone to picking up pebbles and stones (which are not digestible). Watch a teething puppy closely at all times.

Teething puppies also yelp once in a while during play and their gums may occasionally spot blood. They can go off food for a day or so, too. One of the strangest teething side effects occurs in breeds with up-standing ears. If their ears go up early, the ears could flop back down during teething or go up and down several times!

I always avoid playing vigorous tug-of-war with a teething pup although there are conflicting opinions on whether this could actually cause malformations. I just don't want to take chances.

Too much fun and love. Even though it's good for your dog to meet your friends, pups are like small children in that they can be overstimulated and tip over into hysteria — and playing with strangers is automatically more exciting than playing with you. The pup will tire more quickly, yet might fight the need to sleep in order to please these humans. If he's getting too worked up, has reached nap time or seems to be shrugging off drowsiness, put him in his crate and lock him in for a while. Or at the very least, ask your guests to pay attention to you for a while.

Small children can be exceptionally draining on a puppy or even an adult dog in new surroundings. Supervise their play and stop play if your dog shows signs of becoming hyper or signals he needs a break by leaving, coming to you, hiding under the bed or going into his crate. Children or adults who chase down dogs are risking bites and it's not the dog's fault — but rather the inattentive adults.

Biting. Terriers and a few other breeds have a tendency to snap if something happens that they don't like. They must instantly learn that this is totally unacceptable with a very harsh correction.

All pups, however, have to learn how to control their jaws. Dogs have incredibly powerful jaws and amazing control over them. A retriever can bring back a bird without disturbing a feather. As a child, I had a dog who stopped my parents from hitting me by holding their arms and never breaking the skin. A Rottweiler who weighs over 100 pounds can play vigorously with a six-pound Chihuahua with no danger of injury to the tiny dog. For dogs, controlling the power of their jaws is a learned behavior.

By eight weeks, a puppy has grown razor-sharp teeth and jaws powerful enough to draw blood and hurt those he plays with. By eight to ten weeks, he has to learn he can and must control his jaws. If he's still with his litter, they'll teach him quickly. If he's already with you, do you have a friend with an adult female dog? Put them together for a play session and the older dog will teach the pup. If you're alone with your pup, you must be the teacher.

Basically, you teach the same way dogs teach each other. If a pup nips an adult, the adult will yelp, bite back hard enough to cause some minor pain and leave the pup. Play stops for a while. So you cry out dramatically, end all games and leave the pup abruptly. If this doesn't work, rap the pup sharply on the top of his snout as you cry out. If that doesn't work, bite his sensitive ear just hard enough to make him wince or yelp. Then leave him. That will work.

Once your pup is no longer biting you, it's time to teach him a little additional discretion. He needs to learn your body is inside the sock you have over your hand or the long-sleeved shirt you're wearing. Again, yelp, stop and leave. By this point, that should be all that's needed.

Chapter 11

MAKE IT EASY BY GOING TO A PRO

At six months of age, your dog is ready for school, and I urge you to take him there — for your sake as much as his.

I obedience-trained my first dog with the help of an excellent book and it was agony. My Beagle, Penny, played dumb, resisted me and generally made our lessons as unpleasant as possible. Penny learned eventually — sort of. She sort of heeled some of the time, but mostly only when I screamed at her. She sort of sat and lay down the fifth time I repeated the command. She sort of came the fifth or tenth time I called her, stopping to investigate interesting smells along the way, pausing at each until I called her five or six more times. She sort of stayed for about thirty seconds. It was such a battle to even get this far that I believed I had a well-trained dog!

A few years later, I yearned for a big dog, but felt it was impossible because a large dog must be well-trained. Even during the rare moments when I believed I could train the dog, I shuddered at the thought of the effort involved. Then a friend of mine who had acquired a lovely "little" puppy who was growing into what looked like a Saint Bernard found a notice about a new training class in our neighborhood. The teacher was a professional handler who had worked for some famous people and shown dogs at Westminster. If I could train my now eight-year-old bundle of stubbornness, I thought, I could handle a big German Shepherd.

Even the trainer was reluctant to take on an older Beagle, but to our surprise, Penny was the star pupil. She loved obedience class. So did I. In fact, I went on to assist in training classes, run my own and even show other dogs in obedience competition.

I am a firm believer in professional training classes. It teaches you how to handle your dog easily and with much less difficulty than you'll ever have on your own. Dogs learn to obey you despite the distraction of all those other dogs in the class — ideal for making a dog safe and enjoyable in an urban environment. And the bonding you and your dog develop during the training is absolutely fabulous.

Dogs love the training, too! They learn precisely what to do to please you — their greatest desire. They have your individual and total attention every day during your practice drills. There's no scolding, shouting or correction either, just instruction and praise.

Professional training teaches you to coordinate movement, command and demand in a way that produces fast, easy responses. It works on the dog's natural instincts and behavior to get what you want without force. It teaches you hand commands and other extra cues that also help your dog understand you more easily.

Your approval is the most important thing in the world to dogs; you cannot give too much praise.

Training also instills in you the habit of praising your dog the right way. Even though we love our dogs, we tend to be stingy with the praise until we work with a pro.

And the training class insists on total compliance. Alone, you'll find you're a bit of a pushover, very likely to accept partial obedience.

Professional training does not involve scolding. It's command and praise, command and praise. It makes your entire relationship a lot more enjoyable.

Training also takes very little time — usually six to eight weekly classes of one to one-and-a-half hours, and daily thirty-minute practice drills.

Where To Go

Dog trainers are not licensed. Anyone can run an ad and give a class. As a result, there are some very weird training schools out there that are a total waste of money. A friend told me she enjoyed taking her Doberman to school except when she had to "lie across his back" to make him lie down! That's one of the most unique techniques any trainer has ever heard — especially since DOWN is so easy to teach. You teach HEEL first, then swing around, unsettling the dog by getting him out of position and step back at him with a raised hand — the dog lies down automatically.

Find the good guys through animal organizations — local humane societies, AKC-sanctioned show clubs, local chapters of breed clubs and/or obedience clubs. Ironically, the best training classes are low in price — it's the frauds who tend to charge hundreds of dollars. A good course should cost under $100, usually around $10 a class.

Sending your dog off to a pro for training is NOT an option. Your dog learns to obey the pro, but if you don't know what you're doing, you'll have the same badly behaved dog at home. You need the training as much as your dog, if not more. You'll see the proof of this in your first class, when your trainer takes your unmanageable dog and has him heeling and sitting in moments — and you thought he didn't know anything!

I also don't recommend hiring a trainer to come into your home and teach you and your dog privately. The two of you will leave your house perfectly trained, go out onto the street and your dog will be uncontrollable. Learning to pay attention to your every move and command while ignoring all distractions in a class with six, eight, ten, fifteen other dogs is very important part of the lesson.

Basic Training.

A basic obedience class will teach you and your dog HEEL, COME, SIT, STAY (for long and short periods, at a distance from you), DOWN and a couple of fancy flourishes like returning to heel.

Your dog will learn to remain in the heel position right beside your left leg when you walk fast and slow, turn in either direction and stop. He will sit automatically when you stop, unless you request he not be taught this — which is a consideration for a light-colored dog who will be plunking himself down on a city street. He will learn to remain in the stay position, both sitting and lying down, when you leave him — despite dogs on either side of him and a trainer walking all around him and touching him.

At the basic level, all work is done on leash.

Fear of disease. Dogs in obedience classes don't interact enough to catch disease from each other. The people who take their dogs to class are much like you, responsible folks who aren't likely to let their dogs walk around with contagious diseases.

Practice areas. Your daily practices must be outside, but where? If you live in a condo with grassy lawns, you can surely find a quiet area away from people and other animals — just make sure your dog is "empty" before you take him to any place where elimination might be unwelcome. You can also go to a quiet area in a park.

In the heart of a city, you may be able to use a quiet, residential street or a business area during the evening hours. My favorite place to practice has been the roof of my apartment building.

Please go to a pro.

I should say something about attack dog training so I will: **DON'T DO IT!** A trained attack dog is a loaded weapon. The training sharpens the dog's attack instincts, encourages aggressive response to annoyances and, in general, loosens the dog's natural inhibitions to attack. Violence becomes a more "acceptable" response to your dog. With an attack-trained dog, you have good reason to fear his protective instincts.

In addition, dogs are trained to attack when you say a word you and the trainer select. It usually has nothing to do with attacking and is not a common word that would ordinarily be used around your dog. The problem is, it could still be said and it could set off your dog. There have been too many instances of children showing off to their friends by saying the secret word to their pet, only to wind up with small, bleeding bodies.

A trained attack dog does not make a good, secure companion. And it isn't necessary — most dogs have protective instincts and some will put down their lives for you, with no training at all. My Beagle, a breed famous for NOT being protective, once flushed a prowler hiding on my apartment floor. My German Shepherd once overcame her terror of thunder storms to place her trembling body between me and the open door. You will have that; you need no more.

Chapter 12

STREET SMARTS

People who live in a city require a special kind of savvy. Why else is it so easy to spot the visiting country cousins? They're jostled, shoved and cursed because they don't know how to move on a crowded sidewalk; they're robbed because they make it so easy for thieves; they complain of rudeness, rushed service and unfriendliness because they don't understand our brisk efficiency, high-speed way of life and self-sufficiency. Well, a country dog is just as uncomfortable, out of place and even endangered in an urban setting because he doesn't have the basic "street smarts" it takes to survive in the big town. So be sure to give your dog the savvy he needs.

PROTECT YOUR DOG FROM STREET DANGERS

Don't set your dog up for disaster by tying him in front of stores. Dognappers can get a good price for your dog from research labs and a small, friendly dog is easy pickings. Professional dog thieves can nab even large, ferocious dogs quicker than you can get out of a store.

Even if your dog isn't at risk of being stolen, he's still in danger. An amazing number of people think all dogs are darlings who must be touched, even when their owners are gone. These folks haven't got the slightest knowledge of dog language and can't recognize warning signs. Reality check: The friendliest dog will bite when he feels he's trapped — and when the just-one-pat stranger pursues your dog until he's at the end of his leash, he is trapped. He has nowhere to go except into that stranger's face and he'll do it with bared teeth. Once bitten, the stranger will scream "Mad killer!" at the top of his or her lungs, and the police and the judges may be just as ignorant. Your dog could die as a result of this idiot.

Don't expose your dog to this. Never tie a dog outside alone.

Be selective about your dog's friends. Exercise the control of a careful parent over the dog friends your dog makes on the streets if you want to avoid the risk of contagious illness and parasites. Dirty, matted fur or sick-looking dogs should be rapidly bypassed without a sniff. People with the most unwholesome animals are often incredibly persistent, following you down the block while demanding, "Our dogs want to be friends." If you run into any of these folks, lie and tell him your dog is fierce and likely to kill theirs or has a deadly disease.

Be alert for real killers. In one of my neighborhoods, a woman regularly walked her two large dogs off-leash. These dogs were known killers who had destroyed several small dogs. Many dog owners reported her, but because of the weakness of anti-cruelty laws, she simply received summonses for not having the dogs on leash. Whenever I saw these dogs, I picked up mine and RAN in the opposite direction.

Another friend used to run into a dog who would attack hers. When the dog was walked by his male owner, the man could hold the dog back, but when the female owner was out with the dog, he quickly escaped her grip. My friend's dog was ultimately injured quite badly. The only solution to this sort of situation is to change your walking routine and location. Go in the other direction and go out at times when the killer is not likely to be out.

Know when to set your dog free. No matter how well-trained your dog is, never take off his leash when...

1. Your dog might terrify your neighbors and turn one or more of them into "get dogs out of our home" vigilantes. As the fun ending to late night walks, I used to let my German Shepherd, Jenna, free at the corner of our block. I'd fling out my arm and say "GO!" and she'd race to the entrance door — until the evening that a departing guest nearly climbed onto the awning at the sight of an 85-pound dog charging at him.

2. Your dog might become confused and frightened and run off in a panic. I once let my Beagle loose around the corner from our home while she was absorbed in a scent. I continued around the corner; a moment later, I spotted my frantic dog racing straight up the street into the path of an oncoming bus which, fortunately, managed to avoid her.

You can NEVER let your dog off leash if he's hostile to other dogs because in an urban area, you can never be certain another dog won't suddenly make an appearance. Nor can you free any dog with a very strong chase instinct, also called prey drive. Chase instincts trigger automatic lunges after anything that moves by them quickly. These dogs will charge a runner, biker, skateboarder, rollerblader, trotting horse and anything else moving faster than a walk. This could cause the target to take a bad fall and your dog could keep going until well lost.

Always watch for broken glass. The most common injury for city dogs is glass cuts on their footpads, cuts that bleed horrendously, sometimes require stitches and can easily become badly infected. Until you look for it, you have no idea how much broken glass surrounds you. It's in the gutters, on the sidewalks and especially in the parks, right in the grass, on the dirt corners and on the walkways. Get into the habit of scanning the ground just ahead of where your dog is going to walk.

Bitches in full heat should not take walks. Every urban neighborhood has a few irresponsible residents who walk large male dogs off-leash, creating the opportunity for indiscriminate sex on a city street, with you as the supervisor. Even if your bitch doesn't meet a loose dog, there are still many people who have no control over their males and will be pulled down the street after you with their dogs exhibiting all the evidence of their readiness. I've even met strange people who, when told to keep their dogs away because my bitch is in heat, say "I don't mind" and seem perfectly ready to be co-voyeurs with me. None of it is fun. If you haven't spayed, restrict walks to 30-second "do your business" trips during her few days of total receptivity.

PROTECT YOURSELF FROM YOUR DOG

Your dog should never precede you through a doorway. All dogs automatically run in and out of elevators, building entrances and your front door as far ahead of you as they can get. This is highly dangerous! A dog could be pinned and seriously hurt by a heavy entrance door or break free and run into the street. If your dog ever gets into an elevator ahead of you with the leash between you and the elevator starts to move, your dog could be strangled. If your dog races out of your apartment at the wrong moment, a crook could push you back, shut the door and leave your canine protector outside. The best place for your dog at all times is right by your side.

A constant pulling dog puts you in danger. Ambra (Golden mix) could kill this woman.

To teach this important lesson, use the HEEL command your dog learned in obedience class. Whenever you answer your door or go through other doors, put your dog on HEEL and keep him there. Eventually, this will become automatic. Now you see how useful obedience training is.

Pulling you down stairs is also a no-no. Dogs also shouldn't race down stairways pulling you along — that's an invitation to a bad fall by YOU. The lesson is the same as for doorways.

PREPARE IN ADVANCE FOR EMERGENCIES

Doormen and dogs should be friends. If you live in a building with doormen, encourage them to make friends with your dog. Although you shouldn't take advantage and create ill will by asking the doorman to babysit while you run to the cleaners, there could be time when you desperately need the doorman to walk your dog. Here's a "worst case" scenario: You're walking your dog while accompanied by your visiting mother and she suddenly collapses. Do you want to run all the way up to your apartment to take your dog home while your mother lies in the street waiting for the ambulance? Do you want to say "Gosh, I can't come" when the ambulance takes off with your mother, sirens screaming? Or would you prefer to dash to the doorman, hand him the leash and ask him to put the dog in your home while you return to your mother?

Always carry some money. Even if you're just dashing out for a thirty-second walk, stick a ten-dollar bill in your pocket. You never know when your dog might get hurt on the street and you'll need to race him to a vet instantly.

Know where a dog ER is located. Every urban area has an animal hospital or team of vets to provide around-the-clock emergency care. Before your puppy comes home, locate this service and post the location and telephone number prominently near your phone. Write it on a card and put it in your wallet, too. Although there's no need to use these people for regular vet care, you must know where they are before they're needed, because when the crisis arises, there may not be time for research.

Teach a nearby friend how to handle your dog. You never know when a crisis at work, a family medical emergency or some other disaster might prevent you from getting home to care for your dog. As insurance, find a friend who lives nearby who's willing to take over for you. Get your dog used to this friend so he doesn't attack him or her when the friend opens your door. Teach your friend your dog's basic commands plus how to walk and feed your pet. Show your friend where the dog's medical records are kept and, finally, give him or her an extra set of keys.

Post a legal notice about your pets. In a number of states, if you're incapacitated, the law says your pets are to be automatically taken into custody and turned over to the local dogcatcher unless there is specific, written authorization for someone else (by name) to take over your care. I don't need to speculate about the potential dangers of having your dog taken to a shelter, except to say dogs have been put to sleep in this situation.

Write a note saying "In case of emergency or incapacitation, contact (name and work/home phone number) who has my full permission to take responsibility for my pets." Then post this where police or other authorities will find it easily and quickly, such as beside your phone, or on your refrigerator not half covered by pizza delivery coupons.

Obviously, you should discuss this with your friend beforehand; and perhaps you should provide your friend with a more detailed letter on your personal stationery for use if your dog is ever actually taken into custody.

Fire emergency. Many shelters and even some vets offer decals to post on a prominent door or window that notify fire fighters that there is a dog inside. Get one. Put it up.

Keep a special document file for your dog. City pets travel more frequently than their country cousins. They're also kenneled more often and put into other situations where up-to-date health records and other documents are required. Ask your vet for a free file folder (many give them out) or buy one in a stationery or pet store. Enter information about your dog's date of birth, sex, breed, surgeries, vaccinations, every shot, license number, rabies tag number, medications, special dietary or other conditions, plus your vet's name and telephone number.

Never leave a dog tied alone on the street. Barkus (Mutt) Paterson was beaten by a nut with a brick and injured so badly that he spent weeks in the hospital.

DON'T RESHAPE YOUR LIFE TO SUIT YOUR DOG

Create a flexible dog. Dogs love routines and simply adore getting in ruts. If you go along with them, they'll make your life utterly miserable any time that breakfast isn't ready at precisely 8:15 or their night walk doesn't commence at exactly 11:31. Not only will they make it impossible for you to sleep or see the end of a great movie on TV, they can even get vengeful. If you're not home by suppertime, your dog may decide to eat the couch for supper.

You don't live the kind of life that can be so regimented and I'm also sure you don't want to become your dog's slave, either. So quite deliberately vary your schedule while training your dog. Give them the message that they'll get a walk before bedtime, but it could occur early or very late. They'll eat every evening, but it could be at 4:00 PM or midnight.

Chapter 13

MS. MANNERS SPEAKS ABOUT CITY DOGS

Good manners aren't just something nice for city dogs — they're vital! City manners can make all the difference between a dog who's barely tolerated and one who's welcome everywhere. They can go a long way in helping more people accept more dogs in more places. And they can make your life a great deal more pleasant with far fewer confrontations with over-zealous dog lovers and dog haters. Here's how to make your dog a welcome addition to your neighborhood.

CLOSE ENCOUNTERS WITH STRANGERS & NEIGHBORS

How to make your dog invisible. On elevators, your dog should move quietly to a rear corner and sit either right beside you or even behind your legs. People were often surprised to find they'd been on an elevator with a Beagle and a German Shepherd when we started to exit — and I received many warm compliments on how pleasant the ride had been. To teach correct behavior, simply take your dog to the place you've chosen and tell him to SIT. After a while, he'll do the right thing automatically.

There's a time and place for play. In any crowded or busy public area like a building lobby or a street crosswalk, your dog should never frolic with other dogs. If he's obedience trained, you can simply put him into HEEL whenever other animals are around. Remember that people who fear dogs often mistake play for fighting and could become panic-stricken at walking near two happy dogs.

The entire outdoors is NOT a dog bathroom. In this day and age, you are undoubtedly required to "scoop" any time your dog relieves himself, but to non-dog people, just the sight of your dog doing his business can be an irritant — especially if it is in an area of high foot traffic. At street corners, your dog should wait quietly beside you and should never to permitted to relieve himself. Because of the frequent congestion at traffic lights and street corners, your dog should be at heel and ignore any other dogs.

Be considerate of your neighbors. Don't permit your dog to relieve himself directly in front of your building, where people are apt to be entering and exiting. Ban bathroom activity from just in front of the driveway to a parking garage and near the dumpster as well. Look around and give some thought to what would irritate a non-dog lover, then avoid any such activities. Remember, if enough people are irritated sufficiently, you could find yourself living in a no-pets residence!

Naturally, you will also control your dog on park walkways and in or right next to playgrounds as well.

By the way, your dog can always use the gutter. There's absolutely no reason for him to relieve himself on the sidewalk unless you haven't made it clear to him that the gutter is THE place or you've chosen the wrong gutter. When housebreaking, you should always take your dog directly to the gutter. If he starts to relieve himself on the sidewalk, use your foot to nudge him into the gutter.

If he's been trained correctly and is still trying to go on the sidewalk, the problem could be the place you've chosen. I knew a woman who persisted in trying to make her dog use a bus stop. I'm sure you're not that nuts but if your street is extremely busy, take your dog around the corner to a quieter place or take him between two parked cars — even dogs crave a little privacy and don't like to make elimination a high-risk enterprise.

At the same time, never let your dog move too far into the street. Some city drivers don't notice dogs or have such serious psychological problems that they actually will try to hit your dog.

Get that nose out of there! One thing that drives non-dog people crazy is sniffing dogs. For this reason, you need to train your dog not to poke under skirts or into crotches, or stick his head into grocery bags. To stop this, just cup your hand over his nose firmly, shake slightly and command NO SNIFF! Sniffing may be natural to dogs, but it's easy to control.

Teach your dog not to stick his nose into other people's grocery bags or body areas by cupping your hand over his nose and saying No SNIFF!

MAKING WALKS PLEASANT FOR EVERYONE

Keep your dog to yourself. Whenever you and your dog are walking on a crowded sidewalk, pull your dog in tightly against your side and hold him there by picking up all the slack in his leash. This will prevent anyone from tripping over your dog or his leash. Do the same thing when you pass another dog on the street and visiting isn't appropriate. If your dog is the type to get very excited around other animals, reinforce your actions with a stern HEEL!

It's their dog, it's their right. Always keep your dog from approaching another animal when you're asked to do so. It really doesn't matter why — it's their choice. There are plenty of other dogs in your neighborhood for your dog's canine companionship.

Respect dogs at work. Never permit your animal to approach dogs accompanied by uniformed policemen, dogs wearing official coats that indicate they're professionals at work or dogs held in harnesses by disabled people. All these dogs are on duty and any distraction could be dangerous to their handlers.

Oops! While Ebby's walker is window shopping, Ebby has "captured" a passer-by. Pay attention!

Guide dogs for the blind wear both a harness and a leash. When the harness is dropped and the leash picked up, you'll see an instant change in the dog as he goes off duty. At such times, it's appropriate to ask the owner if it's all right to introduce your dog. Never let your dog approach before you speak or the person could become alarmed; he or she is remarkably attuned to his or her dog. I don't know if any of the other dog assistants for the disabled have such a clear signal that they're on duty; when in doubt, avoid. Always assume a police officer with a dog is working.

Don't let your dog break your back. It's annoying to everyone if your dog goes berserk every time he sees another dog and even dangerous to you. If he lunges unexpectedly, he could pull you down or wrench your back. If your dog tends to do this, anticipate his action and put him in HEEL as soon as you spot an approaching dog, take up the slack and if your dog leaps forward, jerk back with a sharp HEEL!, then GOOD DOG.

Don't wear out your welcome. Many drug stores and cigarette/magazine/newspaper shops permit dogs to enter, which is a great convenience, allowing you to run small errands while walking your dog. Don't turn these few remaining dog-welcome places into dog-hating ones by trying to take your dog inside when a flock of commuters are getting their morning papers or at any other time when the shop is very crowded. It's terrifying to your dog to be surrounded by so many legs, upsetting to the customers (some of whom may actually fear dogs) and creates still more no-dogs-allowed spaces.

Two dogs can pass each other without commotion if you pull the leash tight and command HEEL!

Along similar lines, be aware that it's against the law to bring animals into commercial places that sell food. I've seen people sneak small pets into grocery stores and always wondered how they'd feel if a government inspector closed down the entire store because of their pet. The bottom line: Be considerate.

LIVING IN CLOSE QUARTERS

Does your dog fit into your kitchen with you? Many urban kitchens are too small for a busy cook and an excited dog looking for droppings. A scene like this is a recipe for disaster — a falling cook, a badly kicked or scalded dog or some other catastrophe. If your kitchen is small, teach your dog to stay out when people are in it. Tell him to OUT!, take him out and make him stay.

The polite way to entertain guests. Maybe you don't mind your dog jumping all over you (has he shredded your leg, your pantyhose or a delicate fabric yet?), but your visitors certainly include people who most definitely object to having a dog hurl himself at them.

It's easy to teach a dog not to jump on people. Each time he tries, bend your knee and lift your leg as the dog leaps, gently catching him in mid-air and pushing backwards. The dog doesn't associate this with something you've done deliberately — he just decides jumping is no fun. One very strange thing about this is that your dog will cease jumping on you but continue jumping on everyone else until you get a friend to do this. When your friend does it, jumping stops — on everyone!

Whether or not your dog jumps, he may be one of those dogs who gets so excited by the arrival of company that he makes a complete pest of himself, disrupting the visit completely. For those who aren't ardent dog-lovers, this is irritating enough to cut a visit short and avoid future ones. Even those who adore dogs will eventually resent the fact that they're really visiting your dog and not you.

Teach your dog to act with more decorum when guests visit by putting on his leash and commanding HEEL! before you open the door. Keep him there as you usher your guest in and settle him or her in a chair. At this point, on-leash, your dog may greet the visitor and be acknowledged, then he returns to HEEL and when you sit, he lies down and stays. Once he's very calm, let him go. If he becomes annoying, back on-leash he goes. He'll soon learn and all this won't be necessary.

A useful command to teach all dogs is SETTLE or COOL IT! It means "Stop acting like a whirling dervish or a clown and go settle down quietly somewhere." I teach it to dogs very early, before they're obedience-trained, by grabbing them and issuing my command very sternly, holding them until they stop wriggling around. Then I put them down by my feet and hold them there firmly until they decide to stay quietly. Once they understand this, I lighten up, allowing the dog to decide where he wants to settle — so long as he quiets down and leaves my guests alone.

By the way, if you've chosen a very hairy dog, you've accepted that a certain amount of hair is always going to be floating around your home — and you may even have given up wearing dark-colored clothing. But not all guests arrive dressed for hair. When I permitted my dogs on the living room furniture, I used to drape a blanket or sheet over the chair my guest used to protect them from becoming hair-covered. And a few times I had friends remove dark-colored clothing and don one of my robes upon arrival.

Barkers. Depending on where you live, excessive barking can be just an irritant or grounds for eviction. On the whole, urban life isn't suited to an indiscriminately mouthy dog. The ideal dog is mostly silent, barking only for cause — if a stranger comes to your door or walks around in your hallway.

In fact, you cannot completely control any dog's inherited barking patterns, but you can moderate them. With known barkers like most Terriers and Toys, you must begin the day your pup comes home. Don't permit any nuisance barking. If your pup barks when playing, when seeking your attention, when your alarm clock goes off, when the intercom buzzes or the telephone rings, or when there's noise in the neighborhood, stop it at once with a sharp NO! NO BARKING! With a feisty, spirited breed like a Terrier, punctuate your command with a sharp rap on the mouth. And if he keeps barking, hold his mouth shut.

True barkers use real reasons for barking as an excuse to keep mouthing off for the next half hour. As soon as your dog has barked sufficiently, tell him, NO! THAT'S ENOUGH! STOP!

Don't try to control dogs who bark or howl when they hear police, fire or ambulance sirens. The pitch of the sirens is actually painful to some dogs so they cannot control their reactions.

An even worse problem than the mouthy dog is the one who's mouthy only when he's home alone. Some dogs are so quiet when you're home that you may find it hard to believe they don't keep their mouths shut when you're away. Some dogs who don't bark much, like Beagles, have a large repertoire of yodels, loud whines, yowls and "songs" that can be even more penetrating. I discovered my Beagle was noisy by receiving an eviction notice — no complaint, no warning!

There are training remedies given in a number of books — when I got that eviction notice, I went through every book I owned (many) and tried everything suggested. Nothing worked! A trainer I called finally told me about the No-Bark Collar which contains a battery and gives the dog a mild electric shock whenever he barks. Despite the trainer's reassurances, I had grave reservations about using it, but I was out of options. So with great concern, I tried it — and it worked like a charm almost instantly, with no ill effects on the dog.

Later, I used it on my German Shepherd who was barking when I left her home. It stopped her in a couple of days and what's even better, it didn't stop her from barking when there was a good reason to do so; it only stopped the nuisance barking. Normally the dog has to wear the collar for about two weeks. No-Bark Collars aren't available everywhere, but I've seen them in pet superstores and catalogs.

Chapter 14

GAMES DOGS (AND PEOPLE) MAY PLAY

Have you forbidden your dog to lie on the furniture? Is he totally obedient? Are you sure? Try this: As you insert your key into your lock, listen for a soft "thump" — the sound of your dog jumping down from his soft, upholstered waiting place. Whether you hear the thump or not, the moment you enter, go right to the forbidden surface and put your hand on it. I'll bet that many of you will feel you dog's body warmth!

Anyone who says animals are totally without guile has never lived with one. Resting on forbidden surfaces while you're away is just one harmless instance of the great variety of tricks that smart dogs invent. Knowing your dog's games can save you needless worry, help you in training and give you a lot of laughs. I've always found my dogs are at their funniest when they're trying to put one over on me.

Take the case of the vanishing food. Some dogs consider any food left around for other pets to be fair game. The more vigilant you become, the craftier they are at locating and devouring, until you'd swear your dog can teleport food into his tummy while lying quietly at your feet! The solution? (1) Feed all your pets on the same schedule as your foodaholic, (2) Always remove unfinished food from the floor the moment an animal leaves the dish (you can offer nibblers the food again later), (3) Ask your friends to remove their pets' food dishes before you arrive, (4) Feed your cats on the kitchen counter.

Another wonderful trick at least half of all dogs figure out is playing human beings against one another. They'll cuddle up to visitors as if they've found their soulmates and completely ignore you. The result? Flattered guests slip them extra treats and intercede when your dog misbehaves, which he will as it's part of the game. If you fall for your dog's abandonment, your dog gets double points. You'll lavish extra love and treats, too, in a jealous attempt to recapture your pet's true love!

No one can predict what Poodles will invent, but they are the acknowledged masters of manipulation and duplicity. Obedience trainers have dozens of tales of Poodle diversions created when they decide class has gone on long enough. Many Terriers and Toys are nearly as good and some individuals are masters, regardless of their breed — my Beagle was Queen of Tricks.

Just what did my Beagle do?

Ghostly illness. After a two-week vacation, I returned home to find a badly limping, forlorn Beagle. What had my friends done when taking care of her, I wondered? My anger mounted as the pitiful dog hobbled around on three legs day after day. Yet my friends were astonished; they swore they'd never seen a limp and Penny hadn't suffered any injury.

After a week of limping, I carried Penny Beagle to the vet for extensive x-rays. Nothing wrong! Having cost me nearly a hundred dollars, Penny put down her foot and danced merrily along on all fours once again. She had finished punishing me for going off without her!

On another occasion quite late in Penny's life, a masseuse decided to try to relieve the pain of Penny's arthritis. Warning me that she didn't know much about dog anatomy, the masseuse worked carefully and gently. Penny lolled across her lap, a look of ecstasy on her face. I began reading.

Much later, the masseuse rushed up to me, almost in tears. "I didn't mean to hurt her," she said anxiously. "But I've made it worse. Look at her!"

Penny was moving across the floor, dragging one leg. "That's the wrong leg," I said dryly. "She wants you to work on it, too."

Fake ailments tend to appear suddenly whenever your dog feels you've been neglecting him. Although digestive upsets are not unheard of, dogs' favorite illness is a limp. Look for one that appears without any known injury, comes and goes, and switches legs. A poor dog can't remember everything! This type of illness should be suspected if you've just been away, out a lot, or very preoccupied. Verify your suspicions if you haven't seen a switch of legs by feeling the supposedly injured leg for heat or swelling, then manipulating it in various directions. If it really has been hurt, there will be a yelp of pain or at least a wince and an attempt to pull it away from you.

Oh the agony, the pain! Dogs can have a great sense of drama. If your dog ever howls or otherwise acts as if he's dying or in horrendous pain when you're administering medicine, cutting toenails, correcting, giving a bath or doing anything else your dog considers unpleasant, consider the situation carefully: Are you REALLY hurting him? If not, keep going.

I was taken in by this one for quite a long time until Penny forgot herself and started screaming BEFORE I'd begun to close the nail clipper.

Hunger strikes. My Sheltie once spent a week with friends and when I returned, I was told that the dog would no longer eat dog food. "What does she eat?" I asked.

"Steaks," was the answer. "She'll eat dog food or nothing," I responded. The dog actually fasted for four days, then wolfed down her dog meal and everything returned to normal. She probably figured it was worth a try to get an all-steak diet.

Don't fall for it! Don't be tricked into creating table scraps — I know someone who buys deli meats for her dog to mix into his food. Don't feed him an elaborate and expensive special diet. Don't heat his food. No dog will starve himself to death with perfectly good dog food in front of him, but some will try to make you think they will.

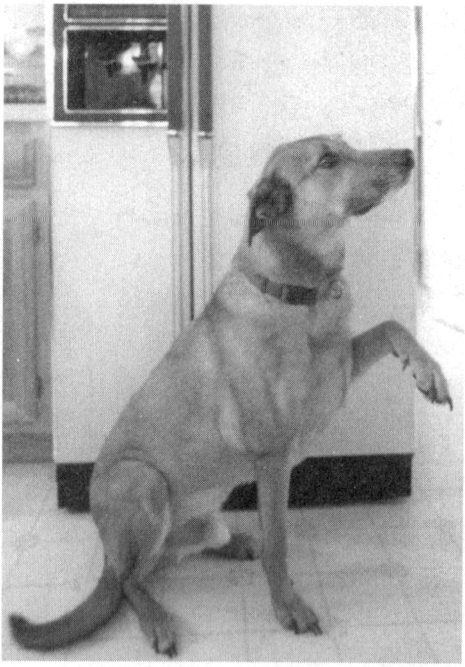

If your dog is looking from you to the refrigerator and turning on the charm, he is still begging.

The letter of the law. A dog lying in a far corner of the room cannot officially be begging. But if his eyes are staring intently at each morsel of food as it moves into your mouth and he is occasionally emitting extremely loud sighs, moans and groans to remind you of his presence, I call that begging and I very sternly tell him to stop.

A dog sitting in front of the refrigerator, blocking you from moving the leftovers inside, is also begging in my book. So is one staring intently at the refrigerator as if it's prey. So is one that fusses at you until you get up out of your easy chair, only to be led to the cabinet housing dog treats.

Dogs are wonderful in the way they obey the letter of the law, then grab off more letters if their methods work. Lying on the corner of the quilt that's dragging on the floor is not lying on the bed, but eventually, the quilt and blanket section of your bed will move down to the floor to become a dog bed. This may even happen while you're sleeping, which makes for some shivering wake-ups.

Resting his head on your lap is not getting up on you, according to the letter of the law. But when his entire upper body moves up on your lap, watch out, because the next step is to move the two back legs up as well.

COME! is not a fly-by, even when accompanied by a fast lick of your hand. The command STAY does not mean it is okay for your dog to creep forward on his belly like a soldier when you blink. A dog who sniffs for twenty minutes before relieving himself is not out on business; he's taking a stroll with his nose.

No matter how cute your dog is while extending the definition of your rules, insist on full obedience — or suffer the consequences!

The fine art of innocence. If you were living with twenty dogs and came home to find a one-dog mess on the floor, you'd shout, "WHO DID THIS?!" and nineteen dogs would hang their heads, looking incredibly guilty. Only one dog would bound around gaily or stare at you wide-eyed and deeply hurt that you could suspect innocent him. He's probably the culprit. Most dogs act guilty even when blameless, but a rare few have a simply marvelous innocent act. When doubting your own sanity ("I could swear there was a piece of pizza on the top of the counter"), believe in yourself and discipline.

A variation of the innocent act used by many more dogs is what I call "The Who Me? Act." This is what you get when you discover your dog blissfully dreaming on the forbidden bed. "Get off that bed this instant; it's not allowed and you know it," you shout. Your dog stirs, lifts his head and gives you that wide-eyed look: "Who? Me? Are you talking to me? I'm not on any bed, am I? Oh, yeah, well, how did I get here?" Keep yelling and hold your laughter or "who me" will take over your home.

Dogs even lie to each other. When I had a Beagle and German Shepherd, the Shepherd's job was protecting the house. She needed a job and the Beagle was useless as a protector — she almost never barked and greeted everyone as a long-lost friend. One day, the Beagle strolled into the living room and found the Shepherd sprawled across the entire sofa, sound asleep. This was the only piece of furniture the dogs were allowed on and there was no room for the Beagle. So Penny went to the door and as I watched, her fur came up in alarm. With a glance at the Shepherd, she turned and began barking fiercely at the door. The Shepherd sprang awake. "That's my job!" she seemed to say and raced to the door barking. At which point, Penny Beagle backed up, turned and jumped onto the couch.

TURNING THE TABLES: TRICKS FOR YOU

If your dog is going to use trickery on you, aren't you entitled to occasionally make your life a little easier by tricking him? Here's my favorite bag of tricks.

The fast shuffle for pill haters. Anyone who has doctored a dog knows that most canines view pills as poison. They devise methods of avoiding them that range from eating an entire meal in three seconds yet leaving the pill in the clean, empty dish in solitary splendor to hiding a pill somewhere in their mouths for hours after you're convinced the tablet has long been swallowed.

There are dozens of methods to get pills into dogs and all work...for three or four pills. Shoving a pill down your dog's throat so far that it falls by gravity is the official way to administer medication — but after the first few times, you'll have to pin the dog down with a body press while working mouth and pill with your four hands.

There's one method that keeps working for years: Cut up a dozen tiny, one-swallow pieces of soft cheese or meat (cream cheese or liverwurst). Stuff the pill into about the eighth piece. Now begin feeding your dog the treats, starting with a large one so he can taste how delicious it is. After that, feed them faster and faster so he is frantically swallowing in order to get the next one. As soon as the pill goes in, shove the rest of the pieces into his mouth at light-speed. This will be so exciting to your dog, he'll never know he just took a pill.

By the way, there's also a wonderful way to give liquid medicine. Buy a medicine syringe at your pet supermarket or pet supply catalog. Instead of a needle, it has a hole at one end, but it fills by pulling back the plunger, like a syringe. You can easily measure the dosage. Then, you stick it into your dog's mouth as far as possible and press the plunger. The medicine squirts back where the only thing your dog can do is swallow it. If you've ever been coated from head to toe in Robitussin, you will understand how wonderful this invention is.

Mice on the furniture. If your dog is using the sofa, bed or chairs while you're out despite your orders to the contrary, it's probably best to adjust yourself to it. But if you want to try to stop it, place set mousetraps all over the resting place.

When your dog jumps up, the traps snap (they NEVER catch the dog) and he might decide that's no fun. But I've got to warn you that I spent weeks coming home to snapped traps and a warm sofa, two different times for two different dogs. Friends report the same.

Another common remedy is to spread newspaper over the surfaces on the theory that dogs don't like the crackling of the paper. I don't know one case in which this worked — and I know several dogs who picked up a lifelong love of shredding paper.

Mice on the toilet paper. If your dog has discovered that toilet paper comes on rolls and it's a wonderful game to run through the house holding the end of the roll, try resting a set mousetrap on top of the roll. This does work.

It might also work for pickpocket dogs who sneak into purses to find loose tissues. I never tried it, but it sounds good.

Smoking hurts. If you smoke, your dog will sooner or later grab for your lit cigarette or leap on you for a cuddle when you're smoking. To avoid setting your dog on fire, teach him early that cigarettes are not fun toys. Don't rely on a NO, make him learn to look to see if you're smoking. Deliberately play with the cigarette when he's on your lap until he grabs for it and then let him get a nose full of smoke. By getting the cigarette so close to his nose, it's possible you'll lightly touch the nose — don't worry; dogs' noses are wet enough not to be burned.

By the way, dogs with squashed-in faces like Pugs, Pekes, Boxers, Lhasas and Bulldogs, have genetic breathing problems. Cigarette smoking can affect their health quite seriously so if you're a heavy smoker, never pick one of these breeds.

FOR YOUR PROTECTION: STREET SAVVY TRICKERY

Here are four easy tricks you can use to help your dog protect you on the street, even if he's the meekest of lambs:

1. **Never tell anyone on the street that your dog is harmless!** Don't say, "He wouldn't hurt a flea," "He'd escort robbers to the silver" or "Nothing will make him bite." You never know who's listening. If you want to allow your dog to approach another animal or be patted by a person and are questioned as to the safety, say something like, "He's all right once I tell him everything is okay."

2. **Teach your dog to bark on command.** As I explained earlier, it's not difficult to teach your dog to bark on command. Once he knows this, use it whenever you're in a situation in which you want to alert someone to your dog's presence and offer a mild threat — for example, when a stranger is acting in an unusual manner or hanging around in front of your door.

   This is also quite effective on the street because when a dog barks, he takes a very erect, alert position which, to a non-dog-person, looks like a guard dog.

3. **Make your dog look ferocious and about to explode.** On the street, if you see someone suspicious nearby, pull the leash up short so your dog is very close to you and it looks like you're holding him in. Then jerk the leash erratically as if your dog is trying to lunge away from you. Say nervously, "Easy boy, it's all right now, calm down, CALM DOWN!" Avoid words that your dog actually associates with calming down and keep an edge in your voice. Your anxiety plus all the nonsense jerking will make your dog nervous and edgy — and to a non-dog-person it will look like you're losing control of a killer.

A Toy breed won't look all that frightening, but your actions should start a Toy barking uncontrollably and give the impression there's a lot of ferocity in those few pounds — the noise alone should make any crook give you a pass; you're attracting too much attention.

4. **Teach your dog to fake an attack.** I mentioned earlier that I played a game with my German Shepherd, letting her off her leash near my building and swinging up my arm while saying GO! On that cue, she happily charged down the block to the building entrance. To anyone around, it looked exactly like an attack.

I don't suggest actually releasing your dog as I did the Shepherd — that's like firing a blank because you don't know that your dog actually will attack. If he does, because he senses your fear, there would be all kinds of problems.

Short of releasing your dog, you can make the threatening person think you're about to let a killer loose. Teach this trick during play with a modification of fetch: Keep the dog on leash and say excitedly "Are you ready to play fetch?" or something similar. Get your dog worked up before you throw an object, then release the leash, throw your arm out towards the object and give some sort of command like GO!

Once your dog has mastered this, if you're ever in a threatening situation, ask your fetch question under your breath so he starts to look very excited, lean down as if you're about to release the leash and yell to the threatener, "I'm going to let him loose, get out of here!" Then say loudly to your dog, "Are you ready, boy? All set?" It's a very foolish crook who sticks around to find out what you do next.

Chapter 15

CITY SCARES & OTHER SPECIAL PROBLEMS

Living in a city with a dog is complex and can generate a number of special problems which simply don't arise in the country. This chapter is designed as a reference for use when snags arise in your relationship with your dog.

FUR, FUR EVERYWHERE

When you chose your dog, you decided you didn't mind grooming and selected a shedder. Now you observe that your rugs are covered with fur, there are fur bunnies the size of a large dog drifting around the house and everyone you meet immediately says, "What kind of dog do you have?" as they pick a clump of fur off your lapel.

German Shepards are among the biggest fur-producers in the dog kingdom. Lorbeer Hugel's Jenna-Far von Brode/Jenna (German Shepard) Farley hides a double undercoat.

Even if you haven't gotten a shedder, you've discovered that an indoor dog tends to leave quite a lot of fur about. And instead of the twice a year schedule of a country dog, yours sheds constantly!

There is a way to manage this...

1. Get a dog-sized shedding comb (they're used on horses, too). It looks more like an old-fashioned straight razor than a comb — usually shedding combs have leather han-

dles and an long metal blade with tiny serrated teeth. You turn the shedder into a loop by pulling the string on the end of the blade through the hole in the handle. It's designed to pull the hair out of the dog's undercoat without hurting the dog at all.

Late at night, when no one can see you, take your dog out on a quiet street or up on your roof and shed him out by combing him all over with the shedding comb. When he's going through his semi-annual shed, you may have to do this every few days. A shedding comb will remove an enormous amount of the hair if your dog is in the process of shedding and reduce the fur load in your house considerably.

2. Keep up with your grooming. Brushing and combing your dog regularly will remove hair before it falls onto your furniture and clothes.

3. Give your dog a bath with a hair trap over the drain. Bathing takes out a lot of hair.

4. Invest in a really good vacuum. I think dog hair has little hooks on it because it is extremely difficult to pick up. Carpet sweepers and electric brooms do zilch. You'll need a vacuum with superb suction.

5. Get more than one of the best lint pick-ups around, so you always have one on hand to clean off your guests before they leave.

6. Protect your furniture by draping light blankets or sheets over it when you're home alone. This is also a good idea for your car.

7. Washing machines and dryers remove hair from linens, blankets and clothes, but be sure to clean the lint catchers every time you wash.

WEATHER WATCH

In the summer, a hot country dog finds relief from the heat by digging a hole down to the cooler dirt, or crawling under the porch, or going into the woods. In the winter, country dogs grow thick, woolly coats which enable some to sleep happily in sub-zero temperatures with nose tucked under tail.

When it gets hot in town, your dog has no naturally cool place in which to retreat, and the temperature in a small home can easily soar. During such heat waves, be sure your dog has a big bowl of cool water and access to a cool, uncarpeted floor. Pull drapes or blinds shut before you leave for work. And if you have a Pug, Bulldog, German Shepard, Golden, Newfie or any other breed intolerant of heat, leave fans or the air conditioner on during the worst weather. In fact, sixty percent of all dog-owners do this during all summer heat waves. Do not take your dog jogging — all dogs are susceptible to heat stroke, which can be fatal.

If you're keeping a Yorkie, Shih Tzu or other natural long-hair in an artificially short cut, treat your dog as extremely heat- and cold-intolerant. Their natural coat acts as an insulator. You've imbalanced their ability to adapt to heat.

Winter also requires precautions. Very thin-coated dogs like Greyhounds, Whippets, Italian Greyhounds and Chihuhuas need coats or sweaters throughout the winter. Dogs with coats like Great Danes and Boxers may or may not be warm enough through the winter — judge by their reactions to the cold.

As I mentioned earlier, city dogs don't grow true winter coats. They're outdoors for only a minuscule fraction of the day and the rest of the time they're in your heated home. I've found many city dogs grow so little protection for those brief shocks of freezing cold during walks that they tend to catch colds and develop bronchitis. My double-coated Beagle was one of these bronchitis dogs. After my experiences with her, I adopted the habit of putting a sweater on all city dogs (except the really furry breeds like Shelties and Collies) whenever the temperature dips into the twenties. By the way, I found sweaters much easier to handle than coats, and although I expected my dogs to eat their first sweaters, they must have needed them because they always jumped into them eagerly.

City snow presents a serious medical problem for dogs, which I'll discuss in Chapter 19.

THE MIGHTY DESTRUCTO

If, despite all your careful training, your dog suddenly becomes destructive at home while you're away at work, there can be several reasons. A number of breeds, particularly Sporting and Hound dogs, can become destructive if they don't get enough exercise. Some Terriers can also do this. If you disregarded my warning about this, you now have to pay the price by providing much more exercise in the form of running, chasing and fast walking. This doesn't go away. Once you determine how much exercise your dog needs in order for the destruction to stop, you must keep it up.

Toys, Poodles and several other breeds don't like to be left alone and may retaliate or dissipate their boredom by demolishing your home. Getting a second dog will NOT cure the problem, only double the trouble. Stern correction may stop a few dogs, but others will decide punishment is worth the price. For these troublemakers, consider the following:

1. Create a pen or dog room in which you can confine your dog. Portable fencing can be used to make a large playpen area, but this will not work for Bichons or Terriers who are great jumpers and climbers...and will escape. If you can empty a small room, you might close the dog in this, but it had better be empty or the dog will destroy whatever is in there.

2. Hire a dog walker. Fortunately this is one of the perks of living in the city, one which I'll discuss in more detail in the next chapter.

3. Take your dog to work with you. Some informal offices, particularly in the artistic fields, don't mind if you have a small, quiet dog that you confine to your office and teach not to jump all over your associates.

4. Hire a pet sitter. Hire a sitter to come in for several hours each day to play with your dog. This can be expensive.

5. Use dog day care. Also costly but available in many cities, often through pet spas and health clubs.

You might create your own solution. One man with a very destructive Chihuahua read about the healthful influences of dogs on lonely old people. That made him think of the elderly neighbor who regularly stopped to visit with his dog whenever they were walking. He suggested she provide the dog with "day care." She said her building didn't permit pets, but the man spoke to the building manager, explaining the dog would only be visiting during the day. The manager approved, the lady was delighted and the Chihuahua basked in double attention.

By the way, some dogs become destructive only when left a certain number of hours. If you notice the house is fine when you come home early but messy if you come home later, try adjusting your schedule so you can stop at home for a brief visit. I used to run home and fetch my Beagle whenever I had to work late.

DOGS WHO CAN'T WAIT

Young pups don't have big enough bladders to control themselves for a long workday. Old dogs may lose this ability as they age. Otherwise, it's a rare dog who can't get through a workday without an extra walk.

If your dog is one of these rare few, you can provide him with an indoor bathroom (papered area) or hire a dog walker. The mature dog who is well-housebroken may be so upset at having to use the house that a dog walker is really a greater kindness.

PARTY ANIMALS

Dogs generally react to crowded parties with extreme responses. Either they're scared out of their minds or think the party is in their honor. Frightened dogs can include many of the Working dogs who make friends slowly and on their own terms. They're simply overwhelmed by all those strangers and want to flee or assume the situation is dangerous and turn hostile.

Scared, unsociable or dominant dogs shouldn't attend your party. Set up your dog's crate in a room and put him in it for the duration. If there is no such room, move him and his crate to a friendly neighbor for the evening. Try not to pick a neighbor who lives right next door or you could have an all-evening barker.

Social dogs can be a tremendous asset to a party. My Sheltie and Beagle both paid special attention to shy people, served as conversation-starters and had a wonderful time conning everyone out of hors d'oeuvres. By the time the last guest left, Penny Beagle was usually lying flat on her side sound asleep with a swollen belly. She'd had a grand time and so had my company.

If you love to give parties, make certain you teach your dog not to charge out the moment a door is opened. I once rescued a dog who had run out and gotten lost in New York City during a party. He managed to get several miles from his home!

JEALOUS DOGS AND JEALOUS OTHERS

Jealousy is not a human vice, it's a basic animal emotion to which dogs are extremely prone. The more devoted your dog is to you, the more likely he is to be jealous of other animals and humans. One of the prices you pay for a one-man dog is that he very much wants a one-dog man or woman.

Be alert for early signs of jealousy. Chelsea (Sheltie) Skelly is ignoring Corey Langevin and looking to the adults for some attention— in some dogs, this could be a warning.

1. Jealousy of others' pets. A dog's house is his territory; all other dogs know this when they come to visit and they're submissive to the dog who owns the territory. If you instantly make a fuss over the visiting dog, you're upsetting the balance of nature — you're signaling both dogs that you prefer the visiting dog over the resident. Naturally, this rouses the jealousy dragon.

If you don't want your dog to greet visitors with a growl and a snap, pay attention to your dog rather than the visitor dog. Say something like, "Look, Fido, Spot has come to see you" as you pet Fido. After Fido has greeted and accepted Spot, you can give Spot a quiet greeting, while you assure Fido that "Of course I love you best, but Spot is nice, isn't he?" If Spot's person also pays some extra attention to Fido, trouble will be avoided.

If you have an Alpha dog or a very strong leader, he'll be uncomfortable when visiting other dogs since this means he must assume the submissive role. He may show this by clinging to you and rebuffing the resident dog's greetings. Again, you don't want to unbalance nature by overdoing attention to your dog — it will only teach him this is a good tactic to get extra attention. At the same time, stay aloof with the resident dog until the dogs sort things out. They may not. Some dogs will simply stay quietly by your feet, ignoring the host dog.

2. Jealousy of your new pet. Introducing a new dog into your household must be done carefully, with an understanding of dog psychology. Never assume your current dog will accept a new playmate easily. Penny Beagle loved other animals so much she was constantly stealing puppies and kittens out of friends' litters. But when the new puppy came home, Penny pretended he didn't exist even while he was chewing her ears. She also suddenly insisted on sleeping with me although she'd never chosen to do so before. All dogs resent a newcomer, and all dogs will compete with other household residents for your attention.

Just as with visiting dogs, your resident dog is automatically the Alpha or leader dog. This may change later, but at first, it's vital that you don't confuse the issue by appearing to give precedence to the new dog. Give your first dog lots of affection and attention. When you pet your new animal, pet your older dog at the same time. After a couple of weeks, you can give solo attention to the new dog if you talk to the older one at the same time. Never bar your current dog from any part of your home where he has previously been permitted to roam freely. Do not let your new dog do anything or go anywhere you don't allow your old dog and do not give your old dog's crate to the new dog — invest in a new one.

If you need to feed a baby several times a day, give your older dog a treat each time you feed the newcomer. It's okay to take your old dog out alone, but do not take your new one out on his own. If the kid needs to see the vet, take them both.

For the first three weeks, bend over backwards to tell your older dog he's still loved, respected and the top dog of the house as far as you're concerned in every way he will recognize.

Don't interfere with the relationship between the dogs. Dog #1 may ignore dog #2 for a while, even growl occasionally. Eventually, he'll accept the newcomer. And also eventually, they'll settle the who's boss issue. For a new baby, this will happen around puberty, at about six months of age. In most cases, dog #1 will stay boss even if he's a Shih Tzu and you've added a Great Dane. But at times, a more subordinate older dog will submit to the rule of a bossier youngster — my Beagle gave way to my German Shepherd. The decision may be made peaceably or with just a few snarls and snaps, but in many cases, there's a frightening fight. It will only last a few minutes, but it will be ferocious. Stay out of it! The issue must decided. No one will be badly hurt and they'll never fight again.

If you get involved, the fights will continue and escalate until you have two mortal enemies in the house. A couple resisted my advice to let their dogs fight it out for over six months — when they finally decided to let the dogs fight, they had to turn the hoses on them to break up the battle.

Both dogs required vet care and now only one dog at a time can be in the house, while the other has to be tied on a run in the back yard — a miserable situation. If there were no backyard, one dog would have to leave. Let them fight the first time this arises.

By the way, for most dogs, cats are not difficult to introduce. A very few dogs don't like cats, and will never exist happily with them. Former racing Greyhounds are sometimes trained to run by using cats, and such dogs will kill cats. Adopt yours from a rescue group that cat-tests their charges, then listen to what you're told FOREVER.

Other dogs will be taught how to respect a cat by the cat — who will always be the boss of the house. Your dog could get a bloody nose in his first few encounters. Then they will resolve their relationship and everything will be fine.

3. Jealousy of a new child. This is a serious problem with potentially dangerous consequences. That's why I recommended you carefully consider your future family size before choosing a breed. Some dogs, particularly Toys, will never truly accept a new baby and cannot be trusted around infants. If a baby is on the way and you own a Toy, I strongly recommend you start searching for a new home for your dog.

People often try to deal with jealousy by telling the dog to take care of the baby. This is fine for dogs who are marvelous with children — German Shepherds and Newfoundlands will raise your kids. But my aunt's Wire Fox Terrier became so possessive of "her baby" that no one was allowed near the new arrival — not grandparents or father. When she growled at my aunt on the second day Kathleen was home, the dog left. Other breeds may be fine with infants but snappy and irritable with toddlers. Choosing the right breed can make all the difference in whether or not your dog can continue to live with your expanded family, enhancing your life together.

Even the most devoted-to-children dog can resent a newcomer who causes unpleasant changes in the dog's life. Plan ahead so the dog doesn't associate the inevitable changes with the baby. Shut the dog out of the nursery several months before birth. Gradually cut back on the amount of attention you give to the dog. Then when the baby does arrive, make a concerted effort to pay some attention to your dog, and insist that visitors the dog cares for do as well.

4. Jealousy of a new love. Very devoted dogs of any breed and many Toys may fail to welcome a wonderful new person in your life who's absorbing your time and attention intensely. Resentment can show with growling, sulking, ignoring you when you want to pay attention to your dog and "acting out," deliberately ignoring the house rules. You've got to be fair and reassure your dog that he still holds a big part of your heart by spending some amount of time with him.

I hope you've planned for this eventuality by not permitting your dog to sleep in your bedroom. If not, suddenly shutting him out will be taken as rejection. In these cases, insist he sleep quietly in his place. But be prepared. I heard about one jealous dog who suddenly decided to sleep on the bed, between the couple who were not sleeping at the time — another who quietly moved up to the side of the bed and watched intently!

5. A new love's jealousy of your dog. This is not uncommon. Other people must understand that your city dog is very important to you and because in a sense he's a child substitute, he deserves the same kind of attention and respect you'd give a child. This certainly isn't "stealing" affection from the new love. Frank, serious discussion is called for here

and perhaps a little education about the needs of a dog. If, after this, your new person isn't able to understand this, perhaps he or she really doesn't have a place in your life.

THE TERRIFYING BIG BANG

Many dogs are terrified of thunder and lightning storms, perhaps because their sensitive hearing is actually hurt by the crashes, possibly because of some physical sensations from the electricity in the air. The best you can do is to give calm reassurance and let him find refuge if he feels he must. Cuddling your dog and crooning, "It's all right, baby" will INCREASE the fear reaction, because he realizes it will get your attention.

Dogs who fear thunder may also be terrified by the July Fourth fireworks and if your city — like several I've lived in — sounds like World War II with amateur fireworks all through the day, your dog might spend many hours in an unhealthy state of high anxiety and fear.

I've seen dogs who hide, very large dogs who try to crawl into your lap, dogs who shake, drool, pant and cry. Terriers and some Herding dogs go into barking fits. Most of them start shedding great amounts of fur, a fear/stress reaction dogs often do at the vet's office as well. All of these are normal so don't be alarmed. Calmly reassure and stay home because your dog is finding safety in your company even if he's hiding in the back of your closet. I know of no way to cure these fears.

If the holiday fireworks cause extreme reactions over an extended period of time, however, consider sedation. Do not use human sedatives, as some are highly dangerous and dosages vary greatly. Speak to your vet and get a dog tranquilizer. Once you've sedated your dog, you must stay nearby and keep and eye on him because the glassy-eyed, zonked-out canine can get himself into big trouble.

Tranquilizing a dog for thunderstorms is NOT an option, since the medication won't take effect until long after the storm has passed.

SPECIAL CITY FEARS

I've known a number of dogs who were frightened of trucks rumbling past them on the street, who reacted to car backfires with the same terror as thunder even when inside the apartment, or who became highly nervous in areas with heavy traffic and congestion. Quite a few dogs are afraid of cars (and get carsick as a result), and I knew one dog with agoraphobia — fear of the entire outdoors. She was the only city dog I've ever known who ran away when her leash came out.

The agoraphobia was the result of two errors — first, the dog's owner kept her inside for several months when she first arrived. Second, when the dog first showed fear, her owner overdid the consolation, which to the dog acknowledged the outdoors was scary and gave the dog extra attention.

We overcame the errors with slow, patient socialization and the right kind of firm and dispassionate assurance. We started on quiet streets at quiet times, and gradually increased level of activity, just as is done with a puppy. It took much longer, however, with many setbacks.

Fear of riding in cars is also often an error. During the first months with you, where does your dog go in the car? I'll bet it's to the vet! Quite naturally, your dog quickly associates getting in the car with shots and all the other uncomfortable vet stuff. No wonder he doesn't like the car! The solution is to make the car a good thing, so over the next couple of weeks, on about four separate occasions, take him to the nearest takeout ice cream shop. Get him a small cup of vanilla ice cream and feed it to him in the car. It won't take more than four trips before he likes it so much he'll start leaping into other people's cars!

Uneasiness can turn into fear and fear can turn into phobias if you confirm your dog's reaction with too much attention. A warm, loving but briskly assured, "Now don't be silly, come on," is always the best reaction to timidity or nervousness on your dog's part.

Your treatment of your dog on the street can also enhance and confirm fears. At home alone with your pet, you're probably like the rest of us — very affectionate and often silly. But also like the rest of us, the moment you go out in public, you put on your Adult Role. To add to the problem, you want to show off what a wonderfully well-behaved dog you have. To your dog, Mommy or Daddy has suddenly become a hard, unloving, stern, harsh Dictator who barks out orders and praises rarely (and then in an inaudible, emotionless voice). Who wouldn't be scared to go any place where you turn into that!

Try to sustain the relationship you have with your dog at home when you're outdoors together.

PHOBIAS

Dogs can develop terrors of the weirdest things. I know one dog who tried to hide on his owner's feet every time his owner drove the car through a puddle — a difficult situation since the owner was driving at the time and the dog weighed over sixty pounds. Another was terrified of the sound of wind-driven rain against the windows of the house. My Golden, Ambra, ran every time I shook out a garbage bag before putting it into the kitchen trash container. Many dogs run from vacuum cleaners; others attack them so fiercely I worry that they'll break their teeth.

Help your dog avoid this problem by exposing him to new experiences throughout his life. Play games that teach him to enjoy surprises. For instance, while you're making the bed, throw the blanket over your dog and ask in a playful, loving voice, "Where's the doggie? There he is!" just as you'd play with a toddler. If he's afraid the first time you do it, whip the blanket right off, laugh and cuddle him as part of the game. Eventually, encourage him to either seek his own way out of the blanket or run around the house with it on.

When something falls unexpectedly and your dog isn't sure how to react, laugh and throw something else as part of the game. Or pick up the object, bat him gently with it and encourage him to sniff it, saying, "Just a silly dish, see?" In other words, show your dog that the right way to deal with something strange is to explore it, not fear it.

Once dogs' fears become terrors, they don't seem to be curable by ordinary dog-owners. Scolding could intensify them just as excess reassurance definitely does. Calmly ignoring them does appear to eventually calm the dogs slightly — maybe they figure if it's not bothering you, maybe it isn't so bad.

For dogs who are severely affected by their phobias or fears which can lead to dangerous results, you might consider consulting with an applied animal behaviorist. These specialists have advanced degrees and should be certified by the Animal Behavior Society. They're few in number but really do know what they're doing. They work with your vet, so start your search through your vet. If he isn't up-to-speed, I provide information on how to find a behaviorist in the Appendix.

OVERSEXED DOGS

Some canines, both male and female, become oversexed, attacking every other animal, leg and pillow in sight. Spaying and neutering often stop this, especially if you do it very quickly after the sexual behavior begins. A friend's Bichon stopped his attraction to everything in sight about three weeks after his surgery.

Other dogs, male and female, have a lifelong attraction to people, cats, pillows and many other objects. It's annoying and downright embarrassing, and guests who aren't used to dogs may be appalled. It needs to be stopped before it has really gotten started or you'll never be able to break the habit. Be very stern the very first time it emerges.

EATING PROBLEMS

Here's another case where humans cause themselves needless worry by assuming dogs are like people. Do NOT expect your dog to gobble up two or more meals every single day. In the wild, canines don't eat every day even when food is plentiful. Dining in the wild is sporadic and many of our dogs carry this into their lives with us. In fact, every dog I've ever lived with has had his own individual eating pattern. The only time for concern is if your dog breaks his own pattern and the change persists for more than two days.

Mostly, I suggest simply going along with your dog's pattern, but there may be situations where this is impossible, or adjusting to your dog might require you to handle feeding in a special way. So let's look at the most common ways in which dogs eat...

Nibblers. Some dogs eat like cats; they like food around constantly so they can nibble.

Because I worried about spoilage, I gave my nibbler one small meal of her canned food each day, which I insisted she eat at once. Then I left her a large dish of dry food to eat whenever the mood struck her.

When my nibbler lived with my compulsive eater, the nibbler quickly realized that the moment she left her dish, the food disappeared. She would lie down with her head on top of her dish, and finally, after several weeks of this, she started eating her food in one sitting.

Compulsives. Some dogs don't know when to stop. They'll literally eat themselves to the point of illness. And they'll quickly balloon up into blimps, much more unhealthy for dogs than people. If you have a compulsive, you've got to control the food. If your dog acts desperately hungry after eating what holds his weight, switch to one of the dietetic foods that allows you to feed more.

Erratic eating. As I mentioned before, this is quite normal for a dog. In fact, even regular eaters can become erratic at times. Dogs will lose their appetites in hot weather as many humans do. Pups can go off their food while teething. And most dogs eat little or nothing when in a strange environment or when something unusual is going on around home — like entertaining visitors or preparing for a trip, a move or a party.

One-man dogs may go on hunger strikes if you leave, even if they're staying with people they know well. This can become serious — my German Shepherd refused food for ten days and lost over twenty pounds. If you suspect this might happen, try leaving your dog for a weekend (missing two days isn't unhealthy). If your suspicions are confirmed, a good kennel might be the solution. Jenna Shepherd starved with three sets of friends, but the very expensive kennel I located managed to keep her eating. If the kennel doesn't work, your dog is either going to have to come with you or you're going to have to go away on two-day vacations.

A few dogs are totally erratic — you never know when they're going to wolf down their food or walk off and take a nap, leaving you constantly throwing good food away. My Golden goes through periods when she eats one meal, skips three, eats two in a row then skips one, etc. The minute I see she's in an erratic phase, I switch to dry food that I can offer, put back up on the counter and offer again later or the next day.

Eating in unusual places. Many dogs take the first mouthful of their meals away from the dish, drop it on the floor then eat it there. I have no idea why they do this nor how to stop it.

Once in a while, a dog starts taking every mouthful away, usually out of the room. In every case I've seen, the solution was to move the dog's dining room. I suspect the area chosen by the humans was too congested, had too much traffic, was too public or had some mystery problem that made the dogs unable to concentrate on their meals. Whatever the reason, I've always cured it by experimenting with different dining areas until one "took."

Eating yucky things. Dogs are not human beings and nothing brings this home more forcefully than their "food" cravings. For instance, some dogs love to strip the bark off sticks and most dogs find paper irresistible, especially tissues. Fortunately, they don't really eat bark or tissues, just create messes.

Garbage is also fabulous from a dog's point of view since, in the wild, dogs are scavengers. Try not to make your garbage too attractive — keep cans tightly sealed and empty quickly whenever odors might lure a dog. At the same time, correct your dog whenever he sniffs or otherwise goes near your garbage. If left to develop his garbage-hunting skills, he'll become a master at getting into the most tightly closed can — and you haven't lived until you've come home to find your garbage spread all over your home, into the farthest corners and, of course, all over your bed.

Eating excrement is so popular among dogs that it has an official name: coprophagia. It used to be thought that coprophagic dogs were missing dietary ingredients, but now it's generally accepted that some dogs do it for their own personal reasons. Scold your dog if he tries, watch him off-leash if he has the tendency. Permitting this habit is dangerous in the city where there are so many risks of disease.

When you take your dog to the country or the park, don't be surprised if he begins grazing like a cow, especially in spring. Dogs like to eat grass on occasion. It apparently cleanses their digestive tract. Alas, the cleaning often includes vomiting — usually after you return home.

One last note about what dogs eat outdoors: Never permit your dog to drink any standing water in an urban and/or congested environment. It inevitably contains chemicals of one sort or another, some of which are slow-acting poisons to canines. Car antifreeze has an sweet taste that actually attracts dogs — and it kills. Don't even let your dog lick the street!

EXERCISING

As we've covered already, all dogs need exercise. Small and medium-sized dogs fill some of their exercise requirements by charging around your home, and these crazy hour races do relieve you of some of the burden of providing exercise. If you've got an indoor racer, wall-to-wall carpeting will reduce neighbor annoyance and give your dog a firmer footing so he doesn't skid into walls every time he runs around a corner.

Most dogs larger than Toys also require active exercise outdoors. One of the best ways to is to play "fetch" in a park or very quiet area at a quiet time of day. Many cities have special areas in parks where dog-owners gather to exercise their dogs together. If you can't get to a park and don't live near a quiet street, the roof of your apartment building is a good place to play as long as you're very, very careful not to throw things off the edges.

If your dog cannot be trusted off-leash, use a retractable, or tie a six-foot length of cord to the end of your dog's leash to give him running room — then be careful not to throw the fetch object beyond his radius of movement.

In addition to fetch games, dogs also need several walks a week. To get the health benefit, however, you have to walk briskly. No strolls, no leisurely start-and-stop down the street.

If you can't give your dog enough exercises, many urban areas have pet health clubs with treadmills designed for dogs.

Chapter 16

YOUR CITY SUPPORT SYSTEM

All urban areas offer a wide range of magnificent supports and life-with-dog enhancements to help you raise and enjoy your happy dog. I know I haven't identified everything available in your neighborhood, but I hope this chapter will give you an idea of how much is out there and point you in the right direction to find what you need. I suspect that almost anything you could ask for is there, if you hunt hard enough.

Training. Every metropolitan newspaper has classified ads for both private and class training programs, but you'll avoid the fakers if you go through your local humane society or dog clubs.

Walking. All urban areas have dog-walking services, but because this is not a regulated profession, be careful about entrusting your house keys and your pet to a stranger. Seek a referral. Go with an established organization rather than an individual who runs a classified ad or posts a notice on a community bulletin board. Ask potential walkers what their qualifications and standards are, and what guarantees they offer for protection of your home and dog. It's also quite proper to ask exactly what you'll get in terms of length of walk, how much running, where the dogs are taken, etc. Finally, watch the dog-walker at work — the pros' strings of up to fifteen dogs are wonderfully disciplined and under good, safe control at all times.

Health clubs for dogs. As I mentioned earlier, these exist in quite a few metropolitan areas. They all offer treadmill workouts and other activities; some even have swimming pools. Most let you drop your dog off en route to work and pick him up on the way home — when he's not doing his workout, he's relaxing in a kennel. Naturally, you want a club that's run by caring professionals. Dogs need to be watched while exercising to be safe. There should be no possibility of dog fights. The place should be clean, without odors. Dogs should be eager to go there and come home relaxed and happy.

Social life. You and your dog can also explore new dimensions to your social life. If you've gotten a pedigreed dog, you're welcome to join and participate in your local breed club. It's an excellent place to learn more about your dog's heritage and meet other dog-lovers. Most clubs have guest lecturers, social gatherings, special programs and a wide array of other activities. They also have shows and competitions.

In any urban area, dog-walkers can provide exercise and play while you're at work.

Now you can even take your dog out to a coffee bar — dog-friendly places recently opened in New York and Chicago. Dogs roam freely off-leash, snacking on such menu items as peanut-carob and wheat-ginger bones. New York City's is called Fido's and is located on West 18th Street. Where these cities go, can others be far behind? Check it out!

Scout out the largest park in your area as well for "park parties," sites where dog-owners gather regularly at specific times, such as just after work or Saturday afternoon. The dogs play together while the people visit. When the big park is far away, you might find a "dog run" in a city garden built by neighbors on an empty lot. Or you may discover that a smaller park has informal, unwritten hours when the dogs come out to play. As you meet other dog-owners, don't hesitate to ask what opportunities exist.

Day care. The New York Dog Spa & Hotel in New York City offers day care on a daily or weekly basis, for around $25 a day. Other cities must have similar programs. Just start calling grooming centers and health clubs for dogs.

Your local SPCA. Large city SPCAs often offer a host of services for dogs and their people, often at bargain prices. Many have medical clinics, vaccination days (when you can only get shots but at rock-bottom prices), special programs designed to enhance your enjoyment of your dog, obedience classes, free literature, grooming programs and more. Check them out!

Groomers. A great many breeds require grooming to continue looking like they should. Some, like Poodles, get hair cuts almost as often as you do. But even with a big, wooly mutt, you might prefer to let someone else fight the bath battle once in a while.

Different dogs require different grooming techniques. Look for a groomer who knows what's needed and how to do it. Since there are no regulations for groomers, it's quite possible for someone who got a lot of compliments on how she cut her Poodle to set up shop. Such people not only don't know what to do with a Terrier but haven't the skills to safely manage many dogs in one small space...or the know-how to clean anal glands, ears and eyes...or the knowledge to keep dogs out of drafts and avoid harm with dryers and other equipment.

Groomers have to know how to do a variety of cuts and treatments — how to pluck Terriers, for example, and how to cut out the faces of Westies, Bedlingtons and Bichons, all of whom rely on a haircut to get the look you know for the breed.

Get referrals and recommendations.

A standard grooming consists of a bath, brushing and combing, clipping or plucking as necessary, nail clipping, and cleaning of the anal glands, ears and eyes. Additional treatments range from special conditioners to nail polish and bows. You control the styling of your dog's fur and you should always be consulted before a groomer shaves the dog down. This is an extreme measure to be taken as a last resort. If you've let your long-hair get very tangled, you may pay extra for the time needed to work out all the snarls, but this is always preferable to making the dog naked — that's very, very unhealthy.

A good groomer should be knowledgeable about your options. Terriers, for instance, are normally plucked to retain a harsh, bristly coat, but I understand that cutting the coat softens it. Your groomer should know all about this. Many bushy dogs need special attention around the eyes and anal area to maintain cleanliness, but cutting out these areas isn't in the breed standards — if you're not showing, however, why not do so. Speak to your groomer about it, if he or she doesn't mention it to you.

Some breeds can be kept in much easier-to-care-for clips than the breed standards demand. Pet Cockers, for example, never wear the to-the-floor curtains of hair on legs and sides that you see in show rings. Pet Shih Tzus, Yorkies, Lhasas and several other breeds can be clipped in a short, curly, easier coat (many of these mat readily so still need regular brushing by you). If you have a trustworthy groomer and find your dog's fur a bit overwhelming to care for, discuss your options — and listen carefully to the groomer's warnings, because changing a dog's coat can change how he reacts to hot and cold.

In cities, some groomers offer pick-up and delivery services, or groom your dog in a van that comes to your door. Many groomers permit you to drop off your dog en route to work and pick him up on your way home. I'd avoid using a groomer who comes to your home — your equipment isn't as good as the professional and your dog will get a better, safer bath and grooming with the professional stuff.

Behaviorists/dog psychotherapists. These are two "growth areas" in the dog world and much as people snicker at the idea of a "dog shrink," there genuinely are times when you might consider calling upon a behaviorist. Applied animal behaviorists are more than trainers. Most have doctorates in animal behavior and a growing number are offering their assistance in helping unhappy dog-owners deal with very bad habits or phobias. The average person who has followed this book and gone to a class with his or her dog generally doesn't run into an unsolvable problem, but there are rare instances when an expert is necessary. In such cases, the root cause could be medical — veterinary behaviorists work with vets, administering tests to make sure there are no physical bases for the behaviors. You can obtain the names of professionals in your neighborhood from your local dog clubs and humane shelters, or by contacting professional associations, listed in the Appendix.

This area is ripe for scam artists, however, so check credentials carefully.

Grief counseling. This is also a growth area. Increasingly, the larger welfare societies are offering a very valuable form of therapy to help you to handle the loss of your dog. For those of us with "roommate dogs," the death of a beloved companion can be devastating, as real and as painful as the loss of a dear friend. Alas, most people remain sympathetic for about 48 hours, then start saying things like, "It was just a dog. How can you still be upset? Just get another one!"

Your grief is real and valid and being able to attend group meetings (led by professionals) where you can let it out and have it honored is very important to your healing. Grief counseling can also help you decide when you're ready for a new dog and what sort of animal you should seek. Take advantage of this.

Pet supplies and bulk foods. Nowadays, with the growth of pet supermarket chains, it's very easy to find a wide array of equipment and supplies at good prices. You can also get bulk foods at low prices. In cities, you can even get home deliveries. But before investing in fifty-pound bags, think about the insect and rodent situation in your home. Large bags will attract pests unless you can store the food in galvanized metal cans with tightly sealed lids. A good pest can chew through plastic!

Photographs and paintings. Would you like a permanent memory of your dog? Get a beautiful photograph from a professional who knows how to work with dogs, or even an original painting of your dog. Again, your local dog organizations can direct you to a photographer, but take time to examine samples of his or her work. You don't want someone who simply takes shots of champion dogs at dog shows because these rarely capture the personality and "heart" of the animal. Look for someone who will truly make a beautiful record of YOUR dog.

Fine artists can paint pictures to order from photographs, and can be located anywhere. There are some truly wonderful artists who capture the complete spirit of your dog. Find them through animal organizations, advertisements and feature articles in dog magazines.

Exotic services. Urban environments can offer you a great many services and products for your dog that you never thought of — and which your dog certainly doesn't need. In New York City, for example, there's a pet bakery specializing in cakes, cookies and other treats made of ingredients that are good for cats, dogs, gerbils and other companion animals! You can also find caterers, party planners and party facilities for pet parties.

You can find clothing stores for your dog — or departments in pet supermarkets or special mail-order catalogs. You can get your dog reindeer antlers for Christmas or a Halloween costume, a bridal dress, whatever you desire. You can also find nice coats, lovely sweaters (which I prefer to coats), boots to help out with city salts during snowstorms and other practical clothing needs.

There are even acupuncturists and Oriental-massage specialists who claim to help animals. Dog health clubs often offer massages.

If you ever think, "wouldn't it be nice if," look around — chances are it's out there.

LEAVING YOUR DOG BEHIND: WHAT CHOICES DO YOU HAVE?

Inevitably, there comes a time when you must go away for several days and leave your dog behind. There are three choices: Leave him with friends, kennel him or bring in a dog-sitter. There are advantages, disadvantages and do's and don'ts for each.

Sending your dog to friends. Although this is by far the most preferred option, I've found it isn't always as successful as I originally believed. Even the best-behaved dog may act up when you leave him behind with people who aren't as sensitive to his communications or needs as you are. And there's nothing so deflating as returning from an exhausting business trip or happy vacation to be greeted with, "What your dog did!" Suddenly, you feel miserable, filled with guilt and forced to scold your dog when you want to hug him and tell him how much you missed him, apologizing and offering to pay damages when you want to regale your friends with tales of your trip.

My Beagle, Penny, always did something disastrous when I left her, sometimes because of stupid friends. Once I heard Penny had eaten the family's dinner roast — it turned out she'd been left alone in the car with the roast for nearly an hour. "What did you expect?" I said in bewilderment. "Well, she's so well-behaved," my friend answered. No dog in the world is that good!

As I mentioned earlier, my German Shepherd went on hunger strikes. She also developed chronic diarrhea every time I left her with friends — and none of them understood her urgent dog-language requests to go outside. A good kennel was actually much better for Jenna; she came home less nervous, weighing the same as she had when I left and looking healthier.

The final straw were the friends who assured me they'd be insulted if I didn't leave my two dogs with them. So I did and went on vacation over 1,500 miles away, planning to return home the week after Labor Day. On Thursday before Labor Day, my friends called to ask, "What do you want us to do with your dog? We've decided to go to Cape Cod for the weekend." Frantic, long-distance telephone calls followed to create emergency stop-gap arrangements for only part of a holiday weekend.

My vacation ended with a non-stop day-and-night drive through holiday traffic in nine states, always racing, racing, racing to get home to dogs who had been alone in my apartment for twenty, twenty-two, twenty-four hours. Totally confused and upset at their treatment, my dogs had done a super number on my home. Don't say it can't happen to you — they were dear, long-term friends!

If you want to leave your dog with friends, take the following steps:

1. **Be sure your friends really want your dog.** Don't coerce anyone into taking him. They won't give good care if they feel he was foisted on them.

2. **Be sure your dog knows and likes your friends.** Dogs react differently to different people no matter how the people feel about the dog. Jenna never particularly liked a large, gruff friend of mine; even though he adored her, she was nervous in his presence. She wouldn't have been happy staying with him.

3. **Make certain your friends understand what your dog is used to in terms of discipline, affection, etc.** Although dogs adapt well to different rules, they can be very unsettled if they're used to lots of loving and go to a place where they're ignored, or suddenly

receive much harsher corrections than you use.

4. **Give your friends a written list of what's allowed in your house, what your dog knows and the words you use to command.** Don't assume they've observed this. I watched one friend go into a rage because when he said, "Down," my Sheltie laid down. He meant "get down off the couch," but my Sheltie thought she was being told to lie down — "Off" was our couch command. Another friend spanked a dog for lying on the bed — but beds were fine to lie on in my house.

5. **Write down what your dog eats — specific quantities, number of meals and approximate times.** Friends don't notice this.

6. **What should go into your dog's suitcase?** His crate, if it isn't too large for your friend's house (your friend will appreciate being able to confine your dog; your dog will be more relaxed with his den along). His dishes, enough food and treats to last 'til your return, a few rawhide chews, a couple of toys, his collar (with rabies and license tags attached), his leash and either your dog's medical folder or a written record of his last shots plus the name and number of your vet.

7. **Handle your departure correctly to create minimum trouble.** Don't make a big thing about leaving, but don't sneak out, either. Say good-bye calmly and tell him to be good with these people who love him, then go. If you get upset, your dog will, too. At the same time, don't keep the taxi waiting while you drop off your dog — plan to visit with your friends for an hour or so until your dog has sniffed the place out and settled in.

8. Finally, just in case your friends decide to go to Cape Cod, line up an emergency replacement — another friend who can step in and take your dog or a kennel that has your dog's records.

Bringing in a dog-sitter. For cats, you can hire a person who comes into your house once a day to feed the cat and clean the litter box. Dogs really need human companionship; a brief daily visit is cruel and not an option. A dog who is left alone for days can develop very destructive, nervous habits, could harm himself, could end up with permanent neurotic disorders.

However, a pet-sitter who moves into your home for the length of your absence is an option. It's rare to find a person who does this for a living — most live-in pet-sitters are people with jobs who want to pick up a little extra cash, or someone whose home is being painted or redecorated and looks for an alternative living arrangement. I find it too risky to turn over my dog and my home to a complete stranger, no matter how many recommendations or references. But I have found business associates and friends who welcome the opportunity to enjoy my air conditioning and piano. Your large-screen TV, superb stereo or simply a vacation from roommates could provide an attractive lure. You might even offer an out-of-town friend a chance to "do" the city.

Make sure that the prospect of living in your home isn't so appealing that a person who really doesn't like dogs is applying for the job. Watch the person interact with your dog during several visits. And watch your dog to see if he likes this person.

Unless your sitter is a good friend, you might arrange a check-up visit by a friend while you're away. Give him or her a letter to be used to fire the sitter if problems are found.

Just as with friends, give written instructions about feeding, walks, commands and house rules. Leave enough food to last the entire time you're gone. Make sure the sitter knows where the dog's medical records are located and how to reach the vet. Leave a number where you can be reached in case of emergencies.

Kennels. Dog neophytes are horrified at the idea of a dog going to a kennel. To them, this is institutional care, never as good as caring friends. I've found they're wrong. A good kennel is actually the best solution. Yes, there are snake-pit kennels and without any government regulation, you have to do your own investigation — long before the need arises, so you aren't rushed in any way and you can be thorough.

First step, references and referrals.

Second step, call the kennel and make arrangements for a tour. Any kennel that limits what you can see should be crossed off your list — "not wanting to upset our residents" is a lie. There's a tremendous amount of traffic in all kennels and dogs find it all an interesting break in a dull day. A good kennel is proud to show you how well your dog will be cared for.

Your investigation should reveal that dogs have roomy enclosures, free from draft but with good ventilation. There should be no odor and no old messes in the enclosures. The dogs will be excited by your visit, but you shouldn't sense hysteria. Most good kennels have a separate sleeping area in each enclosure — a raised, often carpeted or padded bed place — plus an exercise/bathroom area. If the kennel is outdoors, there's an indoor sleeping area where dogs can get out of the weather and the door to the indoors enclosure either faces south or is closed at night and in inclement weather. There should be plenty of water in each enclosure. The dogs should be clean. Toys and / or bedding in the enclosures are a very good sign. The kennel should keep detailed records on each dog — name, age and the basic facts plus exactly what your dog eats and when. They should demand proof that all your dog's inoculations are current.

A really outstanding kennel that I use gives my dogs the brand food I feed and feeds on my schedule. The kennel has a central court where carefully selected dogs play together.

They even hire high-school kids to come in after school and walk the dogs, particularly the ones who are so well housebroken. It bothers them to soil their enclosures.

Good kennels have a much higher overhead than warehouses, so they aren't cheap — but if the journey ends with a happy, healthy dog who's happy to see you but not nervously following you across the room when you get home, isn't the expense worthwhile?

Chapter 17

YOU CAN OFTEN TAKE HIM WITH YOU!

Getting ready for a vacation, considering rental of a seasonal home for weekends, or plotting on how to secure lots of invites to friends' country homes? Don't leave your dog behind — you can generally take him right along. Traveling with a dog can make plans a bit more complex, but it's not impossible. Most dogs enjoy going with you, and seeing something new. Finding accommodations for your dog is becoming easier all the time.

PREPARING YOUR DOG FOR THE ROAD

If you plan to take your dog on public transportation, he will require a good traveling container. This is NOT the same as his crate, as the traveling crate will be mostly enclosed with only holes and a gate-like door.

Traveling containers are available at all large pet stores and in all catalogs. The ones recommended by the airlines are usually the best.

Make sure the container is very sturdy in case it's dropped. It should have ventilation holes on all sides, so no matter how it's packed, your dog can breathe. The door should have a very sturdy latch that can't accidentally be knocked open or broken off, even if the case falls.

The carrier should be tight-fitting so your dog can't get injured by jostling...and so your dog can't injure others by unbalancing the load suddenly. If he can lie down comfortably but not stretch all the way out and stand with a bit of a hunch, that's ideal.

As soon as you get the case, affix permanent labels with your name, home address and telephone number. For each trip, add another label that gives a way to reach you at the destination and state that's what it is: IN PHOENIX, CALL MARY SMITH AT xxxx. Remove this after each trip so there's never any confusion. Plan for your dog to travel wearing his buckled-on collar containing his license, rabies tag and an ID tag, if you have one. Do NOT put his leash on — it could catch and hurt him badly. Carry the leash in your on-board bag.

For trips longer than a few hours, you'll also want to purchase a clip-on bottle that dispenses water to your dog when he licks the opening. Open dishes will spill in the first few minutes of the trip. Bottles are available in professional pet-supply stores.

Get your dog accustomed to his new carrier well before departure so it's not another strange thing on a stressful day. Leave it where he can investigate it. Play with him by tossing his toys inside and encouraging him to go inside to retrieve them, and even feed him inside for a while.

I pad the bottom of the carrier with an old towel, believing my dogs find it more comfortable. Probably not, but it does give them the smell of home, which is calming. I also put a rawhide chew-toy inside for him to play with during the trip.

No matter how you're traveling, feed your dog a long time before you leave to avoid motion sickness. As a general rule, I feed the night before an early-morning departure, at dawn before an evening takeoff. If we leave in the middle of the day, I delay feeding until after arrival. As I mentioned, canines don't have to eat every day, so missing a meal is not harmful, and I offer more Milkbone snacks to ease my own guilt. I also feed easy-to-digest dry food just before trips.

All experts I spoke with are vehemently against sedating traveling dogs, especially if they're separated from you. The medication can actually make the dog more uneasy and leaves him unable to help himself if there's a problem.

PACKING YOUR DOG'S SUITCASE

What does your dog need to take along on your trip?

- **Water and food dish.** He doesn't need "his" dishes, but you certainly need something for him to use. A single dish will work just fine; just empty out the water at feeding time.

- **Toys.** A familiar toy that smells of home and a few new rawhide chews.

- **Treats.** A box of treats that you can also use for snacks when you have to postpone a meal.

- **Brush.** Even if he won't need a grooming while you're gone, bring one along just in case he gets into something.

- **Food.** I like the semi-moist, crumbly hamburgers — they pack easily, aren't too heavy, don't take up much room, and they are good for unsettled tummies, too. Pack enough for the entire trip.

- **License and medical records.** Bring along certificates that prove he's had his shots or information about what was administered when, by whom, and your vet's phone number.

- **Muzzle, if he has one, leash and collar**. Check leash and collar for signs of wear before you leave, and replace if there's any possibility of a breakage.

- **He does not need his bed.** Some people take "home water," believing this will avoid digestive problems. Handlers, who travel with show dogs constantly, laugh at this. Some dogs do get a digestive upset because of all the new experiences; water has nothing to do with it.

GETTING THERE: TRAINS, PLANES, CARS AND ALL THE REST

Buses. Most bus companies now ban pets entirely. I did smuggle a Beagle onto a bus inside a tote bag — I zipped the lid closed 'til I got to a seat in the back of the bus, opened the bag and put it on its side by my feet. My Beagle settled down quietly, and I discovered I was in a hive of dog-lovers who eagerly helped me keep the secret. Except for short trips on uptown buses, however, this is a risky maneuver. There's no way to know if your seat-mate has an enormous fear of dogs and rigidly obeys all rules. If you're discovered, the driver has the right to put you off the bus immediately, perhaps in the middle of nowhere.

Toys can be smuggled in purses, pockets and totes as Natasha (Toy Poodle) Bell illustrates.

Trains. Some trains permit smaller dogs to ride on-board right along with you, provided that the dog is in a closed container that can fit on your lap or at your feet. One summer I went to a beach resort every weekend with a trainload of fellow weekend-house-renters, about a third of whom were smuggling dogs in ice bags, totes and duffles. The entire train cooperated, dropping beach hats and beach towels over dogs and even forming human walls to surround dogs whenever the conductors came through. I suspect the train crew knew what was going on and laughed about it. Usually, conductors aren't so easy-going and they also have the right to stop the train and put you right off if your dog isn't properly contained.

If your dog is too large, he has to ride in the baggage compartment in a railroad-approved container. If you purchased what I suggested, it's acceptable. Dogs are well-treated and many railroads permit you to visit your dog en route. There is, of course, a charge.

Airplanes. Airlines also allow small dogs to travel right with you. The problem is they must ride in the first seats right in front of the bulkhead, so every flight can take only a couple of dogs. Make arrangements when you make reservations — well in advance. I believe they must ride in containers, too, but on every flight where I've seen dogs, they're sitting free on laps or sleeping quietly at their owners' feet, with no fuss.

Large dogs have to go cargo (see why I said portability affects your decision about the size of the dog?), in a container. Some airlines provide the carriers to insure they're safe. The dogs are generally given very special care by the baggage handlers and go into special compartments which are pressurized and heated. In fact, there was a recent news report about a "hero captain" who saved a dog's life by turning around and re-landing when it was discovered the compartment's heater was broken.

Arrangements should be made well in advance. On travel day, you go to check-in with your dog and make final arrangements for his boarding. Upon arrival, he will be brought into a side area near the luggage carousel.

Anyone who has ever had luggage shipped to South American when they were taking a commuter hop from Los Angeles to Las Vegas might logically worry about the safety of shipping a dog on a plane. But professional handlers and breeders ship dogs all the time without trouble and claim that they have never experienced this problem. To be on the safe side, I reclaimed and rebooked my dogs at every point where we had to change planes.

Cars. When we were talking about phobias, I told you how to make your dog adore traveling in cars. While many dogs experience a bit of car sickness, it usually goes away if you drive with a window cracked to let your dog have a constant stream of fresh air and you feed as I've suggested.

To be sure you and all your friends enjoy driving around with your dog and to keep him safe, establish some ground rules:

1. The best place for your dog, like your baby, is in the back seat. I know it looks cute when you see someone driving around with a Fox Terrier on his lap or a Maltese draped around her neck, but if something goes wrong, the drivers won't be able to concentrate on what needs doing and the dogs become free-flying missiles, heading right for the windshield at warp speed.

2. Dogs should not lean halfway out of car windows — they fall out of cars that way and even when they don't, they can wind up with terrible eye afflictions from wind-borne particles slamming into their eyes. I permit a nose out a window and that's all. If too much of the head goes outside, I sternly say HEAD and it goes back in immediately, because the first few times the head went out, the car window went up (VERY CAREFULLY) and squeezed the head between the window and the top of the frame just a little.

3. Dogs should not wile away travel hours by leaping from the back seat to the front and back again. They not only ride in the back, but they stay there. A dog who has been taught proper behavior should not need to be confined by a dog guard — that's the sign of a lazy driver. The exception is large station wagons and four-wheel drives where the back area creates a raised dog playpen. A sudden stop could send dogs hurtling to the front if there's no guard to stop them.

If you have a big-fur dog, travel with old bedspreads, sheets or blankets. Spread them across the back seat so that everyone who gets into the area after your dog does not leave dressed in your dog's fur.

Molly (Mutt) Paterson can easily jump out of this window, whether the car is moving or still.

Any time you travel with a dog, carry at least one gallon jug of water and a water dish, and remember to offer water during stops on long trips.

When you leave your dog in the car, check your windows carefully. Leave them cracked to allow for fresh air, but be sure the dog can't slide out — be careful with this as some dogs can compress their bodies amazingly.

Never leave your dog in a car in the summer or in direct sunlight on warm days in spring or fall. Cars are metal and temperatures can soar to well over a hundred degrees in just a few minutes. Dogs cook in cars, even when windows are open. Even on cool spring or fall days the sun is that hot.

Dogs can also develop heat stroke in summer traffic jams. When you start getting hot, check your dog. If he's panting ferociously or showing other signs of overheating, pull off the road, get the dog out of the car and into the shade (even the shade cast by your car) and pour your water all over his body.

Tasha (Keeshond) Langevin is waiting to be told it's safe for her to exit the car.

I was once in a traffic jam en route to the shore when four dogs in four different cars collapsed within a few hundred feet of each other. Owners were frantically running up and down the line of cars pleading for water. There was no way to get off the throughway, no cops in sight and no nearby houses or any other place to get help. Two of the dogs died.

GOOD NEWS ABOUT HOTELS AND MOTELS

The American Automobile Association and a number of other travel organizations publish travel guides that list all the U.S. hotels and motels that accept pets. The number is increasing and it's no longer difficult to travel anywhere in the country with a dog. A little planning is needed as there aren't dog-okay motels on every street. Keep the numbers rising by making your dog a welcome guest. Ask where you should walk your dog and clean up afterwards, whether it's required or not.

An alternative to taking your pet into the hotel with you is to kennel your dog near your hotel. Disney hotels in both

Florida and California have attached kennels which permit you to visit your dog whenever you wish and even take him out for all or part of a day, then return him in the evening. Other resorts are adding this feature as well. In the absence of such facilities, why not make similar arrangements with a kennel near the resort? Ask the hotel to help, and plan to arrive early enough in the day to investigate the place.

It's possible to stay in a no-pets motel. Get a room on the ground floor (away from the office's direct line of sight) and park right in front of your room. Bring your pet into the room when you're "at home" then return him to your car whenever you leave. Your dog won't mind since the car is "home" to him by this time and most motels will turn a blind eye since this prevents your dog from being destructive. Just watch the temperatures and the sunlight.

Private camping grounds frequently allow pets as well, although most have leash laws and rigid rules about where you can walk your pet. For the most part, state and national parks and forests still do not allow pets as they can be extremely dangerous (and in extreme danger) around wild animals.

Whenever you travel with your pet, be sure to bring along his license, rabies tag and certificates showing he has had all his shots. Make certain the shots are completely up-to-date before you leave.

TRAVEL OVERSEAS CAN BE EVEN EASIER

If you're off to the British Isles, leave your dog at home. The Brits have a six-month quarantine at the end of which, as far as I'm concerned, you no longer have a relationship with your former dog. The law has protected Great Britain from several terrible animal diseases, but it makes clear that no matter how much the British love dogs, they sure don't care for foreign canines.

Other countries, however, welcome dogs and you'll be shocked at how easily you can travel everywhere with yours, including on public and even local in-town transportation. Dogs are even welcome in many restaurants! You'll need proof of proper inoculations. Check with the embassy or mission of the country you're planning to visit to see exactly what they consider proper. Some countries also require dogs be muzzled at times. Again, the embassy or mission can give you all the specifics. Then bon voyage!

Chapter 18

COUNTRY CULTURE SHOCK

Although dogs evolved in rural areas, your dog has been raised in a city. Therefore, it shouldn't be a great surprise to discover that going to the country could create unusual reactions. The wide open spaces often create a form of "culture shock" that requires special care and considerations.

Some dogs, of course, revert instantly to their wild origins. One friend's Cocker Spaniel charged out of her car into a nearby pasture, rolled in a cow flop, ran to the creek and took a swim, then returned to the owner. Within a minute of arrival, she was a wet, smelly mess and happy as a lark. I also know a Saint Bernard who disappeared in the woods for the first six hours of his visit, returning covered with burrs and in his elation, totally oblivious to the fact that his owner was a basket case.

To a city person, this sort of behavior can cause human culture shock. But it's much more common for the city dog to view his first exposure to the country as something like visiting Mars would be to us. The bravest dog may turn timid and fearful, frightened of perfectly natural things.

PREPARE YOUR HOSTS

If you're visiting country friends with your dog, give them a fast education about city dogs before you arrive. Full-time residents of the boonies may never permit dogs inside their houses, expecting them to be tied outside for the duration. Your dog knows nothing about how to handle being tied and would view this as terrifying, cruel and unnatural punishment, worse than being left behind in a kennel. City dogs live with people, as you'll explain to your hosts before you arrive. Of course, you can also reassure them that city dogs are very well-trained.

Ahead of time, you also need to warn your hosts that they should never simply open the door and shoo your dog outside. He doesn't know how to behave. He doesn't know how to avoid getting lost. And he surely doesn't know country critters. You need to supervise your dog's "outs" at least in the beginning.

Country people shouldn't expect your dog to know everything their dogs know. Your hosts need to look to you for guidance in what to expect of your dog.

If your hosts don't know dogs, they may have a great number of misconceptions, and if you want your visit to be pleasant for all, it's important to observe what your hosts don't understand, then explain the facts.

When you first arrive at a non-dog-people home, put your dog on his leash and his best behavior until your hosts are comfortable. Non-dog people may also be very worried about destruction if the humans go out and your dog stays home alone — bring along his crate or confine him to your room to set them at ease.

BE A GUEST WHO'S INVITED TO RETURN WITH DOG

Immediately upon arrival, ask your host where your dog should relieve himself and come prepared to scoop anything that happens in any other place. With non-dog people as hosts, it would be best to always clean up after your dog — they simply aren't accustomed to excrement anywhere on their property.

A TOTALLY NEW WORLD

Don't count on your dog to know anything about the country. Although most dogs instantly know what grass and dirt are for (and will baptize your hosts' flower garden or putting green immediately upon arrival), some city dogs are not even sure where they are to relieve themselves. This is when teaching your dog to go on command can avoid any troubles.

Many city dogs are stunned to find that you expect them to go about in the country all by themselves without the security of you and their leashes. They look out the door, back at you and then out the door again, not sure of their ability to handle it on their own. Go with them at first and if they're still nervous, snap on the leash. Accustom them to freedom slowly.

Majors Roxanna Riordon/Roxie (Browner) West Highland Terrier rules her country and her city home, happy in both enviroments.

This fear of solo journeys could cause your dog to relieve himself on the front stoop or right in front of it, something most hosts will not appreciate. Clean up the mess and next time, take your dog to the correct place.

Soon after arrival, take your dog on a tour of the property, showing him the boundaries of his new territory and allowing him to sniff. It's very unlikely this tour will keep your dog inside the territory, but it will give him a sense of where he is.

City dogs are very naive about country life. They can become lost more easily than country dogs, because they don't understand the necessity of watching where they're wandering. Don't let your dog roam and keep an eye on him when he's outdoors.

Keeping an eye on your dog will also help you avoid problems with country critters which are alien to your dog. Your dog has no knowledge of snakes, racoons (vicious fighters), porcupines, skunks and other common country wildlife.

And don't trust the host's country dog. He's apt to be jealous and could lead your dog astray, then abandon him. If the country dog is a Working Group dog (or mostly a Working Group breed), he could be extremely territorial and see your dog as an invader. Bad fights come from this attitude so take care to introduce your dog to him and give the country dog a lot of attention.

Water. Some dogs, particularly Goldens, Labs, Newfoundlands and other water retrievers, are in nearby water (and previously unnoticed mud puddles) before you've got both legs out of the car. You'll have your hands full keeping these dogs dry. Other dogs find "free" water frightening. Even though all dogs can swim, not every dog wants to swim. Never toss your dog into the water to show him it's okay. This can create a lifetime phobia and a lingering distrust of you.

I don't believe in commanding a dog to enter the water if he's uneasy. Instead, go into the water yourself and drift around close to the edge, talking to the dog all the while. Little by little, he'll come out into the water to you, still standing on the ground. Drift a little farther away and eventually he'll find himself swimming. From that point on, if he likes the water, you've got a swimming companion. Some dogs will never enjoy the water — accept it.

Dogs tend to fear salt water more than fresh because of wave action. Few dogs will willingly swim in surf, and I suggest you respect their preference. Salt water, by the way, must be washed off immediately after a dip, as it can be more uncomfortable and drying to a dog's coat and skin than yours. And if you take a dog to the beach, don't plan to spend the day in the sun — an umbrella doesn't ease the heat of the beach, which can be too much for the average dog. Sand adds to his discomfort, too, and contains sand fleas that like dogs as much as regular fleas.

If you're visiting the country in the winter, the water has become ice, which is far more dangerous to dogs. Dogs handle water just fine — they either avoid it or leap in for a dip at every opportunity. But they don't seem to recognize ice; they think it's land. Every dog I ever had near frozen water strolled onto the ice without a thought, even when it was just thin, new ice around the shore. If that's all it is, fine, the dog can walk out; but if he gets out too far before breaking through, you could very well lose your dog. When there's ice, take great care.

Tie-ups. Although you certainly don't want your dog to be banished to the yard for your entire visit, teaching your dog how to handle being tied up is a good idea. The first few times you tie up any dog, he will immediately wrap the rope or chain around any obstacle and lie down miserably, trapped with just three inches of slack, unable to move.

To teach your dog how to handle this, don't remove the rope and untangle it for him; instead lead him back around all the obstacles until the rope is free. This will mean a lot of bending, pulling and urging your dog to move in complex ways he doesn't at first understand and resists, but he'll learn quickly from this lesson how to get himself free. Then he'll figure out how to avoid getting tangled up in the first place.

When you go to the beach or out for an afternoon of exploring, your dog might prefer being tied up outdoors in a shady yard rather than being locked in your bedroom. Don't leave him tied until you're sure he's at ease in the country. Be sure the rope is very sturdy so he can't break free to hunt for you, and leave him a big bowl of water.

Fighting dogs. In the country, even meek city dogs can suddenly be transformed into aggressive defenders of their new territory. And, as I mentioned, host country dogs might be rather hostile to an invader. If your dog is suddenly more alert, growling whenever he sees something on "his" land or the host dog growls and acts with hostility towards your dog, keep an eye on them. The best way to deal with a dog fight is to prevent it from happening in the first place.

Stairs. I've known two city dogs who literally didn't know how to climb stairs; all they'd ever seen were those few low steps in an apartment lobby. The Sheltie would start up and then crash down from about halfway. The Bichon simply sat down at the foot of the stairs and howled. If your dog doesn't follow you up to the bedroom, you might have to carry him. Slowly encourage him to follow you, praising every moment forward. If he falls off the stairs, have someone behind to catch him. Going up is different from going down. You have to teach both directions.

BRING HIM HOME CLEAN AND PEST-FREE

It's a lot easier to give a dog a bath with the garden hose than it is to do it in a bathtub. And it's easier to prevent fleas from emigrating to the city than getting them out of your rugs and furniture. Whenever the temperature is above freezing, fleas are almost a constant in the country. Ticks are also a possibility.

So before you start for home, give your dog a nice grooming. Start by checking his entire body for ticks; get well down through the fur to really feel the skin. If you find a tick, remove it by saturating a tissue with alcohol then grabbing the tick firmly with the tissue, waiting a few seconds then pulling firmly out. Then bathe your dog and when he's completely dry, apply flea spray or powder; treat the blanket on the back seat of the car, too, and the upholstery on the floor.

I hope I haven't alarmed you with this chapter. One of the most amazing things about dogs is their adaptability. Once they get used to the country, dogs can move from the city to the sticks and back again without any problem. Many "weekenders" have dual dogs — in the country, the dog goes to the door to ask to go out; in town, he waits for his walk. In the country, he charges around the yard in delight, but in the city, he greets the appearance of the leash with joy. Never worry that you're going to "hurt" your city dog by exposing him to the different world of the country — he'll enjoy all your worlds as long as he's with you.

Chapter 19

CITY HEALTH

This chapter is designed to alert you to the special health problems that exist for city dogs. It is not intended to give you a comprehensive primer on dog medicine. There are many excellent canine medical books for dog-owners, and I highly recommend you add one to your personal reference library.

CHOOSING A GOOD VET

Modern canine medicine is too complex for any layman to make significant decisions about what's ailing a dog or how to treat him. When in doubt, always consult your vet.

Vets have come a long way from the era of "if he sneezes twice, put him down." Today, there are a vast array of treatments and even specialities in veterinary medicine. A vet has to be extremely knowledgeable, especially since his patients can't tell him what's wrong. They can't say what hurts or why they feel bad. He has to rely on the owner's observations and his own education and instincts, which are born out of his love for his patients. Choosing a good vet is vital to insuring your dog's health.

To be frank, there are a fair number of bad vets around, people who must be in the field for the money because they have no rapport with animals whatsoever. I've subjected a dog to unnecessary surgery and left vets with thoroughly upset dogs and no treatment because the dog was so hostile that proper examination was impossible.

The one good result of my experiences is that I've discovered it's surprisingly easy to separate a good vet from a bad one. Start by letting your dog tell you — if he's comfortable and relaxed, even when the vet is doing uncomfortable things, then the vet has the right rapport with animals.

Next, let your own instincts guide you. You're your dog's parent, responsible for recognizing things your dog can't tell you and for administering treatments at home. Your vet should be VERY communicative, receptive to all your questions, never making you feel stupid, never rushing you out. He should take plenty of time to be sure you thoroughly understand anything he wants you to do or watch for. He should listen to what you have to say, too, and never dismiss your observations or comments as worthless — they're a primary way for him to find out what's going on.

Finally, a good vet is always thorough, giving a full examination every time your dog visits.

GENERAL CARE: THE ANNUAL CHECKUP

I believe in an annual physical for my dogs, no matter how healthy they look. Because they can't speak, there can be problems you don't recognize. One year, I learned it was time to give my Shepherd daily medication for her dysplasia; another time, I discovered my Beagle had developed a heart murmer. So it was very worthwhile to schedule "spring checkup" when they were due for their annual shots.

A thorough exam consists of checking heart sounds, palpating the abdomen, listening to the lungs, examining coat, gums, eyes, ears and even the pads of the feet. Good vets also look at your dog's fur, usually by casually stroking your dog when you first arrive, since changes in texture and sheen are often the first symptoms of internal illness.

I also request more complete treatment of things I do at home year-round, such as clipping nails, cleaning the ears of flop-eared dogs, cleaning out the anal glands. I bring in a stool sample since even city dogs can pick up parasites.

Every year, your dog needs a basic distemper / leptospirosis / canine hepatitis booster shot. In urban areas, ask your vet if your dog needs anything extra against parvovirus or if a new disease has cropped up that you need to know about. Dogs used to receive annual heartworm blood tests as well, but now I believe most dogs are on a year-round medication.

Some cities no longer require rabies inoculation, but regardless of the law, get the shots every three years. Rabies is on the upswing. It's epidemic in racoons, skunks, foxes, bats and even squirrels in many areas of the country and it's spreading. Out West, they're even finding rabies in horses! Town dogs do get out in the country on occasion and also visit parks with squirrels — get the shot!

BASIC CARE FOR YOUR DOG

What sort of regular care should you give your dog? It's relatively simple:

Brushing. Every dog should be brushed fully at least once a week, although, of course, the fuller your dog's coat, the more attention you need to give to him. Even dogs with extremely short, thin coats still need brushing to stimulate the skin, remove dander and dust, and move the skin oils down into the fur. It's also a time when you can thoroughly examine your dog's body, an important part of caring for him.

Get down through the fur to the skin. When you come to clumps or tangles, carefully comb them out, starting at the end and gradually working your way down the fur length. Try to avoid letting them get so bad you have to cut them out.

While you're grooming, look under the fur for fleas or their tell-tale black dirt specks. Check for ticks (yes, they can be picked up in parks) and keep an eye out for any sort of swellings, sores, painful spots or other irregularities. Some dogs develop hot spots which cause them to itch and scratch until they tear open the skin. You can actually feel hot spots — I find putting cold compresses on them can ease the discomfort to the dog.

Extremities. Clean the eyes, ears and anal glands regularly. Sniff the ears — any odor means go to the vet.

Every time you groom, take a close look at your dog's feet, spreading the pads out and looking between pads for any signs of redness or irritation. Thorns and other sharp things can get caught and cause serious problems. Pads should be smooth, not rough and never show signs of splitting. I rub Vaseline into my dogs' pads when they get rough; it seems to lubricate and smooth them.

Keep the nails clipped short. If your dog has furry feet, cut the hair between the pads several times a year. Both long nails and too much hair can distort the shape of the foot, changing the way your dog places his weight and eventually causing major physical problems.

Every few months, peel back your dog's lips and examine his teeth carefully. As he ages, dark tarter will build up on the base of the teeth and this will have to be scaled off at some point (your dog needs to go to sleep for this procedure) or he'll develop more serious problems. Any unusual color, marking, pitting or mouth odor means you have to go to the vet. A healthy city dog has sweet breath; bad breath is, at the very least, a symptom of severe tooth decay that requires extraction right away. (No, dogs don't get fillings so far as I know.)

By the way, unusual swelling anywhere around the muzzle and jaw area could be an abscess, which is as serious in dogs as it is in us.

Baths. City dog-owners often err on the side of excess when it comes to bathing their dogs. A dog's fur insulates him from heat, warms him in the winter and protects him from wind and rain; it does this so well because it contains natural oils distributed throughout the fur. Every time you bathe a dog, you remove those oils, leaving your dog fluffy and lovely but naked as far as the elements are concerned until the proper balance is restored, which can take some time.

Part of the reason for brushing a dog weekly is to remove dirt and dander so he doesn't need so many baths. The average dog with an easy-care coat needs no more than four baths a year, and even light-colored or dense-coated dogs can get by with spot cleanings and regular brushing for far longer than you might think.

Naturally, a smelly dog needs a bath if he smells when he's dry — almost all dogs smell when wet.

When you bathe your dog, be sure to keep him warm and out of drafts until he's completely dry. Dogs are quite susceptible to the cold at these times. Use a dog shampoo because human formulas aren't good for dogs. A hand-held shower attachment can be immensely useful in rinsing underneath your dog. If your dog is too large to fit into the sink, I find the easiest way to give a bath in the city is to strip down and get into the tub along with the dog. Once he's clean, wrap him in a towel, put him on the bathroom floor, close the curtains and clean yourself.

If you get your dog used to it when very young, you can speed drying by using a hair dryer on a cool setting. If you wait 'til your dog's an adult, he'll never allow that scary, noisy thing near him.

Feeding. When? My adult dogs got one meal a day. For me, evenings were more convenient so that's when they ate. It really makes no difference whether your dog eats in the morning or at night or you divide his daily intake into two meals.

Because the big, nationally known commercial dog food manufacturers have staffs of canine nutritionists, their food is better formulated for your dog than anything you can make at home. Vets will tell you that dried food is fine all by itself, but like many people, I feel I'm feeding better when I use a combination of canned and dry, about 1/4 canned to 3/4 dried. I choose the meaty-looking canned foods, but I've discovered that some of the supposedly top-quality foods are too rich and cause digestive upsets in my dogs.

You don't need to immediately leap to the brands which used to be available only by prescription, either. Many major brands will keep your dog very healthy and happy, at less cost.

By the way, many of those much cheaper "house brands" offered in large supermarkets and pet stores are really top-quality brands which have been custom-packaged for the stores with their own labels. Compare the look and texture of the foods. I pay as little as HALF the price of the national brand for exactly the same food from the same factory.

Dogs have different likes and dislikes. Some like large crunchy nuggets, others like small ones. Some like a bit of gravy (I make that by adding a little hot water from the tap to the canned food I'm using, then mix in the dried food). Some like canned food, some don't. Some like the semi-moist hamburgers, some don't. Some like the vegetables in some of the cans while others eat all the meat and leave the peas and carrots sitting in the clean dish. While you're not about to let your dog rule the house, adapting your purchases and preparations to his tastes seems a fair adjustment to me.

One note about food: Some commercial foods contain brown dye to make them look more attractive to us (dogs don't care what good looks like) and the dye stains the mouth and chin areas of light-colored, fuzzy dogs. Check labels.

Several friends tell me their dogs eat the same food for every meal for their entire lives without problems. I found that many of my dogs eventually got bored with their food and regained their appetites when I switched varieties, mixtures of wet and dry or did something else to give them a change.

I keep a box of semi-moist, individually wrapped hamburger food on hand for emergencies. And if you ever run out of dog food, cooked rice and a can of tuna fish (with oil) makes a tasty, nutritious meal.

Your vet will probably tell you that if you're feeding a good, nationally known brand of food, your dog doesn't need any supplements once he's stopped growing (many vets do recommend a good dog multi-vitamin for growing pups). This may well be true, but I feel I'm taking better care of my dogs when I give them a few extras. About once a month, they get an egg mixed into their food. They never have trouble digesting it despite the experts' claims that dogs can't tolerate raw eggs. On approximately the same schedule, I mix a bit of chopped, fresh parsley into their food, to take the place of that grass they can't get in the city. And about twice a month, I give them a tablespoon of fat from the drain can I keep in the refrigerator — less for small dogs. My personal feeling is that these additions give healthier, shinier coats and stronger bodies.

Several years ago, a vet told me to give my Beagle a child's dose of cod liver oil daily in winter, explaining that dogs require vitamins they get from sunlight for complete health and it's not available in the winter. After thinking about it, I realized city dogs never get all that much sunlight so my dogs get cod liver oil in every supper all year round. They love it!

As I've mentioned several times already, Milkbones are an important part of keeping a dog's gums and teeth healthy. I feed eight to ten a week and make rawhide chews available all the time. Now they have a new dog cookie specially designed to remove tarter. Don't invest in a giant box until you see whether or not your dogs like it.

A good diet is vital. My Beagle didn't get a bad tooth until she was fourteen years old, but a friend who carefully cooked dog food herself and supplied rubber toys owned a dog who lost eight teeth by the age of seven and another who was toothless by the time she was ten.

One additional note: Adult dogs only require one meal a day. If you'd prefer to feed twice a day, be sure to feed half the total to avoid fat-dog problems.

HOW TO TELL WHEN YOUR DOG IS SICK

It isn't always easy to tell when your dog is ailing because dogs frequently hide symptoms and pretend that nothing is wrong. Signs of sickness may be very subtle and even disappear at times, leaving you to wonder if you're simply imagining things. It's better to be too careful when this happens — go to the vet.

What sort of symptoms should you watch for? Overall, look for any abrupt change from the norm. Individual dogs are too unique to rely absolutely on what dogs do in general.

Here are the most common changes to watch for:

Doesn't act "right." Trust your instincts, even when you can't find anything specific on which to base them. You're so close to your dog that if you sense something is wrong, you're probably right.

Changes in appetite or thirst. The disappearance of appetite, a sudden fierce hunger, or a new desire to eat strange things like dirt are all signals that should send you to the vet. Any unusual type of vomiting with no known cause is also a warning signal. Remember, a sudden heat spell or a big change in your daily lives could also cause some of these symptoms. They're alarming if they persist or there's no reason. Sudden, inexplicable changes in thirst are major alarms — go to the vet fast.

Breathing problems. Extreme panting when it's not hot and your dog has never done this before, rasping breath at any time and any other change in breathing can be very urgent and should send you to the vet at once.

Color changes. Get used to the color of your dog's skin and the shades inside his mouth. Any sudden change of color should be viewed with alarm — pale gums can mean internal bleeding, among other things. A bluish tinge to the gums may be a crisis because it can be a sign your dog is suffocating.

A new pot belly or tenderness in the tummy. Unless you've just grossly overfed your dog, the sudden appearance of a pot belly can be a very bad sign, perhaps even of bleeding or fluid build-up. And if you ever pat a normal-looking tummy only to see your dog wince, hurry to the vet at once.

Diarrhea, constipation or any unusual discharge from anywhere. Some dogs get the runs if you blink twice. If you've got such a dog, you quickly get used to his patterns. Other dogs get runny eyes from hayfever, just like people and you'll get accustomed to their seasonal problems. Dogs get quite a few allergies that cause itching, runny eyes and/or noses, sneezing. It's the sudden change in pattern or appearance of things you've never seen before that should alarm you. Don't dally about these symptoms — parvo starts with the runs and can dehydrate a dog to the point of death in only one day.

Cough. Anything that is persistent or causes expectoration requires a vet's attention.

Rough, dry, dull or shedding fur. Your dog's fur can change very quickly if something bad is happening inside. Pay attention to it.

Excessive chewing or itching. Dogs bite and chew at themselves for a lot of reasons — I've known bored dogs to chew themselves into a mass of sores. One year at the Westminster Dog Show, the announcer mentioned that a Terrier had chewed the bushy fur off her legs just a few months before and a breeder who was watching with me said, "Just like a Terrier. She probably said, 'I hate all this bushy fur here' and removed it."

But chewing and itching can be more serious. Dogs often bite or chew an area that's hurting inside.

Some dogs have a flea allergy that makes them so sensitive to a single bite that it starts a cycle of extreme scratching and chewing that eventually leaves the skin raw. Then that irritates the dogs so much that they continue chewing until they turn their entire bodies into hairless, raw wounds. Steroids are required to stop the cycle and let the skin heal.

By the way, a cold, wet nose does ***NOT*** *mean a dog is healthy and a hot, dry nose is not a sign of illness. Many dogs have hot, dry noses at some point every single day and a few dogs have dry, cracked noses all the time.*

SPECIAL CITY AILMENTS

A few medical problems are unique to the city:

Poisoning. Sure, country dogs get poisoned, but the threat of poisoning is much greater in the city. Any juicy tidbit lying in the gutter could be laced with virulent poison, and a wet spot on the street could be antifreeze. In your home, some of your houseplants may well be poisonous to your dog. Sago palm, Dieffenbachia, philodendron, peace lily (also called snowflower), caladium and English ivy are common plants that are very not good for your dog.

If you ever suspect your dog has been poisoned, don't delay by treating him at home — race to the vet. Bring along a sample of what he ate if at all possible. If your vet needs help or you really want to wait, there's a round-the-clock National Animal Poison Control Center hotline (see the Appendix).

Glass cuts. Broken glass is all over city streets and liberally spread around in parks. That's why glass cuts are the most common city injury to dogs. A cut pad is serious and it bleeds profusely. Wrap the foot substantially and apply pressure directly onto the cut to slow the flow. Then hurry to the vet.

Kennel cough. This dry, hacking, nonstop, little cough is not serious in itself but can have some nasty complications. It's also unbelievably annoying, especially at night. Because it's very contagious, your city dog will probably catch it at some point in his life, either at the vet's, the kennel or even on the street. The vet can give you a cough suppressant and see that no complications occur.

Colds and bronchitis. Yes, dogs get them, too, though probably not from people. Keep a dog with a cold warm and quiet; don't stress him with travel or excitement. Take a dog with a productive cough to the vet, as it's probably bronchitis.

If you notice your dog gets respiratory problems every winter, put a coat on him whenever the temperature outside drops below twenty.

Winter salt. The salt used on city streets and sidewalks burns dogs' feet like acid. When they experience it, they may refuse to move, lie down in the dirty slush and even howl in agony. If it's not washed off their feet right away, the salt will cause their pads to dry and crack wide open. Once the snow has been treated, take your dog outside only for elimination and if possible, carry him to the curb. The moment you get back in the house, wash his feet thoroughly.

The only preventative solution is rubber boots, sold in many pet stores and through mail-order catalogs. Boots may look stupid but do prevent a lot of pain and the risk of more serious problems.

Obesity. City dogs are usually much less active than their country cousins and obesity is a common problem. It's serious because obese dogs have more medical problems than obese people. Your dog's weight is ideal when you can feel his ribs but not see them and when his skin is loose, not filled with dog.

Experiment to learn how much food maintains your dog's ideal weight. Never feed what the food manufacturers tell you on their packaging — I think they believe dogs should be blimps or they assume we're all giving our dogs ten miles of road work every day. Their recommendations aren't even close to the right amount.

If your dog has accidentally gotten fat, he needs a diet. No fasting, no starvation diets, however; dogs should lose weight slowly. Cut his feedings back until you see that he's gradually shrinking. If he becomes hysterically hungry, switch to one of the low-calorie foods available in the market — that will let him eat more with fewer calories. Watch out for his treats, too. Many a dog has gotten fat on treats, not meals.

PLEASE DON'T THINK ABOUT BREEDING

Breeding a bitch in the city can be a bitch. Can you imagine what a dozen unhousebroken German Shepherd puppies could do to your home? Well, several breeds like Shepherds are known for having large litters.

Even dealing with a bitch in heat is unpleasant in the city. There's the spotting (puddling in some dogs), the fact that every male dog in town will be dragging his owner in your direction, and the danger of the unleashed males (there are a few in every neighborhood).

Breeding has no significant advantages...

• It is NOT a way to recoup your investment in your dog. Home-bred dogs don't sell for nearly as much as professionally bred dogs, and there isn't always a market when you have puppies. An awful lot of people are "stuck" with unwanted puppies they can't even give away, which is one reason why shelters end up with so many. Even if you could sell all your pups, it's unlikely that you'll do more than net out even on the costs of breeding and caring for the pups.

• Dogs don't need to breed "for their health." This is a total myth.

• There are better ways to teach your children the facts of life than bringing unwanted puppies into the world.

If you're still wavering, consider the time required — to safeguard your dog, you'll need to be sure you're home during whelping. Puppies need to be held, cuddled, spoken to and otherwise given plenty of human attention if they are to become socialized well to humans so they make good pets. Lots of time. Then there's the cleaning up, the trips to the vet for the puppy exams and puppy shots. And you can never predict if your bitch will go down with calcium insufficiency or some other unavoidable ailment, requiring you to switch from mother's milk to bottle-feeding of very expensive "bitch milk" — every two hours for every single puppy. That's round-the-clock!

Finally, a pitch for the humanitarian in you — as I told you in Chapter 6, ten million dogs a year are euthanized in this country (in plain English, they're killed) and there's just one reason: There are too many dogs. One female dog and her offspring can produce 67,000 dogs in just six years! The only way to stop the killing and reduce the incidence of abandoned dogs and their suffering is to reduce the overpopulation. If more people who want dogs would go to shelters and adopt one instead of producing a half dozen puppies in order to get one, we'd start to make inroads on the terrible overpopulation problem in this country. SPAY. NEUTER. Before sexual maturity — new research proves that (a) nothing bad happens if a dog is neutered before he lifts his leg or a bitch is spayed before her first heat and (b) spayed and neutered dogs do NOT get lazy or fat (although unwarranted sexual activity does stop as does most male marking and males tend to be a bit more affectionate).

Please don't breed.

SERIOUS ILLNESS AND OLD AGE

Today, veterinary medicine provides high-tech, high-caliber medical care that treats the most serious of ailments and enables dogs to live much longer than in the past. The biggest animal hospitals have specialities just as in human medicine — everything from cardiology to dermatology. There are dogs on dialysis, dogs who take medication to control epilepsy and diabetes, intensive-care units for dogs, chemotherapy treatment for dogs with cancer, implants for dogs with cataracts, prostheses for dogs who need hip replacements and even little wheeled carts to make dogs with paralyzed hindquarters mobile again.

You can expect to live a long, happy, vigorous life with your dog. You can also expect that at least at some point, medical bills will be significant.

Sooner or later, every city dog-owner yearns for pet medical insurance. And insurance companies regularly come up with pet programs, almost all of which are later canceled. The only insurance that makes a profit for the insurers expressly excludes genetic conditions (no matter when they emerge) and pre-existing illnesses or disabilities. None of the extremely expensive inherited ailments are ever covered. In short, insurance doesn't cover much of the really expensive stuff. Pet insurance is also expensive and has a tendency to go up in great leaps. I heard of one policy that started off at $200 a year and jumped to $1,000 the very next year. Maybe a good policy will appear soon, but investigate thoroughly before investing.

Despite all this talk of expensive medical care, an old pet is not necessarily a sick one. Even when your dog is stiff with arthritis, has glassy eyes covered with cataracts, a few lumpy cysts under his skin, fewer teeth than he began with and very white hair, he can still be a healthy pleasure to live with. He moves more slowly, of course, and needs less exercise. He hasn't much patience with active children or young pets. But he is extremely content to spend his twilight years proving he has learned his lessons so well that aggravation is long forgotten. As he rests quietly beside you, you'll find joy in sharing his serenity and devotion. This very special time together can last for years.

As your dog nears the end, however, do NOT get the next dog. The second dog should arrive well after the end or your old dog could decide the new guy is a replacement and quietly, obediently step aside — he can decide to die. At the very least, a young dog will be upsetting to the old gentleman.

There may come a time when life may be more of a burden than a pleasure for your old friend. Be realistic and listen to others who have clearer vision and judgment, who are not so blinded by love. They will see his pain much more clearly than you, and they can help you face what's really quite obvious. Should the time come when your dog's days are filled with pain, take advantage of the opportunity to be his very best friend and end that suffering quickly and painlessly. It's the hardest decision you'll ever make and only you can make it. Don't let anyone coerce you because you are ultimately the one who must live with it.

Chapter 20

YOU & YOUR DOG IN TIMES OF CRISIS OR DISASTER

Nobody's life is a smooth, peaceful road. We all hit speed-bumps, potholes, flat tires and, at times, catastrophes. Once you share your life with a dog, these difficult times involve him as well as you. Sometimes, the crisis is because something has happened to your dog. At other times, the crisis is complicated by your frantic question, "What should I do with the dog?" Still others could put you in a position where you believe you will have to give up your dog.

This chapter examines the possible crises and disasters that could occur.

MOVING YOUR HOME

A move is a time of great turmoil and stress to you AND your dog. He becomes uneasy long before moving day, when he sees his home is being torn apart and being put into boxes and senses your tension. This alone is enough to cause him to change his eating patterns and develop bowel problems. No matter how busy you are preparing for your move, take time every day to pay attention to your dog and reassure him that everything is all right.

If you're visiting your new home occasionally before the move, take your dog along. Give him an opportunity to sniff it out so it isn't totally alien on moving day.

The final days before moving are pandemonium and during the move itself, strange people are taking your possessions away, walking around everywhere and leaving doors open. It's the perfect time for a nervous, frightened dog to get out and get lost, or get underfoot and trip a mover carrying your Chippendale chair, or worse yet attack the movers!

When I moved three hundred miles with my Sheltie, I took her to our new home the week before we moved and left her with a family we both knew very well. She had a great vacation while I made the move. When she came to the new home, which she'd already investigated, and found all "our stuff" there, she settled in without a problem.

When I made a second move with my German Shepherd and Beagle, I put them both on their leashes before the movers arrived, asked the movers to empty the smallest bedroom first, then put them in there and closed the door. I even put a sign on the door that said "Dogs Inside" so the movers wouldn't open it.

Upon arrival at the new place, the movers happened to bring the Shepherd's crate in the first load. I've already told you how it calmed Jenna and kept her safe from escaping. I looped the other dog's leash over the bathroom door where she too was secure and out of the way.

LOST DOG!

There's nothing so heartbreaking as the sight of a lost dog in a busy city. Usually such animals are absolutely terrified and panicking, racing across and down busy streets in the midst of traffic. Even a knowledgeable dog-lover can rarely catch them.

Yet no matter how careful you are, there could come a time when your dog gets away from you. That's why it's important to have your dog licensed and always wearing his tags. You might even investigate tatoos and microchips, the newest ways of establishing permanent identification of your dog.

If the worst happens, DON'T PANIC! Frantically racing from one spot to another calling your dog's name accomplishes nothing. By the time your dog responds to your call, you'll have moved to another location.

Immediately after losing your dog, try to follow his path (and call since in this case, you're staying behind him all the time). Keep any hint of your fear out of your voice so you don't add to your dog's terror.

If you haven't found your dog after thirty minutes, go home. Call your local shelter, the dog catcher and anywhere else lost dogs are taken. Give a full description of your pet, your name and your phone number. The people who work at these places are invariably caring folk who will very much want to help you. Then STAY OFF THE PHONE so that everyone who now has your number can reach you. I know you'll feel a tremendous urgency to get out there and do something, but at this point waiting by the phone is the best thing you can do.

If there's no news about your dog after three to four hours, set up your own Search & Rescue Team. Get access to a second phone and station a friend by your phone in case your dog is found. Stay off your phone as much as possible and try to arrange for someone to answer it throughout your search.

Next, call in your friends. Start someone calling every shelter and dog catcher in the area on the second phone every two to three hours. The next morning, friends who know your dog well should visit every shelter and examine all dogs, including the ones who have just arrived and those in treatment. Your dog could have slipped past the person watching for him and if he's in the system, he's headed to adoption, transfer or euthanasia. Visit every day you're searching. By the third day, if you have a purebred, call the breed club. Call earlier and enlist them in your search if you haven't a good crew of friends.

Still using the second phone, someone should call all the vets and animal hospitals within a five to ten mile radius (someone could have picked your dog up and taken him further away).

Find a good, sharp picture of your dog that shows his face and body, go to a local quick printer shop and make up a Lost Dog poster. Yes, offering a reward will help. Then with your friends, get those posters up everywhere, in ever shop, on every bulletin board, on light poles. Make a circle around the spot where you lost your dog and extend your postering out for at least a mile.

I wish you luck.

INJURED DOGS

Although I hope you never need it, the best way to deal with accidents and sudden illness is to be well-prepared in advance. How? First, by knowing where the nearest 24-hour emergency service is located. Second, by knowing how to give dog first aid. Third, by having a fully-stocked first-aid kit standing by.

What sort of first aid do you need to know? How to make a muzzle out of gauze. Injured animals bite even those they love because of their fear, confusion and pain. How to move a badly injured dog. How to do CPR and breathing. What to do about a broken bone, a snakebite, a bad burn. How to recognize and treat shock. Get a good dog first-aid book at your library or bookstore or, better, buy a video that shows you exactly what to do. See Appendix for resources. Then practice.

What about a first-aid kit? You need one in your house in an accessible place and, if you have one, another in your car. You can buy a nice kit (see Appendix) or make up your own. Basic ingredients: 2 big rolls of gauze (6′) to wrap a wound or break and make an emergency muzzle, 2″ wide ace bandage, packet of 4″ gauze pads, a big roll of adhesive tape, a scissors, hydrogen peroxide to induce vomiting, a tube of antiseptic ointment, cotton swabs, a tweezer for splinters, pair of chopsticks to make a splint, at least one bottle of water for flushing wounds and burns. Discuss this list with your vet as he might want to add some items.

DIVORCE & CUSTODY

Several people have told me that one of the most painful aspects of their divorces was determining who got to keep the dog. For childless couples, the dog is often their only child and all the problems and emotions affecting and involving children at a time like this affect your dog.

When the relationship is breaking up, the atmosphere is tense, emotional and difficult. Small wonder that your dog picks this up and starts having stress problems himself. His eating becomes erratic, he has bowel upsets, he may "revert" to his childhood and start having accidents in the house. If his problems are ignored, he could very well become sick, as stressed dogs often wind up with serious illness. Just like a child, he needs reassurance, extra attention and support before, during and after the break-up.

Need I say that your dog should not become a weapon to be used by you or your significant other? Trying to make him love one of you exclusively and turn against the other will only be incredibly upsetting — a sensitive dog could be destroyed by this sort of game. He loves you both unconditionally.

Just as pre-nuptial agreements are a good idea, an agreement on who gets the dog when you first acquire him is also a good idea — which you probably won't do. If you haven't, the dog is legally considered "property." If the one who doesn't get the dog gets visiting privileges, try to be cooperative if only for the dog's well-being. If you're the one who loses the dog, consider grief counseling, offered by many local humane societies and very helpful in getting past the pain.

ABUSE

If someone is abusing your dog, it must be stopped. Unfortunately, in many states, the law will not support your efforts very well. Cruelty to animals is not against the law in every state and even where it is, district attorneys are reluctant to prosecute and judges are inclined with let perpetrators off with a slap on the wrist.

Your local humane society can help you determine what the law is in your state and who you must contact to get help in stopping the abuse. In most cases, it's not the police. In New York State, the first state to have anti-cruelty laws, the ASPCA has humane-law-enforcement officers who are empowered to investigate reports of cruelty, seize animals, issue warrants and make arrests. They also work with district attorneys to try to get as many cases as possible prosecuted. I wish I could assure you that there was a good network like this in your area — perhaps you can help create one.

If the law cannot help you, the humane society will be able to provide suggestions and guidance on what you can do.

If you are the one being abused, my heart goes out to you. Recent research shows that some people are afraid to leave their abusers because they're frightened that the dogs left behind will be abused. Please don't let that stop you. As I write, some humane societies are working on solutions to the problem that "safe houses" rarely take pets. I don't know that any have a real program in place, but I can assure you that the caring, compassionate people at your local humane society and breed rescue organizations will move heaven and earth to help you get away and safeguard your dog.

NATURAL DISASTERS

If you live in an area where tornadoes, hurricanes, wildfires, earthquakes, floods, tidal waves or other natural disasters are possible, make these preparations right now.

1. **Where in your house will you put what you need?** Choose a spot you will remember for your dog first-aid kit, your disaster kit, important documents and your reminder checklist. You need to get at this place fast so the attic or the back of a closet are wrong choices.

2. **If you ever have to evacuate, where can you take your pets?** Find this out now. Get a map and draw a circle around your town, extending it out far enough to be away from any danger that might threaten your home. Now, call every motel, kennel, vet and friend in this circle to find out if you can bring your pets there in an emergency. No-pet motels often waive their rules in times of disaster. Do not bother with shelters; they'll be overwhelmed themselves, often taking the entire populations of shelters in the path of disaster. If you don't line up at least two sites in every direction, call your breed club and ask for members who can be of help.

   Now make a list of all the sites you've lined up, under the headings of NORTH, SOUTH, EAST, WEST. Include 24-hour phone numbers, addresses and even traffic directions. Make at least one copy. Put one in your disaster kit, another in your desk and perhaps a third in some other location. Update your list every year.

3. **What will you do if you're not home when disaster strikes?** If you're at work across town or on a trip across the country, someone needs to get to your dog and get him out of danger — someone who lives nearby, as there may not be time to travel, someone completely trustworthy, a nearby friend or, failing that, a neighbor who also has a pet. Talk to this person now. Make sure this person knows your dog and your dog knows him or her. If a stranger runs into your house in a panic, your dog may hide or attack instead of accompanying him or her. Show this person where your disaster kit is located and give him or her a set of keys. Then agree on how you will contact one another if evacuation is necessary. Since you might flee in any direction, the telephone number of a more distant friend or relative might be wisest. Alert this person as to the arrangements.

4. **If you don't have a car, how are you going to evacuate?** Your dog won't be permitted on a public evacuation vehicle as all space will be used for humans. How about the person who's going to take your pet out if you can't be with him? Does that person have a car? If so, arrange to go together. Never rely on someone driving crosstown or renting a vehicle. You may not have time, or it might not be possible.

5. **Create a disaster evacuation kit and put it with your dog first-aid kit, which you'll also take with you.** What goes into your kit? Right on top, put your checklist. Then in an easy-to-carry container, place medications, copies of AKC registrations and medical records stored in a waterproof container, current photos of your pet (in case he gets lost); a one-week supply of food (semi-moist hamburger-style food is most portable); a gallon of water; a bowl to serve for feeding and water — if you're packing canned food, a can opener — a spare leash and collar plus muzzle if you

use one; written information on feeding schedules, medical conditions, behavior problems and the name and number of your vet; pet toys.

6. **Make a checklist of what else you need for evacuation.** When a warning comes, you won't be thinking clearly. Make the list now and put it on top of your disaster kit. What goes on it are the things to take if you have time to get them: Your dog's crate, a bathroom rug for a dog bed, extra gallons of water (you can't have too much), whatever additional dog food you have, the real medical records instead of copies, and in large print, THE DISASTER KIT AND THE FIRST-AID KIT.

If you have advance warning, put your dog's collar and leash on, then put him in his crate immediately. As any sort of natural disaster approaches, your dog is going to become frightened and erratic, and he could try to hide or run away, become very difficult to control. Insure that you have control as far ahead of time as you can. For this extraordinary occasion, putting your dog's leash on before crating him isn't dangerous. Having him escape your grasp when you take him out of the crate is.

The collar should contain your dog's ID and, if possible, who should be contacted if he does become lost while you're away from your home.

Call ahead to your emergency shelter to confirm arrangements for you and your dog. Check with your transport if it isn't your own car. If you can't reach the person, find someone else immediately. If your back-up is any distance away, get together at first warning. If nothing happens, you just had an adventurous visit.

If you're taking your own car, start packing it with your

disaster kit and items from your checklist. If you don't have your car, put everything where it can instantly be loaded into your transport when it arrives.

When the evacuation order comes, leave at once. Your dog will not be accepted in a shelter. He will not be allowed to get into a boat or truck picking up last-minute survivors. Your carefully planned evacuation sites will fill up fast. Roads will become clogged. GO NOW, while both of you can get out and find a place to stay. Better it's a false alarm than you're forced to leave your dog behind. Remember that poor dog on the roof of a flooded house who was rescued by a news helicopter? Don't let that be your dog.

Cocker Spaniel Hesper Marcotte is a gentle, loving, cheerful city dog.

Keep your pet under tight control when you go. He'll be terrified. At such times, he could bite, snap and definitely run away in a panic. Don't let go of him for a minute.

SERIOUS ILLNESS (YOURS)

I hope it never happens, but serious illness could occur at some time in your future. Perhaps you need an operation, requiring time in the hospital and perhaps even in a rehab center. Certainly, you'll be very weak and perhaps not fully mobile when you come home. Perhaps you simply have an ailment that leaves you weak and bed-ridden.

At such times, a dog is a wonderful companion and research studies have even shown that you'll recover more quickly with your dog. But how do you handle walks, feedings, shopping for food, etc.?

Bud Avick is the medium-sized Miniature Poodle, a great charmer with a happy personality, and a fantastic city dog.

Most of the time, you'll rely on family or friends to help you through this time. But what if a friend isn't available? In such situations, people have felt there was no option but to give up their dogs. I don't believe that's necessary! In Southern California, former Olympic champion diver, Greg Louganis, is active in a volunteer organization that helps people with AIDS keep their dogs. Greg and many others provide care in feeding, walking, grooming and whatever else is needed. I am sure a little research will turn up a similar organization for any seriously ill dog-owner in most urban areas. Just keep hunting.

SENIOR CITIZENS AND DOGS

Recent research has shown that people live longer, and stay healthier and more alert longer when they have dogs. Senior citizens with dogs also tend to stay socially involved with others, which lengthens their lives. Because of this, some new things are happening that involve senior citizens and dogs...

- In some areas, public housing's no-pets clause is waived for senior citizens. Some apartment rental companies and condo management organizations do the same.

- A few local humane societies will help seniors adopt dogs, waiving fees and providing counseling to match a senior's requirements and limitations to the right dog.

- Some of these societies guarantee "after-care" for pets adopted by seniors; i.e., your dog will find a good home and continue to lead a good life after you're gone. There are also no-kill sanctuaries with whom you can make arrangements now. They'll pick up your pet when you pass on or go into a nursing home and give him a fine life full of love, even if he isn't adoptable.

- I have even heard of animal-welfare programs that will help seniors pay for dog food and vet fees either during a temporary shortfall or on a more permanent basis.

Chapter 21

SO YOU WANT TO MOVE ON BEYOND JUST A PET?

Are you enjoying your dog so much that you'd like to explore what else you might do together? Can you turn your games into competitions where you'll meet other people and their dogs...and maybe pick up a blue ribbon or gold cup? Can you and your dog become heroes or make the world a better place? Can your dog become a star? What else is "out there" to enhance your life with your dog?

The short answer is "lots."

CHAMPIONS

Your dog need not win at Westminster to receive titles, trophies and honors. All you need do is give your training an objective.

Canine Good Citizen. Your dog can put C.G.C. after his name if he passes a series of fairly simple tests that show he's a well-mannered city dog. You get a certificate to put on the wall, too.

The American Kennel Club's Canine Good Citizen program is conducted by local dog clubs, so check to find out when the next testing program is happening in your area.

What does a C.G.C. do? He accepts a friendly stranger without resentment, shyness or hostility. He sits politely while the friendly stranger pets him. He allows grooming and examination even by a friendly stranger. He walks along beside his handler without pulling or jerking even while walking around three people. Then he sits and lies down on command and stays when told to do so, even when his handler walks twenty feet away. He comes to his handler promptly when called from ten feet away; passes another dog with nothing more than casual interest; doesn't panic, turn aggressive or try to run away when a jogger runs in front of him or a large book is dropped; and he stays quietly when a stranger takes his leash and his handler walks away.

All basic city-dog behavior. Pretty easy. Go for it!

Obedience Trials. These competitions offer your dog the opportunity to demonstrate he has learned his lessons extremely well — as well as some more advanced behavior. He can then put some impressive initials after his name, much like scholars put "Ph.D." after theirs.

Obedience competition is serious business and those letters after a dog's name are significant to dog people. Although standard obedience classes teach everything needed for the first level, it takes added time and training to bring your dog up to a winning level. A professional trainer can show you the fine-turning tricks that win high scores from judges, such has having your dog make a square corner at a turn or look up at you when he sits.

Obedience competitions are conducted and/or registered by a number of organizations. The one all others measure themselves against is the American Kennel Club, but its competitions are limited to registered dogs and dogs on their Miscellaneous list. Other groups include the American Mixed Breed Obedience Registry open to neutered/spayed dogs that cannot be registered with any other organization, Mixed Breed Dog Club of America for members only, the Australian Shepherd Club of America open to all breeds and mixed breeds, States Kennel Club in the South and New

England Obedience News.

Each organization has slightly different exercises, rules, regulations about the handler's behavior in the ring, and show schedules. Contact them for information before you try to enter.

As a rule, dogs compete at three levels and must earn a title at each step before proceeding to the next. Each competition has a maximum of 200 points and your dog earns a title by getting a score of 170 or more points, in three novice rings. The levels are:

1. **Companion Dog** (giving the dog the initials "C.D." after his name) requires everything taught in standard obedience class, done on-leash.

2. **Companion Dog Excellent (C.D.X.)** requires the C.D. exercises be done off-leash and adds retrieving over hurdles and a scent discrimination exercise.

3. **Utility Dog (U.D.)** requires doing exercises off-leash with only hand signals (no voice), directed jumping and standing (getting the dog to obey from a distance), scent discrimination and retrieval exercises.

The PupPeroni Classic Tournaments (previously known as Cycle and Gaines) are considered the "Westminster of Obedience." All competing dogs have already earned a title. There are Eastern, Western and Central regional tournaments, each a two-day event comprised of three shows in the divisions of Novice for C.D. dogs, Open for C.D.X. dogs and Super Dog for U.D. dogs. Your dog must compete in all three shows of his division.

Titles are accepted by all the obedience-title organizations including the AKC.

Field Trials. All serious competitions that test dogs' ability to do the work they were bred for are loosely referred to as "field trials."

1. Sporting dog competitions are actually called field trials and are designed to show off the ability to find game, hold it at point, flush it to the gun and retrieve it on land and water.

2. Hounds compete in advanced scent discrimination (the ability to pick a single object out of a huge pile of identical objects) and tracking, in which they trail a scent over hill and dale, often for miles, with deliberate obstacles like rivers and lakes. Different hounds track a scent that has been carried but never touched to the ground and scents that have been dragged along the ground. It's rather amazing to watch.

3. Newfoundlands have a special competition in the water in which they retrieve "drowning" swimmers, boats and ropes.

4. Herding dogs compete to gather up a mob of sheep and move them quickly into a pen. This is most impressive to see.

All these competitions are designed for outdoor dogs. Training your dog to compete in these trials requires a great deal of country work, and therefore, I doubt that you'd be interested in them. If you are, the AKC can guide you.

GAMES, GAMES, GAMES

There are so many "fun competitions" you can do with your dog that if you hanker to "beat the other guys," there's a game you and Rover will love!

Agility Competition. The Sports Channel is covering agility competition regularly. Watch this exciting, fairly new form of sports competition to see if you and your dog are up to it. The sport consists of running your dog through a course of all sorts of hurdles, tunnels, teeter-totters, A-frames (an up-and-down ramp) and weave poles. The arrangement is new for every event and dogs don't get a chance to preview it. Handlers walk it just before the event to plan their moves. There are separate events for small, medium and large dogs so the tiny Toys don't have to jump like a Rottweiler. Winners have the fastest time with the greatest accuracy. Handlers are running constantly and need to be in pretty good shape, as well as the dogs.

The different organizations running agility competitions have different titles, but each one offers several levels of skill, starting with beginners and ending with the masters.

It's exciting and looks like great fun. I suspect that Agility might be my next hobby. The AKC, United States Dog Agility Association and the North American Dog Agility Council all run sanctioned agility trials so you can find a competition program for your dog, regardless of breed.

Flyball Competition. Flyball is a team sport invented in California. It's a relay race with a team of four dogs who have to watch a tennis ball thrown by a spring-loaded shooter, then run out a line of four hurdles spaced about ten feet apart, retrieve the ball and run back to the starting line. The dogs win points towards titles based on the team times. Each dog in a team earns

5 points for finishing the legs in less than 24 seconds. They're fast!

Flyball winners accumulate the titles of Flyball Dog, Flyball Dog Excellent, Flyball Dog Champion, Flyball Master, Master Excellent and Master Champion. There's also an Onyx Award and a Flyball Grand Champion.

Frisbee Competitions. Is your dog a wily, athletic catching artist? Then perhaps you want to see him on one of those videos they run on TV from time to time of wonderful Frisbee-catching dogs. There doesn't appear to be a national organization for Frisbee competitions but the Internet does reveal a whole bunch of local clubs scattered all over the country.

One club's slogan is "where the fur comes to fly," which gives you an idea that these Frisbee groups could be a lot of fun. Indeed, the websites I looked at listed a wide range of activities with and without dog companions, including ski trips and outings that included competitions.

It looks as if the Frisbee people like to have fun.

HERO DOGS

Some dogs work with their owners in ways that are nothing short of heroic. They do a great service to humanity, at times under great stress. It's only natural that after you see how wonderful your dog is that you might wonder if he might not like the opportunity to be a hero. Alas, there are few opportunities for "hero work" on a hobby level for a canine companion.

Therapy Dog. One excellent form of service to humanity, which you and your dog may be able to do, is to visit the sick, the aged and the infirm to bring them cheer, companionship and fuzzy happiness.

You can't simply walk into a care facility, however, and say, "I'm here with my dog to make sick people happy." Therapy-dog visits are organized and scheduled by your local dog club, shelter or other organization and the dogs are screened or even specially trained.

Your dog will be interacting with many different sorts of people who are fragile and/or ill in often complex environments. Therapy-dog program directors want dogs who are friendly and outgoing, not hyper but somewhat energetic and possessing that wonderful quality of empathy, of instinctively understanding when a human needs comfort and love.

In addition to judging a dog's personality and temperament, dogs are also tested to see if they'll behave well. Some organizations use the AKC Canine Good Citizen tests, while others have devised their own. The Delta Society, a leader in therapy-dog programs requires C.D.G. dogs that have passed screening to take a course that teaches them such things as how to see and avoid interfering with IVs, not to jump on people in wheelchairs, etc. A Delta Dog is accepted into any therapy program and I believe he is also an official "service dog," entitled to ride on public transportation and go other places where other dogs are forbidden.

Once you sign up, you'll be making a commitment to bring your dog in at a fixed time on fixed dates for therapy excursions of a fixed length. It might be two hours a week or two hours a month; in most cases, you have some latitude about the degree of commitment. Whatever you agree to, this appointment should become sacred. The people your dog visits will be counting on seeing him. He will form real relationships with people, and if he suddenly disappears, disappointment could cause medical repercussions.

Therapy dogs do an enormous amount of good. There are documented cases of autistic children responding to a therapy dog when they have never responded to anything else...of senior citizens who are totally withdrawn from the world coming back to pet a small dog...of small and even large miracles. As they interact with the dogs and cats, old people remember pets from their pasts, talk to one another and to the animals. Children with cancer forget their pain when a dog snuggles up next to them. When you think of the good your dog can do, the commitment seems pretty minimal, doesn't it?

Service Dogs. These days, dogs do wonderful work helping not only the blind, but the deaf, the wheelchair-bound and the disabled. There are dogs who can alert people with seizure disorders that a seizure is about to happen. If you're thinking that your dog would make a wonderful helper for a handicapped person, remember one thing — you lose your dog; he goes to live with the person he serves.

In truth, service dogs are very, very carefully selected. They must be very steady, not prone to alarms or fears. They need to have an inbred desire to serve and be able to give tremendous devotion. Service training organizations accept only young dogs, too. You cannot drop off the average dog at a training facility.

Many organizations breed their own dogs and here you might be of help because if they have a breeding program, they need people to foster puppies from weaning to one year old, at which point the dogs are mature enough for intensive training. The pups are fostered because it's vital that the dog be raised in a home with caring people. Although 4-H and other children's organizations are very active in helping to raise these dogs, the groups are always looking for new foster families. Most of the groups have no problem with your having another dog in the house. If you're interested, however, remember that you'll have this dog during his most energetic and troublesome months and then you'll lose him. Can you cope?

As a volunteer puppy-raiser, you are expected to provide love, socialization and teach the basic commands. Often you're asked to deliberately expose the puppy to lots of city life so that when he goes into training, he takes to new experiences calmly. You may be told NOT to teach certain things — Seeing Eye Dogs, for instance, must never jaywalk. Please listen to these instructions because if you ignore them, your pup could be ruined for service.

Search and Rescue Dogs (SAR). Search and Rescue Dogs work in teams that fly all over the world to help in the aftermath of man-made and natural disasters. They search for missing persons and homicide victims near their homes; they may also fly all over the world to help in the aftermath of disasters. Their job is to locate victims, alive or dead. In Oklahoma City, canine searchers recovered 169 bodies and found the last living person buried in the rubble!

The work is highly dangerous for the dogs and their handlers. It's also extremely stressful, physically demanding and emotionally exhausting. But these dogs are true heroes — they go where people can't, use their extraordinary senses to find people that humans can't locate and do all this for the reward of being able to play with a little rag toy.

SAR dogs must be obedient, agile, directable, able to search and able to give a strong alert. SAR people search shelters for candidates, looking for dogs with a high prey drive, boldness and a great willingness to hunt for a tossed toy. Once they find dogs with the right qualities, the dogs require extensive training to work in rubble without killing themselves or others, and the training goes on for as long as they're working. SAR programs are much like the National Guard; most weekends find SAR teams out in the field practicing. Obstacle courses are created with sawhorses, plywood, ladders, rolls of cyclone fencing, pallets and more.

SAR is a massive commitment on your part. You and your dog must attend constant training sessions with your team, perhaps at a place quite far out in the country. And you must be able to drop everything and get on a plane whenever there's another bombing, earthquake, tornado or other disaster. On the job, you work long hours under grueling conditions, often with less-than-civilized accommodations. You and your dog work long past exhaustion, grief and horror. Above all, SAR is a young dog's game. It's so stressful that dogs, as well as humans, burn out.

If you want to pursue SAR, I bow in respect. What a splendid thing you and your dog are undertaking!

BEAUTY CONTESTS AND PROFITS

If people are stopping you on the street to say, "He's so beautiful!" you might start wondering if there's a way to capitalize on your extraordinary dog. Well, there is and there isn't...

Conformation Shows. The dog shows we all know about are called "conformation shows" because dogs are being judged on how well they conform to the standard for that breed. Beauty alone doesn't win.

AKC-sanctioned shows are run all over the country by local clubs. But think carefully about this — showing isn't all it seems to be when you watch from a distance.

I never found showing a way to meet other dog-lovers.

Shows are high-stress events and entrants are extremely competitive. An enormous amount of time is spent getting your dog ready to show and there's not a great deal of visiting between dog-owners or handlers.

Even watching a show can be boring. Judges look at all the dogs carefully then point to the winners, calling out the number of their prizes. There's no explanation of why these particular dogs won.

Unless you have an extremely rare breed, your dog doesn't have a very good chance of winning with you handling him. The real champions are turned over to professional handlers who employ a bag of not-very-nice tricks to outdo one another in the ring. If you don't know the tricks or how to deal with them, you haven't got a prayer.

The handler also has facilities to get your dog into "show condition" which requires a full winter coat. Unless you're willing to turn your air conditioner on and lower the temperature into the 40's for a couple of months, you can't do that.

All this is quite expensive — and what are you going to do with your Champion? If you're still interested, get a professional who knows your breed to evaluate his prospects.

Movie Stars and Models. Those classified ads in dog magazines that offer to turn your dog into a star are, on the whole, as reliable as the model schools offered in your newspaper's classified section. If you truly want your dog to become a movie star or model, go for it directly — a school isn't needed. For movies and the theater, get *Variety* and show up at the casting calls they list. For modeling, go to a canine modeling agency. In either event, you must be a very good groomer and a very proficient trainer. Professionals can be quite unpleasant if your dog delays a shoot by not being on his mark, looking his best and ready to perform in a crowd of strangers while being handled by a model or actor who actually hates dogs. You may have to direct your dog's movements with hand signals instead of your voice. And model dogs have to hold often awkward poses for quite some time while looking happy.

It's a tough world and even Lassie works sporadically with long periods of no work at all.

VOLUNTEERING FOR DOGS

If you'd like to help other dogs enjoy a rich and fruitful life like yours, why not volunteer at a local shelter, sanctuary or breed rescue operation?

Or if your dog likes other dogs, consider serving as a foster parent. Both of you can do wonders in calming a dog who has lost his home or even suffered abuse. Fostering can take many forms — you can simply make a home for a purebred through your local breed rescue organization or you can nurture a puppy who's been torn from his mother long before he's ready for solid food. You can take an injured dog who's just been released from the hospital and administer nursing care. You can even take in an abused or tortured animal whose owner is being prosecuted. With these dogs, however, you need to be prepared for the fact that the judge may return the dog to his original home, no matter what you think or know about what happens to him there.

This is hero work, too.

Chapter 22

A PERSON'S BEST FRIEND TO THE VERY END

As I said at the beginning of this book, having a dog in the city is not cruel or impossible provided you choose and train your dog correctly. As you've seen, the right dog, trained correctly, can be very happy with your lifestyle and environment.

I hope you've also found that training isn't all that difficult or unpleasant. There's a pretty simple solution to almost every problem, and your world can be immeasurably richer and larger with a doggy companion.

To me, the greatest pleasures of living with a dog are the simple ones. It's wonderful to drag home after a really tough day at work to be greeted by a wagging tail and the bouncing exuberance of a creature whose entire being says, "Oh, I'm so glad to see you!" Such affection instantly dissipates the difficulties of city life and banishes those city-loneliness blues.

Dogs help convert strangers into neighbors and your neighborhood into a community. They enable you to let the inner child loose and force you to play again. And when you're lying alone in bed with the flu, wondering if anyone cares, your furry companion will suddenly jump up and settle down against you with a soft sigh while gazing at you sympathetically.

A dog will enrich your life in ways you never dreamed and will never be able to explain to a non-dog person. You have a million wonderful experiences ahead of you and only a few little headaches. Enjoy!

APPENDIX: YOUR RESOURCE DIRECTORY

The listings below in no way reflect any endorsement by the author or publisher. They are simply helpful items I've heard about or run across in my research, which I felt might help you in your research efforts. If I have any experience with what's listed, I include it in this information.

When I was working on this book, I made tremendous use of the Internet and found it a fabulous source of information. But don't accept everything you find on the web without looking at the source. There are many sites put up by individuals that provide a tremendous amount of information — and are a lot of fun, too...but not all of these people are experts.

General information about dogs:
- ASPCA's website: www.aspca.org
- ANI-MED, see "medical" below.
- Ark Online is a magazine format website on animal issues: http://www.arkonline.com
- American Dog Owners Association (ADOA) - 518/477-8469
- Great source for all kinds of information in almost all categories listed here and more: www.K9web.com/dog-faqs/
- Mixed Breed Dog Club of America, c/o Chris Dane, 100 Acacia Ave., San Bruno, CA 94066.
- The Humane Society of the United States, 2100 L Street N.W., Washington, D.C. 20037, website www.hsus.org/ has a wealth of helpful and informative information.
- The Ark Trust gives out the Genesis Awards for animals on stage and in movies. Telephone 818/501-2ARK, website www.arktrust.org
- Publications: *AKC Gazette*, 5580 Centerview Dr., Suite 200, Raleigh, NC 27606, 919/233-9780 — official AKC publication

listing all AKC-approved shows.

- Send for "Pet Facts 97-98" from the American Animal Hospital Association, P.O. Box 150899, Denver, CO 80215, telephone 303/298-1818. Reports on a survey of how dog and cat-owners treat their pets. Costs $100 and is more fun than value.

-Publication: *Dog Fancy Magazine* website
www.dogfancy.com

-Publication: *Dog World Magazine* website
www.dogworld.com

Animal behaviorists:
- Animal Behavior Society, Box 180, Mercer College, Macon, GA 31207, attn. John Wright, Ph.D.
- American Veterinary Society of Animal Behavior, 253 S. Greaser Rd., St. Louis, MO 63141, attn, Debra Horwitz, D.V.M.

Breed Rescue:
- AKC publishes a list of national breed club rescue coordinators in the November issue of their *Gazette Magazine*. You can also find this list on their website at www.akc.org/rescue.htm or call the AKC Customer Service office at 919/233-9767.

- Project BREED (stands for Breed Rescue Efforts & Education) is a nonprofit coalition of volunteers, publishing a directory of hundreds of breed groups and the services they offer: Write them at P.O. Box 15888, Chevy Chase, MD 20825. Please enclose a self-addressed stamped envelope as they haven't much money.

- Greyhound Pets of America — 800/36-1472, website www.adopt-a-greyhound.org

- National Greyhound Adoption Network: 800/446-8637,

will tell you of the Greyhound breed rescue near your home.

- National Greyhound Adoption Program: 800/348-2517.

- Book: *SAVE THAT DOG!* by Liz Palika. They claim it tells you everything you need to know about adopting a purebred rescue dog. Published by Howell Book Library in 1997.

Canine Search and Rescue:
- Contact your local fire rescue squad to ask about an SAR group near you.

- Contact FEMA, the Federal Emergency Management Agency and the Office of U.S. Foreign Disaster Assistance.

Canine Good Citizen Certification: Check AKC website or call or write.

Communication:
- *Understanding Your Dog: Everything You want To Know About Your Dog But Haven't Been Able To Ask Him*, by Michael W. Fox, St. Martin's Press. Fox is a very well-known animal expert and the first edition of this book taught me how to understand my dogs a thousand times better than I ever had before.

Competition: Agility
- North American Dog Agility Council (NADAC) — located at HCR2 Box 277, St. Maries, ID 83861. Have many local clubs with names that hint at the kind of people that belong — Jumping Chollas in the Southwest, Haut Dawg in the South.

- United States Dog Agility Association, P.O. Box 850995, Richardson, TX 75085. 972/231-9700, also look for USDAA homepage on the Web.

- American Kennel Club (given above)

- Australian Shepherd Club of America (given under Obedience)

- Book: *Agility Training, The Fun Sport For All dogs,* by Jane Simmons-Moake, Howell Book House, Macmillan Publishing Co.

- Book: *Enjoying Dog Agility,* by Julie Daniels, Doral Publishing.

- Publication: *Clean Run Productions,* 35 Walnut St., Turners Falls, MA 01376, 800/311-6503, website info@cleanrun.com

- Publication: *Agility Spotlight, The Magazine for Dog Agility,* P.O. Box 2851, Santa Clara, CA 95055, website AgilityMag@aol.com

Competition: Flyball

-North American Flyball Association (NAPA), http://muskie.fishnet.com/~flyball

- For *Finish Line* newsletter which lists all tournaments and a seeding list of every team in North America, send $20 to Melanie McAvoy, 1002, E. Samuel Ave. Peoria Hts., IL 61614, 309/682-7617, website melmcavoy@worldnet.att.net

- Book: *Flyball Training...Start to Finish,* by Jacqueline Parken and *On Your Mark,* by Mike Russell (available from Direct Book Service, 800/776-2665).

- Book: *Flying High,* by Joan Payne

- Website called The Flyball Home Page is located at http://muskiefishnet.com/~flyball

Competition: Frisbee

Couldn't locate a national organization but did find several clubs that seems to offer a full calendar of all sorts of get-togethers, outings, competitions and outings combined with competition. Sounds like fun! The most informative website I located is the Washington D.C. club, National Capital Air Canines (tag line, "where the fur comes to fly"), 2830 Meadow Lane, Falls Church, VA 22042, telephone 703/532-0709, website http://www.discdog.com/

Competition: Obedience

- American Kennel Club, 5580 Centerview Drive, Raleigh, NC 27606, or 51 Madison Avenue, New York, NY 10010, 212/696-8276.

- American Mixed Breed Obedience Registry (AMBOR), 10236 Topanga Blvd., Suite 205, Chatsworth, CA 91311, website ambor@aborusa.org

- Mixed Breed Dog Club of America, c/o Chris Dane, 100 Acacia Ave., San Bruno, CA 94066.

- Australian Shepherd Club of America (ASCA), 6091 Hwy 21, Bryan, TX 77803, 409/778-1082, website asca@myriad.net

- States Kennel Club, P.O. Box 189, Hattiesburg, MS 39403, 601/583-8345.

- PupPeroni Classic Tournament: Quaker Professional Services, Pet Food Division, P.O. Box 049001, Suite 23-1, Chicago, IL 60604.

- Magazine: *Bloodlines*, 100 E. Kilgore Rd., Kalamazoo, MI 49001, 616/343-9020. United Kingdom obedience rules.

- Magazine: *Front and Finish*, P.O. Box 333, Galesburg, IL 61402, 309/344-13333 — general obedience-related information in newspaper format.

- Magazine: *Off Lead,* 204 Lewis Street, Canastoga, NY 13032, 315/697-2749, website 104501.1527@Compuserv.com — a monthly.

- Book: *Successful Obedience Handling: The New Best Foot Forward,* by Barbara Handler (video is also available).

- Book: *Theory, Footwork, Handling and Attention: Novice, Open and Utility,* by Terri Arnold with Ann Paul.

Lost Dogs:
- The Progressive Animal Welfare Society (PAWS), an organization based in Seattle, has excellent help in how to find a lost dog on their website at http://paws.org/

Medical Help:
- ASPCA National Animal Poison Control Center website: www.napcc.aspca.org
- ANI-MED: The nation's largest telephone-based pet-care information resource is operated by the ASPCA — just dial 610-254-7900. Pre-recorded information on over 100 topics prepared by specialists, available 24 hours a day 7 days a week. Designed to compliment professional care.

- American Veterinary Medical Association's website: www.awma.org

- Chinese medicine for your dog — read *Four Paws, Four Directions* by Cheryl Schwartz, D.V.M., published by Celestial Arts, Berkeley, CA.

- Pet Emergency First Aid video covering how to make and use a muzzle, snakebites, burns, drowning, breathing problems, CPR, treating shock, fractures and more. Available from Apogee Video, 159 Alpine Way, Boulder, CO, toll-free telephone 888-388,9966, website http://apogeevideo.com — cost approx. $20.

- Dog First Aid Kits: A company named VSI sells a kit for approx. $20 over the Internet at http://www.petfirstaid.org/ — toll-free telephone 800/831-7245. I understand The ASPCA also offers a kit (www.aspca.com), and I'm sure many of the pet-supply supermarkets and catalogs also offer kits.

Spay/Neuter:

- 800-321-PETS — Friends of Animals operates this toll-free hotline to help you find a vet near your home who offers low-cost procedures. There are over 1,000 cooperating veterinarians nationwide.

- 800-238-7729 reaches SPAY USA, another toll-free method of locating a nearby vet who offers low-cost spay and neuter.

Therapy Dogs:

- Delta Society, 289 Perimeter Rd. East, Renton, WA 98055, 800/809-2714, website deltasociety@cis.compuserve.com. (Delta also puts out a magazine called *Interaction*).

- Therapy Dogs International, 88 Barley Rd., Flanders, NJ 07836, 973/252-9800, website: tdi@gti.net

- Book: *Therapy Dogs - Training Your Dog to Reach Others*, by Kathy Diamond Davis.

Vacations:

- Farm Sanctuary in upstate New York is a 175-acre haven for animals rescued from slaughterhouses and factory farms. Spend your vacation in a cabin on-site and help care for the animals, cost about $50-60/week. Call 607/583-2225. (I suspect your dog is not welcome.)

- Dogs are welcome at an increasing number of bed & breakfast inns, however: *The Washington, D.C.-Baltimore Dog Lover's Companion* published by Foghorn Press lists several that go to great lengths to make your dog a happy guest.

J

K

L

M

N

O

P